UNITED NATIONS OFFICE ON DRUGS AND CRIME
Vienna

ADDICTION, CRIME AND INSURGENCY

The transnational threat of Afghan opium

UNODC
United Nations Office on Drugs and Crime

Acknowledgements

This report was prepared by the UNODC Studies and Threat Analysis Section (STAS), in the framework of the UNODC Trends Monitoring and Analysis Programme/Afghan Opiate Trade sub-Programme, and with the collaboration of the UNODC Country Office in Afghanistan and the UNODC Regional Office for Central Asia. UNODC field offices for East Asia and the Pacific, the Middle East and North Africa, Pakistan, the Russian Federation, Southern Africa, South Asia and South Eastern Europe also provided feedback and support. A number of UNODC colleagues gave valuable inputs and comments, including, in particular, Thomas Pietschmann (Statistics and Surveys Section) who reviewed all the opiate statistics and flow estimates presented in this report.

UNODC is grateful to the national and international institutions which shared their knowledge and data with the report team, including, in particular, the Anti Narcotics Force of Pakistan, the Afghan Border Police, the Counter Narcotics Police of Afghanistan and the World Customs Organization. Thanks also go to the staff of the United Nations Assistance Mission in Afghanistan and of the United Nations Department of Safety and Security, Afghanistan.

Report Team
Research and report preparation:
Hakan Demirbüken (Lead researcher, Afghan Opiate Trade Programme, STAS)
Hayder Mili (Afghan Opiate Trade Programme, STAS)
Jacob Townsend (UNODC Country Office in Afghanistan)
Mapping support:
Umidjon Rahmonberdiev (UNODC Regional Office for Central Asia)
Odil Kurbanov (UNODC Regional Office for Central Asia)
Editorial support and publication:
Raggie Johansen (STAS)
Suzanne Kunnen (STAS)
Kristina Kuttnig (STAS)
Supervision:
Thibault Le Pichon (Chief, STAS)

The preparation of this report benefited from the financial contributions of the United States of America and Turkey to the Afghan Opiate Trade Programme, and of the European Commission through UNODC Project GLOE69RU.

Disclaimers
This report has not been formally edited. The contents of this publication do not necessarily reflect the views or policies of UNODC or contributory organizations and neither do they imply any endorsement. The designations employed and the presentation of material in this publication do not imply the expression of any opinion whatsoever on the part of UNODC concerning the legal status of any country, territory or city or its authorities, or concerning the delimitation of its frontiers or boundaries.

Photos: © UNODC, Alessandro Scotti

NOV 1 3 2009

TABLE OF CONTENTS

COMMENTARY BY
THE EXECUTIVE DIRECTOR

In September, UNODC published its *Afghan Opium Survey 2009* with detailed estimates of cultivation, production, labour force, revenues and domestic prices.

This Report is a sort of a sequel: it presents a perspective that is both deeper in scope and broader in geographical coverage. It looks at the multiple consequences of Afghan drugs as they move through neighbouring states, along the Balkan and Eurasian routes, ending up in Europe, the Russian Federation, even China and India. This analysis is proposed to help the international community appreciate the fact that *we all* are part of the Afghan drug problem: hence, *we all* must work for its solution, addressing *all* links of the drug chain: (i.) assistance to farmers to reduce <u>supply</u>, (ii.) drug prevention and treatment to curb <u>demand</u>, and (iii.) law enforcement against <u>intermediaries</u>.

These intermediaries are not only shady characters linked to international mafias. They are also (i.) <u>white collar Afghan officials</u>, who take a cut by protecting the drug trade, as well (ii.) the <u>religious fanatics and political insurgents</u> who do the same to finance their cause.

By looking, with unprecedented detail, at the *Health, Security and Stability* dimensions of the Afghan drug problem, this report shows what more needs to be done at a time when, within the country, market forces have reduced domestic cultivation by 1/3 in the past 24 months. Let us begin with the health question.

A. *Addiction*

The catalogue of casualties caused by Afghan narcotics is gruesome. We need to go back to the dramatic opium addiction in China a century ago to find comparable statistics.

- Every year, <u>more people die</u> from Afghan opium than any other drug in the world: perhaps 100,000 globally.

- The number of people who die of heroin overdoses in NATO countries <u>per year</u> (above 10,000) is five times higher than the total number of NATO troops killed in Afghanistan <u>in the past 8 years</u>, namely since the beginning of military operations there in 2001.

- The number of addicts in the Russian Federation has multiplied by 10 during the past 10 years, and they now consume a staggering 75-80 tons/year of Afghan heroin. <u>More Russian people die from drugs</u> per year (at present 30,000-40,000, according to government estimates) than the total number of Red Army soldiers killed during the Soviet invasion and the ensuing 7-year Afghan campaign.

- Despite major efforts to cope with drug trafficking, the Islamic Republic of Iran is swamped by Afghan opium: with its estimated 1 million opiate users, Iran faces one of <u>the world's most serious opiates</u> addiction problem.

- Central Asia, once only a conduit for Afghan heroin, is now a major consumer – a habit that is resulting in an <u>HIV epidemic</u> caused by injecting drug use.

These numbers show that Afghan opium is not a home-made Marshall Plan, to replace (inadequate) foreign development assistance with (illegal) domestic revenues. Nor is it the result of a country short on controls and long on corruption. Rather, these numbers suggest that the Afghan opium trade is a well-funded threat to the health of nations. And what about security?

B. Crime

While in recent years opium has generated up to $1 billion per year to Afghan farmers, the global heroin market is worth many times that much ($65 billion). Not idly, President Karzai pointed out to me that: *"we take 3% of the revenue and 100% of the blame"*. This report documents the extent to which benign neglect, incompetence and corruption enable narcotics to move from one of the poorest (landlocked) countries in the world, to the main streets of the richest nations in Europe and (growingly) Asia. Here are the hard facts to document this systemic failure.

- While 90% of the world's opium comes from Afghanistan, less than 2% is seized there. This is a major law enforcement defeat, as it is incomparably cheaper and easier to detect and interdict an illicit activity at the source, rather than at destination (Colombia, the other major drug-producing country, seizes 10 times more of its dope than Afghanistan: as a consequence, on the high street, purity has decreased and prices increased)

- Most of the Afghan borders with Pakistan are wide open, enabling low-risk smuggling back and forth across the Durand Line, especially in Balochistan. Almost no drugs are seized in the Federally Administered Tribal Areas (FATA) although thousands of tons transit the region. Abuse of the Afghan Trade Transit Agreement (ATTA) as well as exploitation of centuries-old kinship ties, have turned the Afghanistan/Pakistan border – already known for the unimpeded movements of insurgents-- into a massive illicit free trade zone of drugs, chemicals precursor, money, people and weapons.

- The rates of interception of the opiate flows in the Islamic Republic of Iran (20%) and in Pakistan (17%) are more significant, but are not matched in other countries or regions (except China).

- Countries of Central Asia are only seizing around 5% of the 90 tons of heroin that cross their territory, on the move to the Russian Federation.

- The Russian Federation, the foremost (national) heroin market, consumes 20% of the Afghan heroin production, but seizes a meagre 4% of the flow reaching its territory.

- Even worse, countries of South-Eastern Europe, including EU members like Greece, Bulgaria and Romania, are intercepting less than 2% of the heroin flow.

There is something basically wrong with global counter-narcotics. Why are global seizures of cocaine (from Andean countries) twice as high, in absolute and relative terms, than for opiates (from Afghanistan)? To understand the menace resulting from this law enforcement failure, let us look at the threat Afghan drugs pose to stability.

C. Insurgency

The Taliban's relationship with opium has gone through stages, each a manifestation of an opportunistic response to the situation on the ground – within, but especially beyond, Afghanistan.

- When in power (in the second half of the 1990s), the Taliban tolerated opium cultivation and facilitated its export. In the process, through a direct taxation on farmers (*ushr*) they generated about $75-100 million per year to fund a regime without alternative sources of foreign exchange.

- In the summer of 2000, as a Security Council embargo loomed, Mullah Omar banned opium cultivation (but not its export). Thanks to the regime's near total control of the territory, farmers had no option but to respect the decree (*fatwa*). In the fall of 2000, they refrained from planting; the spring 2001 harvest was close to zero.

- Ever since their return as insurgents into southern Afghanistan (in 2005) the Taliban – and other anti-government forces – have derived enormous sums of money from the drug trade. Although the amounts are subject to debate, some order of magnitude estimates are possible.

In 2006-2007, the drug-related funds accruing to insurgents and warlords were estimated by UNODC at $200-400 million a year. This estimate included incomes from four sources: levies on opium farmers; protection fees on lab processing; transit fees on drug convoys; and taxation on imports of chemical precursors. The proposed sum, a surprise to many observers, was in line with the high opium prices at that time and the unprecedented levels of cultivation (never repeated).

Ever since, the opium economy of Afghanistan has changed its shape and nature: crops, prices and revenues have declined; additional sources of revenue have materialized for the Taliban; also insurgents outside Afghanistan have started to benefit in their own right. In total, there have been pluses and minuses.

- During the past four years (2005-2008) the Taliban have made <u>$450-600 million</u> in total from taxing opium cultivation and trade in Afghanistan. Year over year the amounts have changed as both cultivation (hectares) and prices ($/kg) in the middle of the period were much higher than in earlier and later years.

- At the same time, Afghanistan's opiate exports have shifter towards a greater share of refined products (at present 2/3 of the raw opium output is turned into heroin and morphine compared to 3/4 a few years back). This has allowed the Taliban to tax higher value-added commodities (refined products) and other drug-related activities: lab processing, trafficking and the import of precursors – a business worth around $3 billion in 2007 in Afghanistan alone.

- Furthermore, the Taliban and other al-Qaeda linked groups have been taking a share of the $1 billion opiate market in Pakistan.

As a consequence, the estimation of the revenue derived by insurgents in Afghanistan has become more complex, as the taxes imposed on licit economic activity have to be taken into account and added: a source of money that did not exist in 2006-2007 when the anti-government groups did not control the territory in southern Afghanistan as widely and permanently as they do now. Furthermore, the lines between the ideologically-driven Taliban, the criminal groups in the business for profit, and the government officials taking a cut for greed, have become blurry. Pinning all the blame on anti-government forces diverts attention from the broad range of profiteers, at home and abroad. In short, the Afghan drug economy generates several hundred million dollars per year into evil hands – some with black turbans, others with white collars.

A perfect storm spiralling into Central Asia

The most sinister development yet is taking shape outside Afghanistan. Drugs are funding insurgency in Central Asia where the Islamic Movement of Uzbekistan, the Islamic Party of Turkmenistan, the East Turkistan Liberation Organization and other extremist groups are also profiting from the trade. The Silk Route, turned into a heroin route, is carving out a path of death and violence through one of the world's most strategic, yet volatile regions. The perfect storm of drugs, crime and insurgency that has swirled around the Afghanistan/Pakistan border for years, is heading for Central Asia. If quick preventive measures are not put into place, a big chunk of Eurasia could be lost – together with its massive energy reserves.

This report provides a diagnosis of the transnational threat posed by Afghanistan's opium that only an international and truly comprehensive effort can address.

Antonio Maria Costa
Executive Director
United Nations Office on Drugs and Crime

ABBREVIATIONS AND ACRONYMS

ABP	Afghanistan Border Police
ADB	Asian Development Bank
AEF	Afghan Eradication Force
AGE	Anti-Government Elements
AIDS	Acquired Immune Deficiency Syndrome
ANA	Afghan National Army
ANDS	Afghanistan National Development Strategy
ANF	Anti-Narcotics Force (Pakistan)
ANP	Afghan National Police
AREU	Afghanistan Research and Evaluation Unit
ASNF	Afghan Special Narcotics Force
ATTA	Afghan Transit Trade Agreement
CARICC	Central Asia Regional Information and Coordination Centre
CCZ	Customs Control Zone
CIS	Commonwealth of Independent States
CNPA	Counter Narcotics Police Afghanistan
CNTA	Counter Narcotics Training Academy
CNTF	Counter Narcotics Trust Fund
CSTO	Collective Security Treaty Organization
DCA	Drug Control Agency
DEA	Drug Enforcement Administration (USA)
DFID	Department for International Development (United Kingdom)
EC	European Commission
EA	Enforcement Affairs
EU	European Union
FAO	Food and Agriculture Organization
FATA	Federally Administrated Tribal Areas
FDCS	Federal Drug Control Service
GCC	Gulf Cooperation Council

GPI	Good Performance Initiative
HIV	Human Immunodeficiency Virus
ICG	International Crisis Group
IDS	Individual Seizure Data
IDU	Injecting Drug Use(r)
IMF	International Monetary Fund
INCB	International Narcotics Control Board
INCSR	International Narcotics Control Strategy Report
INL	Bureau of International Narcotics and Law Enforcement Affairs (USA)
IOM	International Organization for Migration
ISAF	International Security Assistance Force
MCN	Ministry of Counter Narcotics (Afghanistan)
NDCS	National Drug Control Strategy
NGO	Non-governmental organization
NWFP	North West Frontier Province
PKR	Pakistani Rupees
ROCA	Regional Office for Central Asia (UNODC)
SECI	Southeast European Cooperative Initiative
TARCET	Targeted anti-trafficking regional operation enhancing communication, expertise and training (UNODC - Rainbow Strategy)
TIR	Transport Internationaux Routiers
TTP	Tehrik-e-Taliban
UNAIDS	United Nations AIDS Programme
UNAMA	United Nations Assistance Mission for Afghanistan
UNDP	United Nations Development Programme
UNDSS	United Nations Department of Safety and Security
UNODC	United Nations Office on Drugs and Crime
USAID	United States Agency for International Development
WCO	World Customs Organization

KEY FACTS

- In the world over 15 million people use illicit opiates (opium, heroin and morphine) annually. The value of the global opiate market is estimated at US$ 65 billion.

- In the 1990s, production shifted from South-East Asia (mainly Myanmar) to Afghanistan which at present provides over 90 per cent of global supply.

- More than 60 per cent of drug treatment demand in Asia and Europe relate to opiates that are, especially heroin, the most deadly drugs. Deaths due to overdose are, in any single year, as high as 5,000-8,000 in Europe, and several times this amount in the Russian Federation alone.

- The world consumes some 3,700 tons of illicit opium per year (1/3 raw and 2/3 processed into heroin) and seizes 1,000 tons. Illicit opiate trade flows have never been previously known: this report breaks new ground by estimating them by country (and regions).

- Every year, the equivalent of some 3,500 tons of opium flow from Afghanistan to the rest of the world, via its immediate neighbours: 40 per cent through the Islamic Republic of Iran, 30 per cent through Pakistan, and the rest through Central Asia (Tajikistan, Uzbekistan and Turkmenistan).

- The main opiate consumer market is Europe (about 19 per cent of global consumption, with a market value of US$ 20 billion), the Russian Federation (15 per cent), the Islamic Republic of Iran (15 per cent), China (12 per cent), India (7 per cent), Pakistan (6 per cent), Africa (6 per cent) and the Americas (6 per cent).

- The world only intercepts one fifth of the global opiate flows every year, with very mixed performances at the country level. The Islamic Republic of Iran has the highest seizures rate, at 20 per cent. Next are China (18 per cent) and Pakistan (17 per cent). In the two main source countries, Afghanistan and Myanmar, seizures represent only 2 per cent each of the world total.

An equally insignificant 2 per cent is seized in South-Eastern Europe, the last segment of the Balkan route to Europe. Along the Northern route (Central Asia - Russia), the interception rate is also low (4-5 per cent).

- Due to dramatic production increases in Afghanistan after 2005, some 12,000 tons of opium are now stock-piled, in unknown locations. According to UNODC estimates, only a fraction (maybe 10 per cent) is kept by Afghan farmers. The rest is likely in the hands of criminal (traders) and insurgent groups.

- Of the US$ 65 billion turnover of the global market for opiates, only 5-10 per cent (US$ 3-5 billion) are estimated to be laundered by informal banking systems. The rest is laundered through legal trade activities (including smuggling of legal goods into Afghanistan) and the banking system.

- This report assesses the relationship between the drug economy and insurgency in Afghanistan and Pakistan. When the Taliban were in power (in the late 1990s) they extracted US$ 75-100 million a year from taxing opium. In the 2005-2008 period the cumulative revenue from opiate farming and trade accruing to Taliban insurgents is estimated at US$ 350-650 million, or an annual average of US$ 90-160 million in Afghanistan alone. This estimate does not include insurgents' potential revenues from other drug-related activities (labs, imports of precursors) in Afghanistan and from the US$1 billion opiate trade in Pakistan. Also not included are revenues extracted by insurgents from licit activity that takes places in areas they control.

- Precursor trafficking converges on southern and western Afghanistan and, so far, has not received as much attention as the outflow of opiates. Although growing, seizures remain low.

EXECUTIVE SUMMARY

Global opium production increasingly shifted from South-East Asia to Afghanistan during the 1990s. This trend increased in the first decade of the twenty-first century to the point that Afghanistan's supply of opium exceeded world demand. Afghanistan is now the source for more than 90 per cent of the world's deadliest drug. This generates a yearly income estimated at US$ 65 billion, most of which is pocketed by criminals outside of Afghanistan. More than 60 per cent of all drug treatment demand in Asia and Europe is related to opiate abuse. The Afghan drug trade spreads crime, corruption, addiction and HIV. It is a major source of revenue for insurgents, criminals and terrorists. It undermines governance, public health, and public security within Afghanistan and along trafficking routes. In short, it poses a major transnational threat to health and security.

In line with its mandate to ensure evidence-based policy, the United Nations Office on Drugs and Crime (UNODC) is carrying out a programme to analyse the scale and transnational impact of the Afghan opiate trade. Its principal objectives are to:

* analyse the dimensions and flows of the Afghan opiate trade;

* identify the links between drugs, crime and insurgency and the impact on health, development, security and the rule of law;

* provide information and analysis to stimulate a policy response.

This report presents the first findings of the programme. They reveal:

1. How the flows of Afghan opiates are distributed in the world.

2. The extent to which regional insurgency or instability is fuelled by the Afghan opiate industry.

In addition to UNODC's own expertise, research material and fieldwork in Afghanistan and neighbouring countries, information from a variety of other sources were used for the preparation of this report, including experts and officials from a number of government agencies and other international organizations, as well as secondary literature.

1. How are the flows of Afghan opiates distributed in the world?

Law enforcement agencies have generally been able to track the evolution of opiate trafficking <u>routes</u>, mostly through data on seizures and arrests. However, to date, there has been no systematic assessment of the <u>actual volume of opiates flowing</u> to various destinations across the world. That information is essential for developing a better understanding of the patterns and dynamics of the global Afghan opiate trade. The task is challenging and must be treated as work in progress, and this report presents a first estimation of global Afghan opiate flows.

With production increasing over the last decade, market destinations for Afghan opiates diversified. While illicit opiates continued to be exported to the lucrative European market, they also increasingly started to go towards the potentially large market in China, emerging markets such as Central Asia and the Russian Federation, and even to more remote regions such as sub-Saharan Africa and the USA. While world demand for opium and heroin is more or less stable, demand has been increasing in countries along trafficking routes, bringing with it increased health risks, including higher rates of HIV infection.

Global potential opium production, 1980-2009

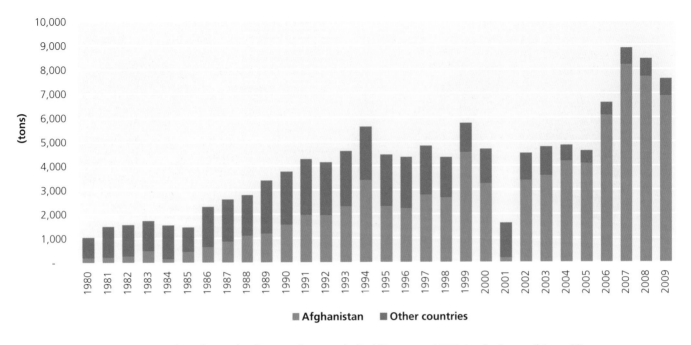

Source: UNODC *World Drug Report* (figure for 2009 based on 2009 Survey results for Afghanistan and 2008 data for the rest of the world).

The world consumes approximately 3,700 tons of illicit opium per year (raw or processed into heroin)

According to 2008 UNODC estimates, there are around 15.4 million opiate users in the world. The overwhelming majority (11.3 million) are heroin users and the others (4.1 million), opium users. Global heroin consumption is estimated at 340 tons of pure heroin per year (equivalent to 2,600 tons of opium) and raw opium consumption is estimated at 1,100 tons per year, bringing global opiate consumption to around 3,700 tons of opium equivalent per year.

Close to half of all global heroin consumption is estimated to take place in Europe (including the Russian Federation). Excluding Russia, European users account for a quarter of global heroin consumption. Russian users rank second with about a fifth of the total, and Chinese users come next with more than a tenth. Heroin consumption figures for Africa have some limitations, but available estimates suggest that the continent may now account for some 7 per cent of global heroin consumption. Pakistan, India and the Islamic Republic of Iran account for one twentieth of total consumption each.

As regards opium, global illicit consumption is estimated at close to 1,100 tons per year, used by some 4 million users. The lion's share, over 42 per cent, is estimated to be consumed in the Islamic Republic of Iran.

Opium production has doubled since 2006

For some 15 years (1990-2005), global annual opium production amounted to an average of 4,700 tons, and seizures to some 900-1,000 tons per year. The 3,700 tons remaining after seizures were sufficient to meet the estimated world

demand for illicit opiates and the illicit market was more or less stable. However, as of 2006, opium production almost doubled compared to the 1990-2005 average, due to a sharp increase in Afghanistan.

Major stockpiles of opium

Major overproduction during the 2006-2009 period can be estimated at over 12,000 tons of opium, enough to satisfy more than two years of world consumption. Stockpiles are probably in remote regions of Afghanistan, in neighbouring countries, or along trafficking routes. Speculation as to why so much opium is being withheld from the market ranges from economic reasons (a hedge against falling prices) to more sinister scenarios (a funding source for further insurgency or terrorist attacks).

Every year, some 375 tons of Afghan heroin (and morphine) enter the world market

The total quantity of (pure[1]) heroin consumed (340 tons) or seized (about 90 tons) in the world amounts to some 430 tons per year. Opium from Myanmar and the Lao People's Democratic Republic yields some 50 tons of heroin and the rest, some 380 tons of heroin/morphine, is produced exclusively from Afghan opium. About 5 tons are consumed and seized in Afghanistan itself, and the remaining 375 tons enter the world market.

UNODC estimates that around 110 tons of heroin are exported to Europe, about 100 tons to Central Asia (the majority destined for the Russian Federation), some 25 tons to Africa, 15-17 tons to China, and some 15-20 tons to the

---

1 Throughout this report, the term "heroin" refers to pure heroin which is equal to the purity of heroin produced in Afghanistan (70 per cent).

**Global heroin consumption (340 tons)*, 2008
(share of countries/regions)**

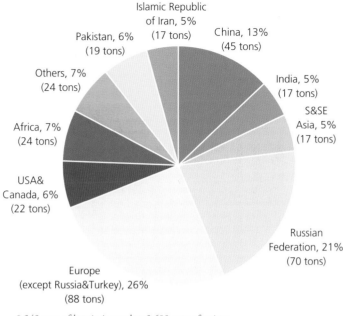

* 340 tons of heroin is equal to 2,600 tons of opium.
Source: UNODC.

**Global opium consumption (1,100 tons), 2008
(share of countries/regions)**

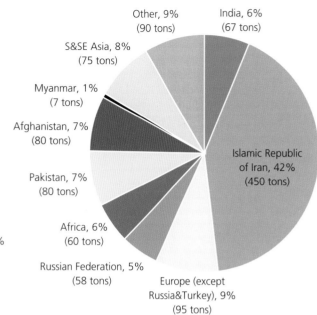

Source: UNODC.

Estimates of opiate stockpiles for the period 2006-2009*:

- Total global opium production: 31,000 tons.
- Total global opiate demand and seizures (in opium equivalent): 19,000 tons
- Total opium surplus: 31,000 – 19,000 = 12,000 tons

* Figure for 2009 based on 2009 Survey results for Afghanistan and 2008 data for the rest of the world.

USA and Canada. The remainder is smuggled to other destinations such as the Middle East.[2]

First, heroin is trafficked to Afghanistan's immediate neighbours, Pakistan, the Islamic Republic of Iran and the Central Asian countries of Tajikistan, Uzbekistan and Turkmenistan. Some 40 per cent (150 tons) of Afghanistan's heroin is trafficked to Pakistan, which is one of the main transit countries for Afghan heroin destined for Iran, India, Africa, Europe, the USA, Canada, China and East and South-East Asia. About 30 per cent (105 tons) enters Iran and 25 per cent Central Asian countries (100 tons). It is possible that the remainder, some 20 tons (5 per cent) of Afghan heroin, is being smuggled into India. This hypothesis requires further research, due to current data limitations.

Does 75 per cent of the heroin consumed in the USA and Canada come from Afghanistan?

A total of 22 tons of heroin is estimated to be consumed in the USA and Canada. Until now, it was thought that the majority of this heroin originated in Latin America and Mexico. But with the amount of opium reportedly produced there, not more than 10 tons of heroin can be produced annually, half of which goes to the north. Either some 17-20 tons of heroin are being trafficked from Afghanistan (or its neighbours) to North America, or Colombia and/or Mexico are producing more opium than previously reported.

30 per cent of all Afghan heroin is trafficked to Europe, primarily via the Balkan route

The primary supply line for the European market is the "Balkan route", flowing from the Islamic Republic of Iran to Europe. Between Iran and Europe, Turkey is the central hub from which narcotics are shipped onward to Bulgaria, Greece, Albania and Romania. Wholesale heroin importation into Turkey is almost exclusively from Iran, although a small amount is trafficked from the Syrian Arab Republic.

Of the estimated 110 tons of Afghan heroin that reach Europe every year, around 80 per cent (85 tons) is trafficked along the Balkan route. The rest comes via the Russian Federation (Central Asia-Russia), the Black Sea route (Iran-Azerbaijan-Georgia-Black Sea), Pakistan (by air), Africa (by air and sea) and South-East Asia (by air). In recent years, probably due in part to increasing instability in the Caucasus, heroin trafficking via the Black Sea route seems to be increasing.

2   All the findings on opiate flows rely heavily on opiate demand statistics provided in UNODC *World Drug Reports* and are subject to change as efforts to improve demand data progress.

Individual heroin seizures reported during the period 2002-2007

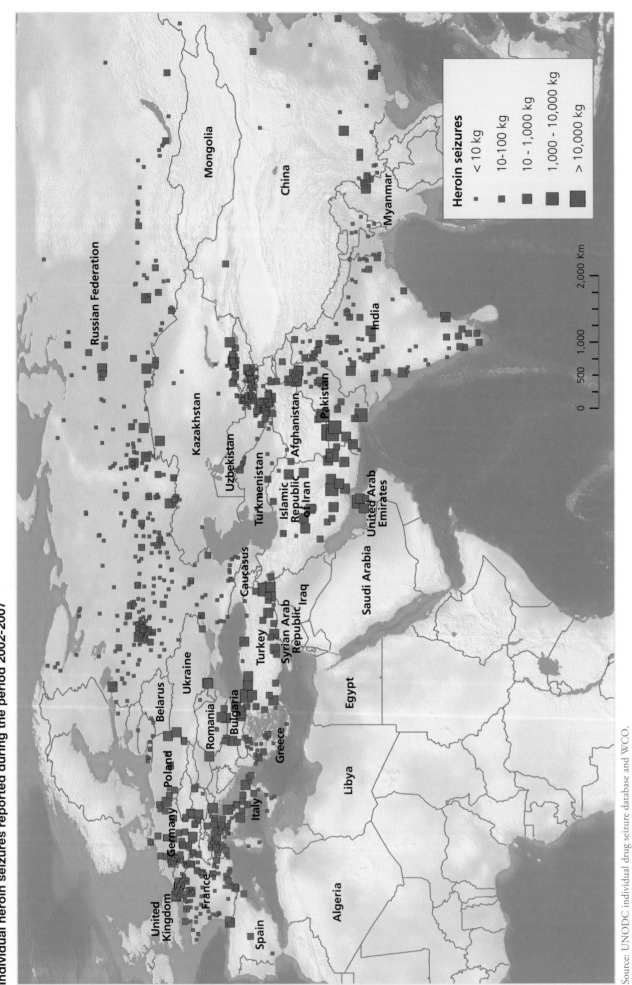

Heroin seizures

- < 10 kg
- 10-100 kg
- 10 - 1,000 kg
- 1,000 - 10,000 kg
- > 10,000 kg

Source: UNODC individual drug seizure database and WCO.

20 per cent of all Afghan heroin is trafficked to the Russian Federation via Central Asia

The estimated 75-80 tons of Afghan heroin flowing to Russia are trafficked from Afghanistan via Central Asian countries. The Central Asian heroin route crosses Afghanistan's borders with Uzbekistan, Turkmenistan and particularly Tajikistan. Most of the heroin (almost two thirds, or 50 out of 75-80 tons) is then trafficked through Kazakhstan by road to Russia. As the last and only northbound transit country for Afghan opiates, Kazakhstan may be as important as Tajikistan on the Northern route. Demand for Afghan heroin has increased dramatically in Russia, and the country has now become more a destination than a transit area. Indeed, there appears to be very limited heroin trafficking from Russia to Europe.

A quarter of the Chinese heroin market may now be supplied by Afghan heroin

New avenues of Afghan opiate distribution have emerged. It appears that the Chinese opiate market is no longer supplied exclusively from Myanmar's declining opium production. Afghan heroin apparently began to be trafficked to China in 2000, mainly via Pakistan, but also across China's borders with Central Asia.

25 per cent of the heroin market in China may now be supplied by Afghan heroin

From 1998 to 2008, Myanmar's opium production declined by more than 70 per cent while opium production in the Lao People's Democratic Republic decreased by more than 90 per cent. The Chinese heroin market is no longer supplied exclusively from the "golden triangle", but may now be supplied also by Afghan heroin, which is trafficked via Pakistan, Central Asia, Africa and Gulf countries.

On the basis of tentative estimates, Afghan heroin may now command a 25 per cent share (15-17 tons) of the Chinese opiate market. This trend, combined with increased regional trade and migration, may result in a growing market share for Afghan heroin in China in the years to come.

Other countries traditionally supplied by the "golden triangle" may also increasingly see Afghan heroin entering their domestic markets.

The case of India

With an estimated 0.8 million heroin users, India is one of the largest opiate markets in South Asia. Some 15-20 tons of heroin may be consumed in India every year. But the exact source of supply is unknown.

What is the source of opiates consumed in India?

Based on demand estimates, heroin consumption in India is estimated at 15-20 tons per year. Data show that heroin is also trafficked from India to various destinations in Africa, North America and Europe. Since there appears to be very limited heroin trafficking from Myanmar to India, this would suggest that heroin comes from Afghanistan or is produced in India itself.

Similarly, while illicit opium consumption in India is estimated at 70 tons per year, official reports from India state that no opium is trafficked into the country. This would suggest that opium for illicit domestic consumption is supplied by local production in India.

Some 30-35 tons of Afghan heroin may be trafficked to Africa every year

Demand for heroin in Africa seems to have been increasing since 2004. A substantial amount (some 20 tons) of heroin is shipped through seaports and airports to Africa from Pakistan every year. The rest, 10-15 tons of heroin, seems to be trafficked to Africa from the Islamic Republic of Iran, the Gulf States, India and South and South-East Asian countries (except China) every year. Traffickers from West Africa and Nigeria in particular are known to operate in Pakistan and in some Central Asian countries, among others. These networks further smuggle Afghan heroin to the USA and Europe, using countries in Africa and other regions as transit points. Afghan heroin is also smuggled into Africa to meet demand on the continent, which is tentatively estimated at around 25 tons per year.

On average, little more than 1 per cent of opium production is seized in Afghanistan

Between 2002 and 2007, a total of 395 tons of opium equivalents of heroin, morphine and opium were seized in Afghanistan. This corresponds to 1.3 per cent of the total amount of opium produced during these years in Afghanistan (29,600 tons). By contrast, during the same period, the Islamic Republic of Iran seized 2,063 tons (7 per cent of Afghanistan's production) and Pakistan 1,057 tons (3.6 per cent of Afghanistan's production) of opium equivalent.

Between 2002 and 2006, on average, 20 per cent of the estimated global opiate flow was seized in the world every year. A closer look at drug seizures relative to drug flows reveals some interesting facts, and some weak links. Seizures as a proportion of the estimated opiate flow affecting Afghanistan, Africa, Myanmar and South-East Europe (except Turkey), East, South and South-East Asia (except China) and India are quite low (1-3 per cent), compared

Estimated heroin flows from Asia to the world (in tons)

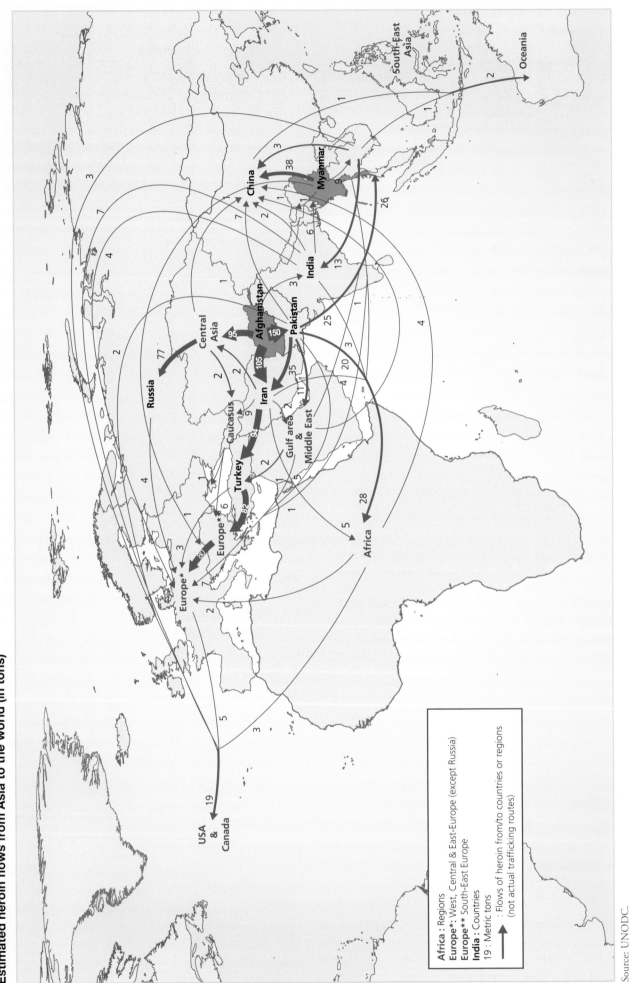

Africa : Regions
Europe*: West, Central & East-Europe (except Russia)
Europe** South-East Europe
India : Countries
19 : Metric tons

: Flows of heroin from/to countries or regions
(not actual trafficking routes)

Source: UNODC.

Annual heroin/morphine and all opiates flows and seizures in the world since 2002*

Country/Region	Heroin and morphine			All opiates (heroin, morphine and opium) in opium equivalent		
	Estimated flow (tons)	Average seizures* (tons)	Per cent of estimated flow intercepted	Estimated flow (tons)	Average seizures* (tons)	Per cent of estimated flow intercepted
Afghanistan	380	4	1%	3,500	61	2%
Pakistan	150	26	18%	1,135	189	17%
Islamic Republic of Iran	140	17	12%	1,713	291	20%
Turkey	95	10	10%	768	69	9%
South-Eastern Europe (Bulgaria, Greece, Albania, Romania, Serbia, The former Yugoslav Republic of Macedonia, Bosnia, Croatia, Montenegro)	90	1.5	2%	724	10.5	2%
Rest of Europe (except Russia)	105	9	9%	828	74	9%
Midde East& Gulf countries (except I.R. of Iran)	14	0.5	4%	114	4	4%
Central Asia	95	5	5%	790	39	5%
Russian Federation	77	3	4%	627	23	4%
Africa	35	0.3	1%	305	2.3	7%
Myanmar	60	1	1%	920	12	2%
India	37	1	3%	328	11	3%
China	55	9	16%	398	73	18%
Rest of S & SE Asia	30	0.7	2%	285	16	6%
Oceania	2	0.3	13%	19	2.5	13%
USA and Canada	24	2	9%	168	17	10%

* Seizure averages for 2002-2006.

with the ratio for other countries, such as the Islamic Republic of Iran (20 per cent), China (18 per cent) and Pakistan (17 per cent).

Precursor chemicals are a key but overlooked link in the chain

A large quantity of controlled and non-controlled chemicals is required to produce heroin from Afghanistan's opium crop – around 13,000 tons per year. None of these chemicals are produced in Afghanistan. They are diverted from licit channels in Europe, the Middle East and Asia, and then smuggled to Afghanistan. The most essential precursor chemical for producing heroin is acetic anhydride, of which an estimated 1,300 tons are required annually for that purpose in Afghanistan. Only 1 per cent of that quantity was seized in the country in 2008.

Precursors are trafficked across all Afghanistan's borders, but the southern and western borders are particularly targeted. Smuggling into Afghanistan takes place at the borders with the provinces of Nangarhar, Hilmand, Kandahar and Nimroz, which in many places are unmanned and not

monitored. Smuggling from the Islamic Republic of Iran takes place over its long borders with Afghanistan, particularly those with the provinces of Nimroz and Farah.

Regional distribution of opium poppy cultivation in Afghanistan (hectares (ha))

Region	2002 (ha)	2009 (ha)	Change 2002-2009 (ha)
Central	96	132	+36
East	21,909	593	-21,316
North	691	0	-691
North-east	9,054	557	-8,497
South	39,220	103,014	+63,794
West	3,076	18,800	+15,724
Total	**74,046**	**123,096**	**+49,050**

Opium poppy cultivation trends in Afghanistan, 2002-2009 (at province level)

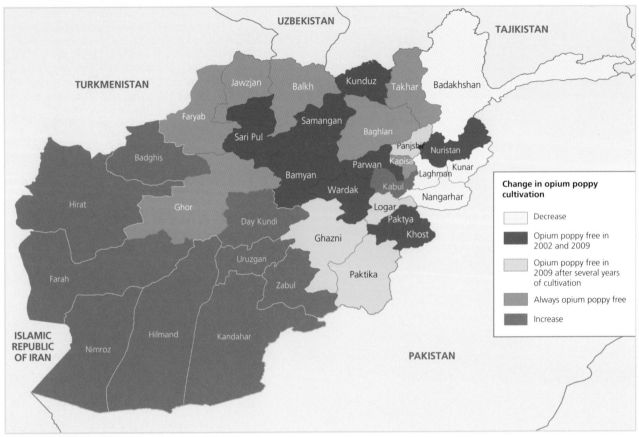

Source: Afghanistan opium surveys, 2002-2009, UNODC.

Opium poppy cultivation in Afghanistan, 2009 (at province level)

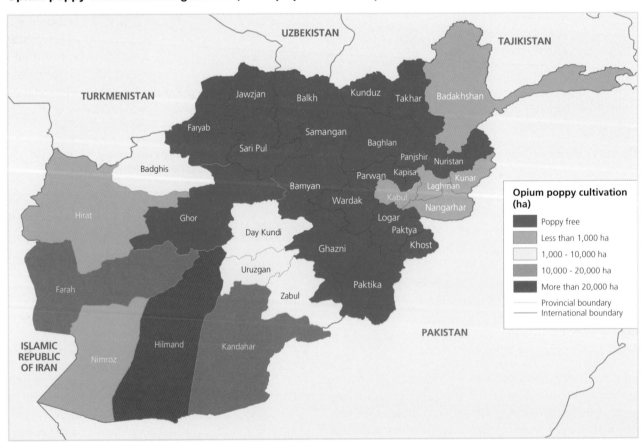

Source: Afghanistan opium survey, 2009, UNODC.

Number of insurgent attacks in Afghanistan, January 2003 - July 2009

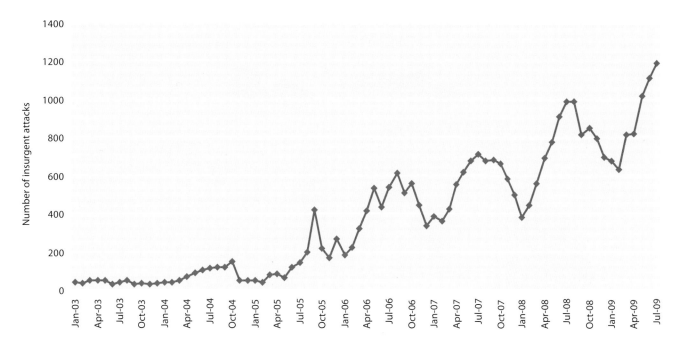

Source: United Nations Department of Safety and Security.

Prices for acetic anhydride have nearly tripled in Afghanistan in recent years. As a result, trafficking acetic anhydride is now more profitable than trafficking opium. It also carries less risk of interception since law enforcement officials are focused on opiates.

98 per cent of Afghan opium production is concentrated in the unstable South and West

In recent years, opium poppy cultivation in Afghanistan has been concentrated in the south-west of the country where government control is weakest. Regions of highest instability are also the regions of highest cultivation. Just five provinces account for 98 per cent of the country's entire opium output. In 2009, the southern province of Hilmand alone accounted for 60 per cent of all opium poppy grown in Afghanistan. Much of the rest of the country (20 provinces out of 34) has become poppy free.

2. To what extent is regional insurgency/instability fuelled by the Afghan opiate industry?

Instability in Afghanistan and the region has an impact on the narco-industry, and vice versa.

In the past, during the Soviet occupation of Afghanistan, opium was used as a source of funding for the *Mujahideen*. Later it helped fuel internecine warfare between the *Mujahideen* competing for political power. Between 1995 and 2000, the Taliban regime tolerated the drug trade and earned some US$ 75-100 million annually from taxing it. In the post-Taliban period, it was a source of revenue for warlords.

As the Taliban regrouped in the south of the country and

in the border region between Afghanistan and Pakistan, they resumed the levying of taxes on agriculture, including, crucially, opium cultivation. More recently, there is evidence that they are moving up the value added chain of the drug trade, linking up with criminal groups and reaping profits from drug production, trafficking, and the smuggling of precursor chemicals. There is growing evidence of the emergence of Afghan narco-cartels.

Since 2005, there has been a conspicuous increase in the number of security incidents in Afghanistan in parallel with the sharp rise in opium production. The nexus of drugs, crime, and insurgency has become stronger, also spilling over into neighbouring countries, particularly Pakistan. As a result, the transnational threat posed by Afghanistan's opium has become more acute.

The value of the world opiate market is estimated at US$ 65 billion per year

An estimated 11.3 million heroin users pay around US$ 56 billion to drug dealers every year. The value of the global opium market is estimated at around US$ 7 billion. Consequently, the combined opium/heroin market is worth some US$ 65 billion per year. This number is higher than the GDP of more than 120 countries in the world.

Europe represents the largest share of the global opiate market, with some US$ 20 billion, followed by the Russian Federation (US$ 13 billion) and the USA plus Canada (US$ 8 billion).

Much of the money generated by the global opiate trade is injected into the world's formal economies every year through the spread of money-laundering and the criminalization of legal assets. It also fills the coffers of international organized crime groups and finances insurgent and extremist groups active in conflict zones throughout the world. Nowhere is this synergy more evident than in Afghanistan where insurgents and drug traffickers have joined forces and presently control parts of the southern drug corridors into the Islamic Republic of Iran and Pakistan.

Global opiate market value (US$ 65 billion/year)

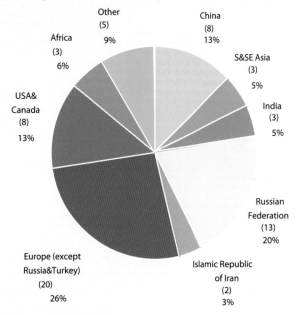

In Afghanistan, Taliban insurgents draw some US$ 125 million annually from the opium farmers and traders

Taliban insurgents in Afghanistan benefit from the drug trade at various points in the value chain and through several mechanisms. This research has focused on the traditional taxes levied in Taliban-held areas, as well as the transit and trade levies that derive from drug trafficking which have been applied fairly systematically across southern and western Afghanistan since 2005. Estimates of Taliban insurgents cumulated revenue from these over a four-year period (2005-2008) range from US$ 350-650 million in Afghanistan. This translates into an average annual income of US$ 125 million (range: 90-160) and excludes potential wages and taxes related to precursor importation and processing facilities, among others.

The funds generated from the drugs trade can pay for soldiers, weapons and protection, and are an important source of patronage.

Beyond the opiate economy, Taliban insurgents levy taxes on all forms of trade and agriculture. Although opiates are the highest-value drugs on the market, cannabis may also contribute to funding the insurgency.

The value of the opiate trade in Pakistan is estimated at US$ 1 billion annually, some of which likely goes to Pakistan-based insurgents

In Pakistan, the value of the Afghan opiate trade (including local consumption and transit trafficking to other countries) is estimated at around US$ 1 billion per year, with undetermined amounts going to insurgents active in the country. Despite the fact that it is a confirmed transit region for opiate flows out of Afghanistan, there were almost no seizures in Pakistan's Federally Administered Tribal Areas (FATA) bordering Afghanistan between 2002 and 2008. The twin insurgencies in Pakistan and Afghanistan are based all along the border between the two countries and FATA is a sanctuary for extremist/insurgent groups like the Pakistani Taliban, Al-Qaeda, and the Haqqani network. Much like in Afghanistan, Pakistan-based insurgents reportedly levy taxes on licit business and trade in this region (including supplies destined for the coalition) and there is growing evidence that this extends to the opiate trade.

The value of the European opiate market is at least 20 times bigger than that of Pakistan

With a figure of US$ 20 billion per year, the value of the Afghan opiate trade in Europe (Russia excluded) is no less than 20 times the value of the opiate trade in Pakistan (US$ 1 billion). The economic power accruing to criminal organizations running trafficking operations to Europe via the Balkan or the Northern routes dwarfs insurgents' benefits in Afghanistan and/or Pakistan. As a whole, Europe's stability is not threatened by the opiate trade, but the very large revenues they extract from the drug trade have given these groups the means to achieve considerable influence in some countries along trafficking routes.

Trans-border ties

Transnational organized crime groups, with kin on both sides of the same border, as well as a diaspora farther up the trafficking route, are also major players and beneficiaries of the illicit opiate trade.

The relation between the narcotics industry and the insurgency in southern Afghanistan is amplified by the role played by tribalism in both drug trafficking and insurgent networks. The strongest overlap between the insurgency, tribal networks and the drug trade is found in the southern and eastern parts of the country, and extends into Pakistan's tribal areas across the Afghan border. Since 2005, there has been a notable increase in insurgent activity and an extension of the area under insurgent control, particularly along the restive Pashtun tribal belt on the Afghanistan-Pakistan border.

Cross-border tribal links, for example among Baluchi and Pashtun groups, facilitate the drug trade. Most Afghanistan-based criminal groups appear to operate locally, but the existence of diasporas in transit or destination countries such as Pakistan, the Islamic Republic of Iran and Central Asia and further afield, for example the Gulf area, has allowed some trafficking organizations to expand their networks beyond the immediate region.

Pashtun tribes on the Afghanistan/Pakistan border

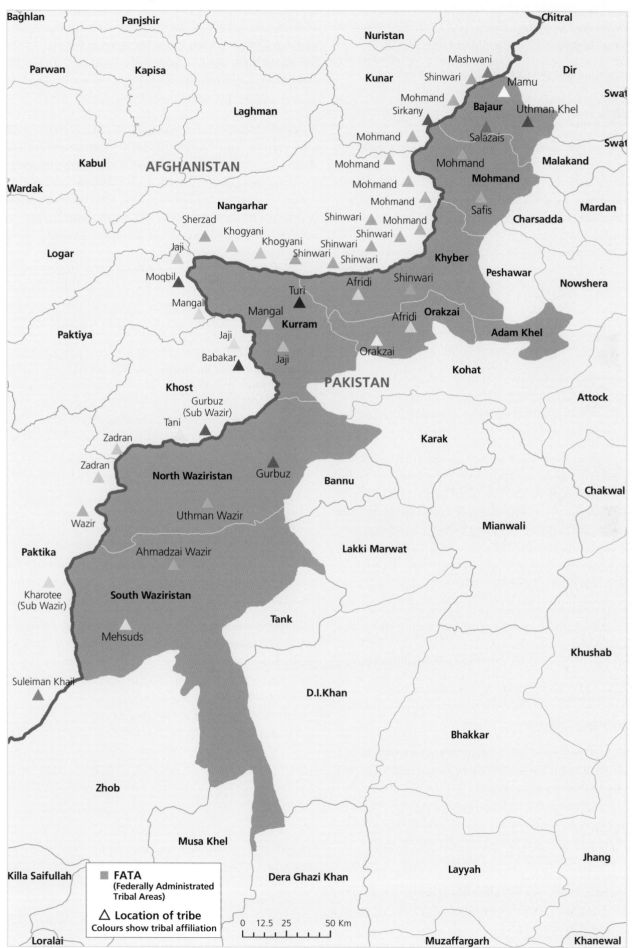

Source: UNODC and other sources.

Family and tribal connections also form the basis of the parallel or underground banking system known as Hawala, a system used by both traffickers and insurgent movements to move money world-wide without detection.

Corruption oils the links in the supply chain

Corruption oils the links in the opiate supply chain from Afghanistan to Europe and Asia.

At the source, in Afghanistan, corruption buys protection against eradication, facilitates illicit shipments, and guarantees impunity for drug traffickers. According to the World Bank, Afghanistan has been in the top 2 per cent of the most corrupt countries every year between 2002 and 2006. Corruption helps explain why, in 2008-2009, only 10,000 hectares of opium were eradicated in Afghanistan (around 4 per cent of the crop), less than 2 per cent of drugs were seized, and almost no major traffickers were brought to justice.

Corruption also undermines trust in public institutions and officials, and steals badly needed development assistance.

Average Afghans face corruption on a daily basis. In some areas in the south of the country, there is growing support for the Taliban, which is viewed as a solution to the prevailing corruption and crime.

The Afghan drug trade thrives against a background of economic hardship in Afghanistan and the broader region, but with conditions varying substantially between countries. In Afghanistan, despite six years of reconstruction and development assistance totalling billions of dollars, unemployment rates remain very high, a large proportion of the population still does not have access to basic services and 80 per cent of people have no electricity.

Poverty and economic stagnation are not only a catalyst for corruption; combined with weak governance and rule of law, they also drive ordinary citizens to take the risks associated with the production, processing and transportation of drugs. In Afghanistan, this combination of factors is also aiding insurgent recruitment.

Concluding remarks

Between 2002 and 2008, Afghan farmers earned a total of about US$ 6.4 billion from opium poppy cultivation, and Afghan traffickers approximately US$ 18 billion from local opiate processing and trading. During the same period, the transnational trade in Afghan opiates produced a total turnover of US$ 400-500 billion. Arrests figures suggest that around 1 million traffickers may be involved in bringing opiates to over 15 million opiate users across the world every year. The source of the trade is in Afghanistan, but its bulk takes place outside that country.

The last seven years have shown that extricating Afghanistan from the stranglehold of the opium economy is a long and gradual process, rife with setbacks and disappointments. The country may thus remain the world's primary illicit opium producer for the foreseeable future. At the same time, there has been tangible progress, for example in the increasing number of poppy-free provinces, decreasing opium poppy cultivation during the last two years, and greater regional counter-narcotics cooperation.

The difficulties in eliminating opium production in Afghanistan and the transnational threat posed by the Afghan opiate trade suggest that solutions cannot be found in Afghanistan alone. This is a shared responsibility that requires a multilateral response. That is why UNODC has launched a number of regional and international initiatives, such as the Paris Pact and the Rainbow Strategy. These efforts must be actively supported and expanded to continue strengthening a strategic response that is based on (a) a growing understanding of the patterns and dynamics of the transnational Afghan opiate trade, and (b) a targeted, sequenced and cost-effective mix of interventions.

This report is designed to contribute to that process. It also highlights the need for further research on:

- opiate demand, purity and prices;
- links between drugs, crime and insurgency in Afghanistan and Pakistan;
- international money flows connected to the Afghan opiate trade;
- transnational organized crime along the Balkan and Northern routes;
- growing penetration of Afghan opiates into East and South-East Asia;
- precursor chemical trafficking routes and procurement methods.

This research will enhance our understanding of the deadly flows of Afghan opiates and inform policies to protect public health and security among affected countries.

INTRODUCTION

In the framework of its Strategy for 2008-2011[1], UNODC has been developing monitoring and analysis programmes[2] for a number of priority transnational criminal markets and threats. With its severe consequences for crime, health, governance and security at the national, regional and international levels, the global trade in illicit Afghan opiates represents one of the biggest transnational drugs and crime threats the world has been facing over the last decade. Over the years, UNODC has undertaken a number of surveys and studies on various aspects of the issue, with a view to support countermeasures and initiatives at the national and international levels, such as the Paris Pact. To complement these efforts and to help place them in an analytical framework on the scale of this transnational problem, UNODC started, in September 2008, a programme to monitor and analyse the global trade in Afghan opiates and the threats it creates.

The main objectives of that programme are:

1) to gain a better understanding of the dimensions, patterns and dynamics of the global trade in Afghan opiates;

2) to identify and analyse its links with, and impact on, security and rule of law issues, including insurgency, organized crime, governance, corruption, money-laundering and other socio-economic issues; and

3) to provide analytical information that helps formulate strategic responses commensurate with the scale of the threat and aimed at dismantling the global Afghan opiate market.

This report presents the first findings of the programme.

As global opium production increasingly shifted from South-East Asia to Afghanistan during the last two decades, the global market share of Afghan opiates grew considerably. The Afghan opiate market now spans the globe and poses a threat for all the countries straddling trafficking routes as well as those hosting destination markets.

The social consequences of drug trafficking are devastating, particularly in states that lack resources to treat drug abusers and raise public awareness of the dangers associated with drug abuse, including HIV infection. Areas with high drug abuse rates are located along well-established opiate trafficking routes, from Afghanistan to destinations such as the Russian Federation or Western Europe. This is consistent with the idea that drug demand can be created through a "spill-over" effect along the supply chain. More than 60 per cent of all drug treatment demand in Asia and Europe is related to opiate abuse and a large number of drug-related deaths can be linked to the abuse of opiates produced in Afghanistan. Not only does drug addiction increase the spread of infectious diseases, it also leads to rising crime rates, can undermine public institutions and negatively impact national security.

There is a need to determine the magnitude of opiate flows into transit and destination countries in order to better respond to the threats. However, a number of basic facts about the supply and demand for Afghan opiates remain unknown, even for established trafficking routes and destinations, and new outlets seem to be emerging in Africa and China. This first report provides a comprehensive analysis of the global situation with regard to the Afghan opiate drug market, its size, flows and emerging patterns.

1   Strategy for the period 2008-2011 for the United Nations Office on Drugs and Crime (E/CN.7/2007/14).

2   These programmes are actually subprogrammes of a larger Trends Monitoring and Analysis Programme designed to implement results 2.1.1 and 2.1.2, in the result area Threat and Risk Analysis.

While thousands of tons of opiates (in opium equivalent) are trafficked out of Afghanistan, a comparable flow of precursor chemicals – crucial for processing opium into heroin – is smuggled into the country every year. The dynamics of precursor trafficking into and through Afghanistan are explored in section I, starting with an overview of suspected precursor trafficking routes on the basis of official seizure information, and detailing interactions across Afghanistan's borders.

The opium economy in Afghanistan is a relatively recent phenomenon that grew out of the civil war and the resistance against the Soviet Union military intervention in 1979. For many years, opium income was used to finance the war efforts against the Soviet troops in Afghanistan. Later on, it helped fuel internecine warfare between the seven largest *Mujahedin* groups, which started competing for political power. The Taliban regime that followed tolerated the drug trade and earned some US$ 75-100 million annually from taxing it between 1995 and 2000.[3] After the dramatic drop in poppy cultivation and the fall of the Taliban regime in 2001, the new Afghan government promptly prohibited opium production, but was not able to stop the resumption and growth of the opiate trade in Afghanistan.

The first part also looks at the source of the threat, opium poppy cultivation in Afghanistan. It provides an overview of the scale of the problem and analyses trends in Afghan opium production between 2000-2009.

Links between international drug trafficking, organized crime, money-laundering and politically-motivated violence have been directly related to the Afghan narcotics industry. The value of the global opiate market is around US$ 65 billion per year. This trade incorporates a combination of indigenous/national, regional and international actors. Transnational organized crime groups are the main beneficiaries of this trade, which they supplement with other forms of crime such as arms trafficking and human smuggling. Insurgency groups in countries straddling drug routes from Afghanistan to destination countries have also become important financial beneficiaries and facilitators of the opium economy. Groups based in Afghanistan, Pakistan or Central Asia may gain access to only a fraction of the value of Afghan opiate exports, but this is still enough to support logistics, operations and recruitment.

The substantial increases in insurgent visibility and mobilization since 2005 coincide spatially and temporally with the concentration of opium production in the south. The continued concentration of poppies and processing in the south are good illustrations of links between insurgents and the drug trade. However, as opium poppy cultivation concentrates in the south, insecurity increasingly does not, spreading outward to areas that were previously stable, such as parts of north and north-west Afghanistan.

The second part of the report examines the regional implications of the trafficking of Afghan opiates and associated transnational threats, particularly insurgencies in Afghanistan, but also across the border in Pakistan. Based on fieldwork, official data and open sources, it analyses the views of analysts and law enforcement officials in Afghanistan and Pakistan.

All actors involved in destabilizing Afghanistan are directly or indirectly linked to the drug economy. For its part, the Taliban-led insurgency is content to reap dividends from the drug economy to finance war expenditures. Their ability to provide protection to farmers and traffickers (preventing interdiction and eradication efforts) delegitimizes the national government as it links them with cultivators' livelihoods, thereby (re)consolidating political influence in areas under their control.

For all the threats, ethnic and tribal links are important contextual factors. There is evidence that these facilitate smuggling and the movement of militants across Afghanistan's porous borders. They may also widen the pool of potential recruits or sympathizers for both organized crime and insurgency. There also appears to be a link between opium cultivation, the shape of organized criminal networks and tribal identities; a link which is also analysed in the second part of the report.

The Afghan opiate trade represents a transnational threat, not only for countries on drug trafficking routes and final destinations, but also as a factor of international insecurity. Complementing other analytical efforts on the Afghan opiate trade, it is hoped that this report will help shed light on the scope and main characteristics of the global Afghan opiate trade and its security implications, regionally and internationally.

Remarks on data sources and limitations

This report is a synthesis of information from a variety of sources, including information provided by Member States and the World Customs Organization (WCO), fieldwork undertaken in Afghanistan and neighbouring countries in 2008-2009, as well as data from secondary literature and expert opinion, including law enforcement and government officials. To obtain background information on the insurgency and suspected drug and precursor routes, the researchers interviewed headquarters and field officials of Afghan Customs, the Afghan Border Police, the Counter Narcotics Police of Afghanistan, the Ministry of Counter Narcotics of Afghanistan, the Anti Narcotics Force of Pakistan and officials from various United Nations agencies and diplomatic missions, along with a number of other key informants.

Estimating the scope of the global flow of Afghan opiates requires data on global opium/heroin demand. The lack of systematic statistics hinders comprehensive assessments of the extent of opiate abuse. For the purpose of this report,

---

3   Kimberly L. Thachuk, Transnational Threats: smuggling and trafficking in arms, drugs, and human life, Praeger, 2007.

opium/heroin demand was calculated on the basis of prevalence data provided in UNODC *World Drug Reports* and compared with global opium production data.

Global heroin and opium seizures were used to identify heroin/opium trafficking routes, and to help estimate the size of the heroin/opium flows in each country. For that purpose, UNODC Individual Drug Seizure and World Customs Organization databases for the years 2000-2008 were used. In addition to the seizure data, information was drawn from official country reports such as ARQ (Annual Report Questionnaire) responses provided to UNODC.

Available demand data was used as the key variable to estimate the size of the heroin/opium flows in the world. The robustness of demand data varies from region to region and country to country and are subject to revisions and changes. Most countries still lack structured or organized data collection systems capable of producing scientifically sound demand, supply and seizure statistics. Accordingly, the statistics and estimates provided on heroin/opium demand and opiate flows should be viewed as work in progress and the best current approximations, given the available data.

The annual profit of the Afghan Taliban from opiate trade was calculated on a combination of quantitative data from survey results (UNODC Afghan opium surveys) and qualitative information. These estimations are subject to change as additional data and information become available.

1. THE OPIATE TRADE

A. GLOBAL DIMENSIONS AND FLOWS

1. Overall magnitude of the problem

Opium is the source material for the manufacture of morphine and heroin, and more than 90 per cent of the world's heroin is manufactured from opium produced in Afghanistan.

Opiates are trafficked from Afghanistan to destinations worldwide via routes flowing into and through the neighbouring countries of Pakistan, the Islamic Republic of Iran, and the Central Asian countries of Tajikistan, Uzbekistan and Turkmenistan. The implications of the opiate trade for Afghanistan and the world are grave and far-reaching. The Afghan opiate trade fuels opiate consumption and addiction in countries along drug trafficking routes before reaching the main consumer markets in Europe (estimated at 3.1 million heroin users), contributing to the spread of HIV/AIDS and other blood-borne diseases.

As most production and processing occurs in the south and west of Afghanistan, greater proportions of heroin are smuggled into the Islamic Republic of Iran (105 tons) and Pakistan (150 tons) than through Central Asia (95 tons). The Islamic Republic of Iran also receives an additional 35 tons of Afghan heroin from Pakistan. A portion of the heroin trafficked into Iran is distributed domestically (14 tons), but the bulk travels onward to Europe and the Middle East. In Pakistan, opiate traffickers operate routes to Iran, China, India and throughout Asia, but also to North America, Europe and other destinations. As in Iran, a significant domestic market absorbs a portion of the heroin trafficked through Pakistan (20 tons). The third opiate gateway out of Afghanistan is Central Asia, also known as the northern route. This route emerged relatively recently following the break-up of the Soviet Union. It handles around 25 per cent of Afghanistan's heroin, the majority of which is destined for the Russian Federation. The markets in Pakistan and Iran are larger than the market of Central Asia, where users consume some 12 tons of heroin per year.

Beyond the main traditional opiate markets of Europe, there are strong indications that Afghan opiates are affecting various countries in the Middle East, Africa, South and South-East Asia and even in the Pacific region. Before 2002, Myanmar and the Lao People's Democratic Republic were the main heroin suppliers for many of these markets. Following the sharp decrease in opium production in Myanmar and Laos, Afghanistan took over.

China, a huge market which traditionally sourced its heroin exclusively from Myanmar, is now a destination country for Afghan opiates. Significant amounts of Afghan opiates are assumed to be trafficked to India, but the scale of the flow remains unclear.

As the following sections of this report indicate, Afghanistan's production more than satisfies global demand. Since 2006, the average opium production stands at around 7,200 tons in Afghanistan (7,900 tons worldwide). As there is no indication of a dramatic increase in global heroin consumption, this amount far exceeds total global demand, to the extent that another 16 million drug users would be needed to absorb it. Thus, even if opiate production in Afghanistan were to cease immediately, there would still be ample supply. It is estimated that opiate stocks equivalent to more than two years' global supply are currently stored in Afghanistan and possibly also in transit and destination countries.

Afghan opiates have become a truly global commodity; one which doubles as a transnational threat to international security and global health.

2. Demand and supply

Heroin demand

There are an estimated 11.3 million heroin users in the world. Of this, four million are estimated to live in South and South-East Asia and Oceania. The majority of these users reside in China (2.2 million) and India (0.81 million), and use heroin produced mainly in Myanmar.

The countries or regions in which mainly Afghan heroin is used host approximately 7.2 million heroin users. In Europe, the main destination for Afghan heroin, there are 3.1 million heroin users. Within Europe, the Russian Federation accounts for 1.5 million users, while the remaining 1.6 million users are distributed among other European countries. There are currently 1.5 million heroin users in the Americas. While some Afghan heroin is trafficked to the USA and Canada (1.3 million users), Afghan heroin is not currently being trafficked to Latin America, where the number of heroin users is estimated at approximately 0.2 million. The number of heroin users in Africa seems to have been increasing since 2004 (0.8 million), reaching 1.23 million in 2007.

Table 1 gives the estimated level of regional heroin consumption per user per year, as reported in the UNODC 2005 *World Drug Report*. While these estimates are the best currently available, one has to be aware that they are not based on direct research. This reflects the absence - for most countries - of any structured or organized data collection system to arrive at scientifically sound per capita consumption estimates. Therefore, heroin consumption estimates should be treated with caution.

Other limitations with the available data complicate an understanding of the situation at the retail level or with regard to wholesale heroin purity. All calculations and trend observations in this section are drawn from the data available to UNODC as well as other sources such as country reports[1] and individual studies.

In addition to the above findings, there are a few other country studies on heroin consumption and purity:

Pakistan

There remain significant data limitations and methodological concerns with regard to consumption estimates for Pakistan.[2] In line with the UNODC 2005 *World Drug*

Table 1: Average heroin consumption per user per year (pure heroin)

Region	Consumption (gram)
East Africa	24.2
North Africa	28.0
South Africa	11.5
West&Central Africa	17.0
Caribbean	13.5
Central America	25.2
North America	17.0
South America	10.0
East&South-East Asia	25.2
Near&Middle East/ South West Asia	25.2
South Asia	19.8
East Europe	33.3
West&Central Europe	57.9
South-East Europe	30.6
Oceania	56.5

Source: UNODC

Report and country studies from Afghanistan and the Islamic Republic of Iran, the regional average pure heroin consumption rate of 35 grams was used per user per year for Pakistan. However, in order to broaden our understanding of heroin consumption levels in Pakistan, more information, including on heroin purity at the street level, should be collected and monitored.

Central Asia

UNODC's Regional Office for Central Asia conducted a similar study of selected drug treatment centres in 2008. According to this data, the average heroin consumption per user is 1-1.5 gram per day. The cost of one gram of high-quality heroin (around 70 per cent purity) is around US$ 10-15 in Central Asia. But the typical cost for one gram of heroin ranges from US$ 1.5 – 2 at street level. Hence, this would indicate that street level heroin purity is between 7-10 per cent ([1.5/15] * 70) in Central Asia. Based on daily consumption (1-1.5 grams per day), the total annual heroin consumption per user is estimated at 365-550 grams (at 7-10 per cent purity) per year, the equivalent of 25-55 grams (midpoint 40 grams) of pure heroin.

---

1   Annual Reports Questionnaire (ARQ).

2   In 2007, UNODC implemented a small survey of treatment centres in Pakistan to determine the average opiate user profile. According to this survey, heroin users in Pakistan consume an average of 1 gram per day and some 365 grams annually (purity levels were unavailable). The average retail price for

heroin was recorded at US$ 2 per gram. The price per gram of high-quality heroin (around 70 per cent purity) is around US$ 5 in the Peshawar region, bordering Afghanistan. The purity of retail heroin in Pakistan can thereby be estimated at a maximum of 25-30 per cent ([2/5] * 70). Based on this, the average pure heroin consumption per user is estimated at around 150 grams ([2/5]*365) annually, which is very high compared to other consumer markets such as Europe (57.9 grams per year).

Table 2: Estimated number of heroin/opium users and opiate consumption in the world, 2008

	Region/country	Heroin users	Opium users	Heroin consumption (tons)	Opium consumption (tons)	Total opiate consumption (tons of opium equivalent)
Major distribution destinations of Myanmar and Laos heroin production	Myanmar	66,000	67,000	1.3	7.0	20.1
	China	2,254,000	119,000	45.0	12.0	458.2
	India	871,000	674,000	17.0	67.0	239.8
	Oceania	32,500	52,000	2.0	5.0	23.4
	Asia (except India, China, Myanmar)	852,000	1,118,500	17.0	75.0	245.0
	Sub total	4,075,500	2,030,500	82	166	986.6
Major distribution destinations of Afghan heroin	Afghanistan	47,000	146,000	2.0	80.0	91.8
	Pakistan	547,000	145,000	19.0	80.0	213.8
	Iran (I. R. of)	391,000	531,000	14.0	450.0	547.0
	Central Asia	283,000	60,000	11.0	33.0	112.2
	Russia	1,490,000	166,000	70.0	58.0	548.6
	Turkey	25,000	25,000	0.8	9.0	14.4
	Europe (except Turkey and Russia	1,614,000	271,000	88.0	95.0	711.0
	Americas	1,538,000	82,000	26.0	29.0	212.0
	Middle East and South Asia (except Iran, Pakistan and Afghanistan)	63,500	491,000	1.6	16.0	27.2
	Africa	1,240,000	172,000	25.0	60.0	235.0
	Sub total	7,238,500	2,089,000	257	910	2,713
	Total	**11,314,000**	**4,119,500**	**340**	**1,075**	**3,700**

Source: UNODC *World Drug Reports.*

Russian Federation

UNODC's Russian Federation country office and the National Research Center on Drug Addiction (NRC) of the Federal Agency on Health and Social Development implemented a survey on drug treatment centres to understand the average heroin consumption per day per user in 2009. According to the survey results, average heroin consumption per user per day is around 1.87 gram with 5 per cent purity[3] or 0.13 gram of pure heroin (70 per cent) per day per user.

The regional average figures presented in table 1 were used for countries where average heroin consumption and purity levels were not available. Data on specific purity levels and heroin consumption rates are required to fill those gaps and better assess the level of drug consumption in a given country.

Total estimated heroin/opium consumption in the world

Total global heroin consumption is estimated at 340 tons while opium consumption stands at some 1,080 tons per year.

Table 2 shows the number of opiate users in major production, transit and destination countries/regions. The number of opiate users is further divided into two groups corresponding to the two main opiate supply sources in South-East Asia (Myanmar and the Lao People's Democratic Republic) and South-West Asia (Afghanistan).

Figures 1 and 2 illustrate the distribution of heroin users and heroin consumption in the world. The percentage distribution of heroin users and heroin consumption for countries/regions are nearly identical. The exception is Europe which has the highest consumption rates per user at 50-52 grams/year while in other regions it is around 20-40 grams/year.

3   The typical price for one gram of heroin (5 per cent purity) is US$ 37.

**Fig. 1:   Heroin users in the world, 2008
(share of countries/regions)**

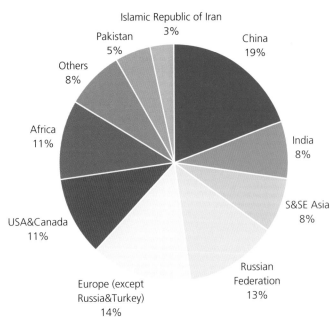

Source: UNODC.

**Fig. 2:   Global heroin consumption, 2008
(share of countries/regions)**

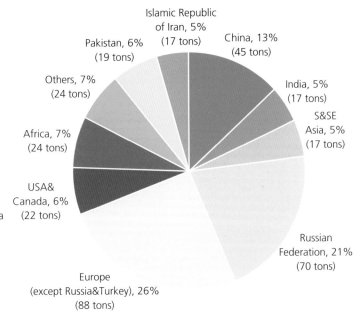

Source: UNODC.

Heroin users in Europe (excluding Russia) account for 26 per cent of total global heroin consumption. Russian users rank second with 21 per cent, while Chinese users follow with 13 per cent. Heroin consumption and the number of heroin users in Africa have reportedly been increasing since 2004, and African users may now consume 7 per cent of the heroin on the market. Pakistani users consume 6 per cent and Indian, South and South-East Asian, and Iranian users 5 per cent each of total consumption.

Opium demand

Global opium demand is estimated at 4 million users consuming 1,000-1,100 tons of opium per year. 16 per cent of users are in India, 13 per cent are in the Islamic Republic of Iran, and 29 per cent are in other East, South and South-East Asian countries. Around 7 per cent of the opium users are in European countries (the Russian Federation and Turkey not included).

Opium users in East, South and South-East Asia (excluding India and Myanmar) consume around 75 tons of opium annually. All the opium for these subregions is supplied from Myanmar or sourced from local production.

According to official reports[4] provided by the Indian Government, heroin flows to India from Myanmar, Pakistan and Afghanistan. However, there is no reported raw opium trafficking to India from these or any other countries. This could indicate that all the opium required to meet India's demand (67 tons/year) might be converted from licit opium cultivation in India itself. To produce this amount of opium, at least 1,300 ha of opium poppy (the average opium yield per hectare in India is 58-62 kilograms) are required. In

2007, around 6,000 hectares were under licensed opium poppy cultivation in India. Either 20 per cent of the licit production is diverted into the illicit market or there is illicit opium poppy cultivation in India. If neither of these hypotheses is correct, then the drug abuse survey results provided by the Indian Government to UNODC should be reviewed or the methodology reassessed.

The annual opiate prevalence rate for the Islamic Republic of Iran is 2.8 per cent, indicating some 1.36 million opiate users (heroin = 390,000, opium = 530,000 and other opiates = 440,000) in that country. According to the *Drug Control in 2008* report from the Islamic Republic of Iran, the average opium consumption per user per month is 74 grams, which amounts to an annual consumption of 451 tons of opium. Thus, it is estimated that Iran accounts for 42 per cent of global opium consumption.

While most of Iran's opium seizures took place in the Kerman, Khorasan, Isfahan, Fars and Yazd provinces between 2005-2007, seizures occur in almost all provinces. This indicates that opium consumption is widespread in the country.

In Africa, an estimated 170,000 opium users consume some 60 tons of opium (mainly in Egypt) per year. However, given that neither UNODC nor World Customs Organization (WCO) seizure data indicate opium trafficking to Africa from any other region, it has to be assumed that the source of much of the opium is local production. Some 2,000 – 5,000 ha of opium poppy cultivation are needed to generate 60 tons of opium, depending on yield.

With regard to Egypt, national authorities have expressed doubts that the national data, shown in the 2005/06 house-

4   Annual Reports Questionnaire (ARQ).

Fig. 3: **Opium users in the world, 2008 (share of countries/regions)**

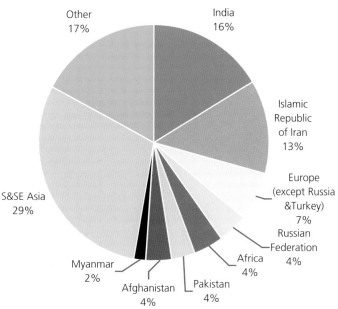

Source: UNODC.

Fig. 4: **Global opium consumption, 2008 (share of countries/regions)**

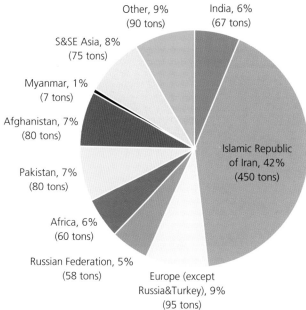

Source: UNODC.

hold survey of Egypt[5] were a fair reflection of the extent of opiate use in this country.[6] As a result of the survey methodology, it cannot be excluded that the positive responses included persons who used to experiment with opiates in the past, but are no longer involved with opiates use. Out of the total number of drug users (all drugs), 75 per cent consumed drugs regularly or were dependent drug users, whereas 25 per cent used them 'for trial and amusement' purposes. Applying the 75 per cent ratio, the prevalence of opium consumption could fall to 0.4 per cent. Extrapolating results from a national student survey in Egypt[7] (out of 18,349 students interviewed, 48 reported lifetime use of opium and 15 of heroin, that is, 0.3 and 0.1 per cent, respectively) to the national level would result in far lower annual prevalence rates of opiate use among the general population (0.14 per cent, including 0.1 per cent using opium). Based on the latter results, total opium consumption would amount to some 12 tons, equivalent to 400-1,000 ha under poppy cultivation. Due to the big difference between these two estimates, opium consumption in Egypt should be studied more closely. The main conclusion, however, is that illegal opium poppy cultivation is taking place in Egypt.

Opium production

Between 1990 and 2005, the total quantity of opium produced globally was more or less stable at 4,000-5,000 tons. During that period, it exceeded 5,000 tons only twice: in 1994 and again in 1999. Since 2006, a production level at around 8,000 tons has remained well above the 5,000 ton mark, as a result of the massive increase in opium production in Afghanistan.

Production in Afghanistan increased from around 200 tons in 1980 to 3,300 tons in 2000, reaching a peak of 8,200 tons in 2007 before dropping slightly to 7,700 tons in 2008, and to 6,900 in 2009. Expressed as a proportion of the global illicit opium production, Afghanistan's share rose from around 20 per cent in 1980 to 70 per cent in 2000, and to more than 90 per cent since 2006.

Since 1996, while opium poppy cultivation has decreased in South-East Asia (Myanmar and Lao People's Democratic Republic), Afghanistan has filled and over-compensated for the production gap left by Myanmar in the global opiates market.

To calculate the potential amount of opium/heroin production between 1995 and 2008, for Afghan opium, a conversion ratio of 7:1 was used, and for Myanmar and Laos, of 10:1.[8]

5   National Centre for Social and Criminal Research, Prof. Imad Hamdi Ghaz and Fund for the Control and Treatment of Addiction and Abuse, *National Study of Addiction, Prevalence of the Use of Drugs and Alcohols in Egypt (2005-2006)*.

6   275 opiate users out of 40,083 persons interviewed, equivalent to a prevalence rate of 0.7 per cent, of which some three quarters used opium, according to a breakdown found in student surveys.

7   National Council for the Control and Treatment of Addiction, Fund for the Control and Treatment of Addiction and Abuse, Prof. Jumaa Yousuf, *Use of Neuroactive Substances among University Students, Preliminary Indicators,* Cairo 2007.

8   The details of the method used to estimate the amount of opium converted into heroin is given later in this chapter.

Fig. 5: Global potential opium production in Afghanistan, South-East Asia and the rest of the world, 1990-2009

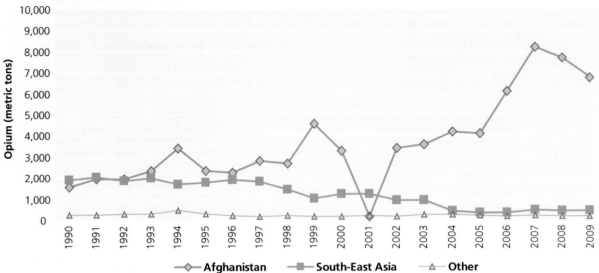

Source: UNODC *World Drug Report* (figure for 2009 based on 2009 Survey results for Afghanistan and 2008 data for the rest of the world).

Fig. 6: Global potential opium production, 1980-2009

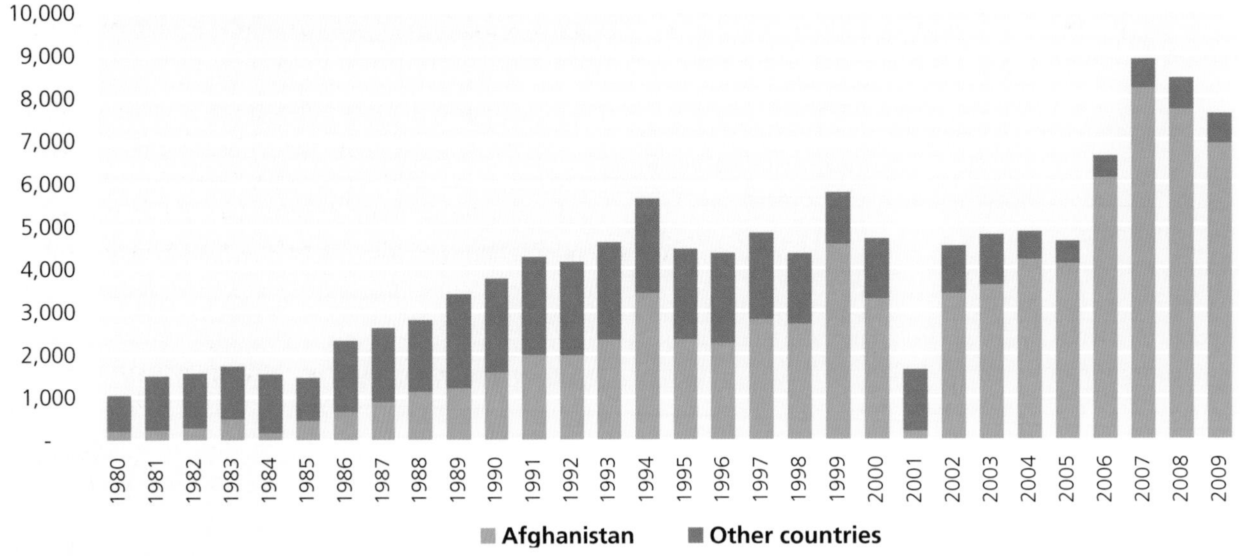

Source: UNODC *World Drug Report* (figure for 2009 based on 2009 Survey results for Afghanistan and 2008 data for the rest of the world).

Table 3: Average annual opium production for the periods 1990-2005, 2002-2005 and 2006-2009

	Average opium production, 1990-2005 (tons)	Average opium production, 2002-2005 (tons)	Average opium production, 2006-2009 (tons)
Afghanistan	2,966	3,825	7,333
South-East Asia	1,429	655	405
Other countries	246	214	184
World total	4,641	4,693	7,922

Table 4: Average annual potential opium/heroin production in the world, 1995-2005

	Afghanistan	Myanmar & Laos	Other	Total
Average opium production (tons)	3,300	1,200	210	4,710
Average amount of opium converted into heroin (tons)	2,315	1,107	160	3,422
Average amount of opium exported as raw opium (tons)	985	93	50	1,078
Amount of heroin produced (tons)	331	111	16	457

Opiate consumption vs. supply

In theory, the increase in supply should be matched by a corresponding rise in demand. However, global demand for heroin has been largely stable in recent years. There is neither data to suggest a sudden increase in the number of heroin users worldwide, nor significant changes in prices or purity levels.

Heroin retail prices have been stable since 2000, with no major changes observed in Europe. Likewise, there are no indications of a dramatic increase in the purity of the heroin seized worldwide – which would be an indication of improved supply – during the same period.

Fig. 7: **Heroin retail prices in Europe (US$), 1990-2006**

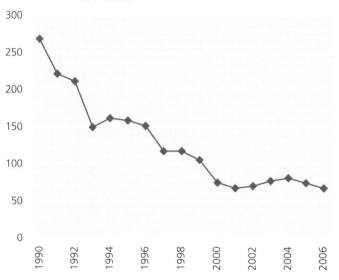

Total global heroin and opium consumption in opium equivalent is estimated at 3,700 tons per year. Between 1995 and 2005, the average total opium production was 4,700 tons, which would yield an average of 460 tons of heroin and 1,100 tons of opium annually. Between 2002 and 2008, average annual seizures were 90-95 tons of heroin and some 250 tons of opium. Annually, the total amount of opiate seizures, in opium equivalent, was thus 1,000-1,100 tons. This indicates that 4,700-5,000 tons of annual opium production are enough to meet global heroin and opium demand (including seizures).

Between 2006 and 2009, the average annual global opium production was around 7,900 tons. This means that a surplus of almost 12,000 tons of opium was produced between 2006 and 2009, an amount equal to approximately 2.5 years of global heroin consumption. The surplus accumulated since 2006 may have been stockpiled anywhere between the production point (Afghanistan) and destination countries.

Table 5 shows the average opium production in Myanmar and the Lao People's Democratic Republic for the period 2002-2008. Based on estimates of heroin production in

Estimates of opiate stockpiles for the period 2006-2009*:

- Total global opium production: 31,000 tons.

- Total global opiate demand and seizures (in opium equivalent): 19,000 tons

- Total opium surplus:
  31,000 – 19,000 = 12,000 tons

* Figure for 2009 based on 2009 Survey results for Afghanistan and 2008 data for the rest of the world.

these countries, 540 tons of opium yield around 50 tons of heroin along with 40 tons of raw opium. Total heroin demand per year in South and South-East Asia and Oceania amounts to 80-85 tons. Since the average amount of heroin seized in those regions is approximately 10 tons per year, a total of 90-95 tons of heroin is needed in those regions each year. In order to meet this high demand, 40 tons of Afghan heroin – in addition to the heroin produced in Myanmar and Laos – is needed per year.

The total estimated opium demand is around 1,000 tons per year and total average opium seizures per year amount to 200-250 tons. With 4,700 tons of opium (average opium production in the world between 2002-2005), it is possible to satisfy global demand for both heroin and opium (including seizures).

Table 5: **Average annual opium production in Myanmar and Laos in 2002-2008**

	Myanmar	Laos	Total
Average opium production (tons)	500	50	550
Average amount of opium converted into heroin (tons)	460	46	506
Average amount of opium exported as raw opium (tons)	40	4	44
Amount of heroin produced (tons)	46	5	51

3. Opiate seizures

The table below shows the amount of heroin, morphine and opium seized in the world between 1996 and 2006. At the time of writing, seizure statistics for 2007 and 2008 were under quality control review. For some countries, there is no seizure information for years prior to 1996.

Between 1996 and 2006, global heroin seizures increased by 88 per cent. Opium seizures increased by 116 per cent and morphine seizures saw the largest increase of 279 per cent. During the same period, 22 per cent of the global opium production was intercepted on average.

Table 6:   Global opiate seizures, 1996-2006

	1996	1997	1998	1999	2000	2001	2002	2003	2004	2005	2006	% Change 1996-2006	Average
World total opium production (tons)	4,355	4,823	4,346	5,764	4,691	1,630	4,520	4,783	4,850	4,620	6,610	+52%	4,636
Total heroin seizures (tons)	29	33	32	36	54	54	49	54	61	58	54	+88%	47
Total morphine seizures (tons)	12	20	23	24	27	11	25	44	39	32	45	+279%	27
Total opium seizures (tons)	174	196	179	239	213	106	97	133	212	342	376	+116%	206
% of heroin seizures (in opium equivalent) in total opium production	6.5%	6.9%	7.4%	6.3%	11.5%	33.2%	10.8%	11.3%	12.6%	12.6%	8.1%		11.6%
% of total opium production seized as morphine (in opium equivalent)	2.7%	4.2%	5.4%	4.1%	5.7%	7.0%	5.5%	9.1%	8.1%	6.9%	6.9%		6.0%
% of total opium production seized as opium	4.0%	4.1%	4.1%	4.1%	4.5%	6.5%	2.1%	2.8%	4.4%	7.4%	5.7%		4.5%
% of total opium production seized as opiate (in opium equivalent)	13.3%	15.2%	17.0%	14.5%	21.8%	46.7%	18.4%	23.2%	25.0%	27.0%	20.7%		22.1%

Fig. 8:   Global opiate seizure trends, 1996-2006

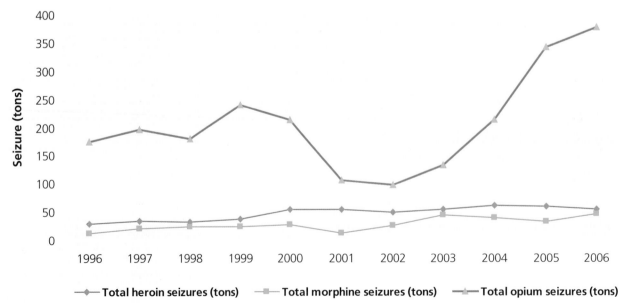

Source: UNODC.

Fig. 9: Distribution of heroin seizures in the world, 2006

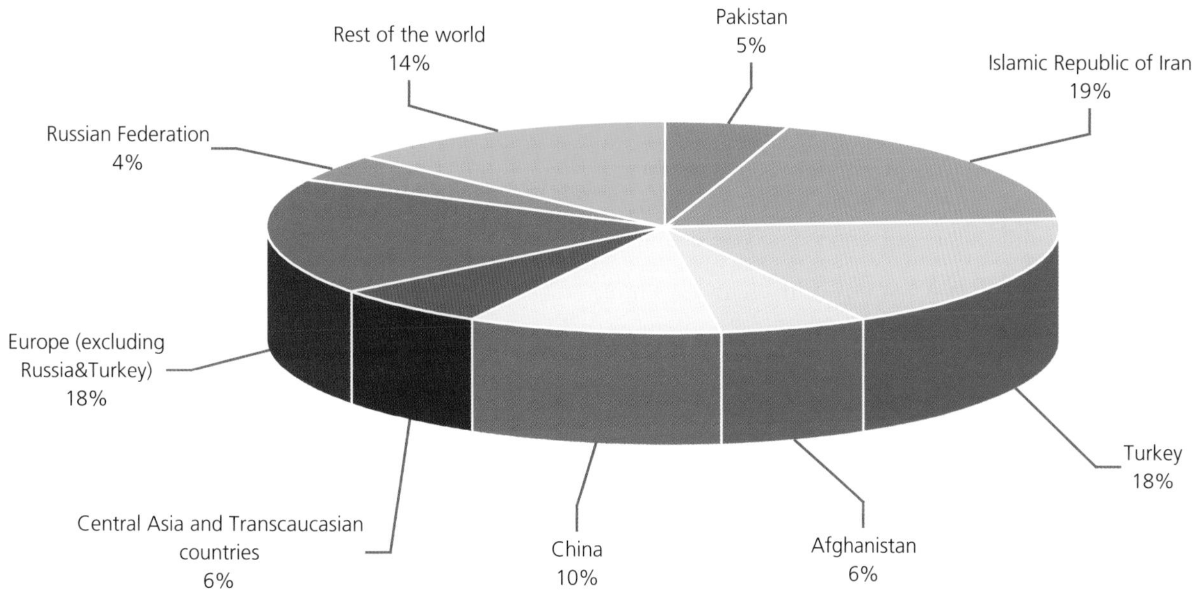

Pakistan 5%
Islamic Republic of Iran 19%
Rest of the world 14%
Russian Federation 4%
Europe (excluding Russia&Turkey) 18%
Central Asia and Transcaucasian countries 6%
China 10%
Afghanistan 6%
Turkey 18%

Source: UNODC.

Heroin seizures

In 2006, almost half of global heroin seizures took place in three countries: The Islamic Republic of Iran, Turkey and China.

One well-known heroin trafficking route to West and Central Europe runs from Afghanistan via the Islamic Republic of Iran, Turkey and South-East European countries (Bulgaria, Greece, Albania, Romania, Serbia, the former Yugoslav Republic of Macedonia and Croatia). Known as the Balkan Route, it represents the shortest route to the lucrative European markets. Between 1996 and 2006, as opium production increased in Afghanistan, commensurate increases in heroin seizures were observed in the Russian Federation (13,483 per cent), Central Asia and Transcaucasian countries (2,461 per cent), Iran (1,225 per cent), Turkey (133 per cent) and Europe (51 per cent).

In stark contrast, and although Pakistan borders Afghanistan and is an important destination and transit country for Afghan heroin, Pakistan's heroin seizures decreased by 52

Table 7: Countries/regions seizing significant quantities of heroin (kg), 1996-2006

Country/ Region	1996	1997	1998	1999	2000	2001	2002	2003	2004	2005	2006	% change between 1996-2006
Pakistan	5,872	6,156	3,364	4,974	9,492	6,931	5,870	6,364	3,488	2,144	2,821	-52%
Iran (I. R. of)	805	1,986	2,894	6,030	6,189	4,001	3,977	3,327	4,715	5,554	10,663	+1,225%
Turkey	4,422	3,506	4,651	3,862	6,338	3,999	2,583	4,705	8,847	8,195	10,312	+133%
Afghanistan						N/A	1,292	815	2,388	7,771	3,600	N/A
China	4,347	5,477	7,358	5,364	6,281	13,200	9,291	9,530	10,836	8,936	5,800	+33%
Central Asia and Trans-caucasian countries	144	2,126	1,076	1,361	3,251	5,154	4,708	6,827	6,310	3,883	3,688	+2,461%
Europe (excluding Turkey & Russia)	6,764	7,017	7,227	8,309	13,911	12,375	10,620	10,071	11,101	9,188	10,191	+51%
Russian Fed.	18	24	443	695	984	1,287	842	3,248	3,897	4,676	2,445	+13,483%
Rest of the world	6,136	7,056	5,304	5,634	7,687	7,199	10,909	9,788	11,719	15,844	7,737	+26%
Total	28,508	33,348	32,317	36,229	54,133	54,147	48,800	53,860	60,913	58,419	53,658	+88%

per cent between 1996 and 2006. It appears that in Pakistan, heroin seizures are inversely proportional to supply trends in Afghanistan.

In 2006, the Islamic Republic of Iran and Turkey seized some 10 tons of heroin each. In contrast, Turkey's neighbours, Bulgaria (700 kg) and Greece (300 kg), together only seized one ton of heroin that same year, despite the fact that most of the heroin that flows from Turkey to Europe passes through Bulgaria and to a lesser extent Greece.

Particularly after the year 2000, heroin seizures have sharply increased in the Russian Federation, reflecting rising levels of opium production and opiate trafficking from Afghanistan. Similar increases were not seen in countries bordering Russia, however. In 2006, approximately 170 kg of heroin were seized in Belarus, Ukraine, Latvia, Finland, Norway and Estonia, whereas 2,400 kg of heroin were seized in Russia. This may be an indication of limited heroin trafficking from Russia to Europe via those countries, bearing in mind that the majority of heroin trafficked to Russia is consumed domestically.

In the Middle East, between 1996 and 2006, heroin seizures sharply increased in Qatar (from 3 to 722 kg) and the United Arab Emirates (21.6 kg to 533 kg). This may indicate increases in heroin trafficking to this region and/or more effective law enforcement.

The decrease in opium production in Myanmar was accompanied by a decrease in heroin seizures there. The total amount of heroin seized was 500 kg in 1996, but decreased to 190 kg in 2006. Similar patterns were observed in countries bordering Myanmar, such as Thailand and the Lao People's Democratic Republic.

Morphine seizures

Pakistan (72 per cent) and the Islamic Republic of Iran (23 per cent) accounted for 95 per cent of global morphine seizures in 2006. In Pakistan, morphine seizures have been steadily increasing, reaching more than 32 tons in 2006.

In Pakistan, the vast majority of morphine continues to be seized in Balochistan province (Chagai district), close to the border with Afghanistan's Hilmand province.

Most of the morphine in the Islamic Republic of Iran is seized in Sistan-Balochistan province, which borders Balochistan province (Pakistan) and Nimroz province (Afghanistan).

Opium seizures

Globally, the amount of opium seized increased from 174 tons in 1996 to 376 tons in 2006, a 116 per cent increase. The main reason is the huge volumes intercepted by the Islamic Republic of Iran.

Between 1996 and 2006, the amount of opium seized increased by 108 per cent in the Islamic Republic of Iran and by 20 per cent in Pakistan. At the same time, seizures decreased by 22 per cent in Central Asian and South-Caucasian[9] countries. Opium seizures in Afghanistan have been steadily increasing since 2002 (there is little comprehensive data available on drug seizures there before 2002). A total of 2,604 kilograms of opium was seized in Europe (including Turkey), amounting to 0.7 per cent of the global total in 2006.

Turkey and European countries have traditionally reported very few opium seizures. Moreover, there is no evidence of morphine/heroin labs in these countries to refine opium. Therefore, it appears likely that a significant portion of the opium trafficked from Afghanistan to Iran is consumed domestically.

The vast majority of global opium seizures takes place in Iran. While Iran's proportion of global seizures is 83 per cent, it hosts a quarter of the estimated global opium users.

In contrast, and despite the fact that 27 per cent of global opium users live in India, seizures there account for 1 per cent of total opium seizures worldwide.

In 2006, Afghanistan seized almost 8 per cent of all opium seized in the world, but this only accounted for 0.5 per cent of the opium produced there. Some of the opium/heroin produced in Afghanistan never enters the international distribution chain because it is consumed by opium poppy farmers and opiate users in country.

Table 8: Global morphine seizures (kg), 2001-2006

Country	2001	2002	2003	2004	2005	2006	Per cent of global seizures in 2006	Change between 2001-2006
Islamic Republic of Iran	8,668	9,521	13,063	12,878	6,939	10,606	23%	+22%
Pakistan	1,825	6,839	27,778	21,256	22,197	32,658	72%	+1,690%
Rest of the world	923	8,341	2,882	5,043	2,872	2,014	4%	+118%
Total	11,416	24,702	43,723	39,177	32,008	45,277	100%	+297%

9   Azerbaijan, Armenia and Georgia.

Map 1:   Morphine seizures reported in Pakistan, 2002-2007

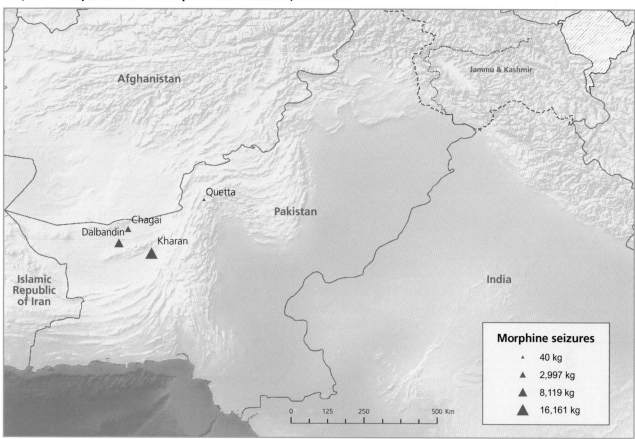

Source: UNODC/WCO. Note: The boundaries and names shown and the designations used on this map do not imply official endorsement or acceptance by the United Nations. Dotted line represents approximately the Line of Control in Jammu and Kashmir agreed upon by India and Pakistan. The final status of Jammu and Kashmir has not yet been agreed upon by the parties.

Map 2:   Morphine seizures reported in the Islamic Republic of Iran, 2002-2007

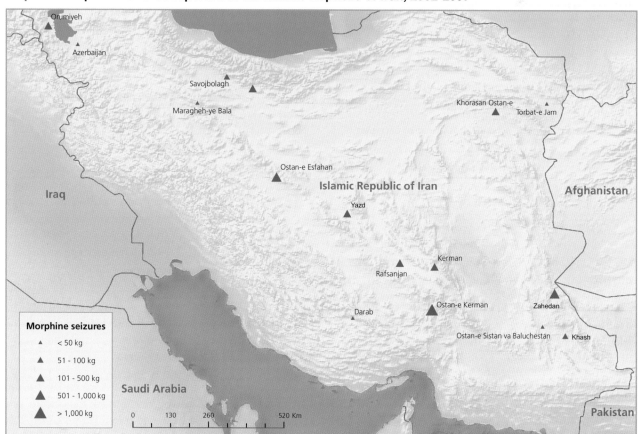

Source: UNODC/WCO. Note: The boundaries and names shown and the designations used on this map do not imply official endorsement or acceptance by the United Nations.

Table 9: Global opium seizures (kg), 1996-2006

Country/region	1996	1997	1998	1999	2000	2001	2002	2003	2004	2005	2006	% change between 1996-2006
Islamic Republic of Iran	149,577	162,414	154,453	204,485	179,053	81,061	72,856	97,575	174,091	231,352	311,306	+108%
Afghanistan	N/A	N/A	N/A	N/A	N/A	N/A	5,582	8,412	21,446	90,990	29,423	N/A
Pakistan	7,423	7,300	5,021	16,319	8,867	5,175	2,686	5,786	2,495	6,437	8,907	+20%
Central Asia and Trans-caucasian countries	7,318	9,954	5,055	9,552	10,870	4,956	3,126	3,032	4,689	2,787	5,740	-22%
Rest of the world	9,682	16,332	14,471	8,644	14,210	14,754	12,686	18,727	9,672	11,441	20,503	+112%
Total	174,000	196,000	179,000	239,000	213,000	106,000	97,000	133,000	212,000	342,000	376,000	+116%

Source: UNODC Delta database.

Fig. 10: Distribution of opium seizures in the world, 1996-2006

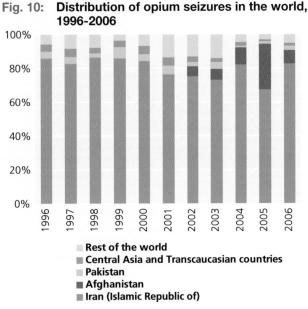

Rest of the world
Central Asia and Transcaucasian countries
Pakistan
Afghanistan
Iran (Islamic Republic of)

Source: UNODC Delta database.

Estimated amount of opium converted into heroin:

Through a combined analysis of seizure and consumption figures, it is possible to calculate the amount of opium converted into heroin or used as raw opium.

According to UNODC illicit crop monitoring surveys in Myanmar, the Lao People's Democratic Republic and Afghanistan, 10-11 kg of opium from Myanmar and Laos are needed to produce one kg of brown heroin, whereas in Afghanistan, 7-8 kg are required.

Between 2002 and 2006, heroin accounted for 95 per cent of opiate seizures in the regions of South and South-East Asia and Oceania. The total estimated heroin consumption in these regions amounts to 80-85 tons (equivalent to 800-

850 tons of opium from Myanmar). The total estimated opium consumption is around 100 tons (excluding India, which does not receive opium imports according to the Government). This means that 90-95 per cent of opiate consumption in the region is in heroin form.

In countries where mainly Afghan opiates are consumed, 72 per cent of Afghan opiate seizures were in heroin form between 2002 and 2006. In addition, some 257 tons of heroin (equivalent to 2000 tons of opium) and 900 tons of raw opium were consumed in these countries during the same period, which indicates that almost 70 per cent of opiates ([2000/2900]) consumed in these countries is also in heroin form. Calculations based on seizures and on consumption thus result in similar heroin consumption ratios.

4. Global opiate flows

The findings in this section were calculated by examining a range of indicators, such as demand statistics provided in the previous section together with the opiate seizure databases of the World Customs Organization (WCO) and UNODC, as well as the Annual Reports Questionnaire (ARQ) and individual country reports. During the estimation period, experts from specialized global organizations such as the WCO were consulted and provided inputs. Similarly, all concerned UNODC field offices were consulted regarding the estimations of heroin and opium consumption in their respective regions.

A trend analysis of both opiate use and seizures data for the 1990-2008 period was carried out to track the pattern and estimate the magnitude of opiate flows in the world. The total heroin consumption was calculated for each country, then combined with official seizure data and balanced

Table 10: Average opiate seizures between 2002 and 2006

		Heroin (tons)	Morphine (tons)	Opium (tons)	Total opiate (tons)	Per cent of heroin seizures in total opiate seizures	Per cent of opium seizures in total opiate seizures
Major distribution routes of Myanmar and Laos heroin production	Myanmar	0.50	0.39	2.80	11.7	76%	24%
	China	8.88	0.16	1.36	91.8	99%	1%
	India	1.04	0.07	2.13	13.2	84%	16%
	Oceania	0.26	0.00		2.6	100%	0%
	Asia (except India, China, Myanmar)	1.57	0.02	0.34	16.2	98%	2%
	Sub total	12.25	0.64	6.62	135.5	95%	5%
Major distribution routes of Afghan heroin	Afghanistan	3.13	0.77	33.48	60.8	45%	55%
	Pakistan	4.14	22.15	5.28	189.3	97%	3%
	Islamic Republic of Iran	5.65	10.60	177.44	291.2	39%	61%
	Central Asia and Transcaucasian countries	5.09	0.00	3.63	39.3	91%	9%
	Russian Federation	3.02	0.01	1.36	22.5	94%	6%
	Turkey	6.93	2.94	0.24	69.3	100%	0%
	Europe (except Turkey and Russia	10.43	0.02	0.74	73.9	99%	1%
	Americas	4.48	0.03	1.36	33.0	96%	4%
	Middle East and South Asia (except Iran, Pakistan and Afghanistan)	0.55	0.00	0.24	4.1	94%	6%
	Africa	0.32	0.01	0.05	2.3	98%	2%
	Sub total	44	37	224	786	72%	28%
	World total	**56**	**37**	**230**	**921**	**78%**	**22%**

Source: UNODC Delta database.

against total production. Production, consumption and seizure data were analyzed together.

For example, the size of estimated heroin flows from Afghanistan or Pakistan to the Islamic Republic of Iran should be similar to the amount of heroin consumed and intercepted in Iran and the destination and transit countries receiving heroin via Iran. To begin with, heroin/opium demand in the main destination regions/countries was calculated. Then, by drawing on seizure statistics from each country, the amounts of heroin/opium flowing between the countries were estimated.

As this report aims to provide global insights as well as orders of magnitude, the flows represented on maps should be considered broadly indicative rather than definitive flow outlines. Flows may deviate to other countries along the routes and there are numerous secondary flows which may not be represented.

Moreover, trends respond rapidly to changes in law enforcement and demand. Opiate flow estimations would there-

fore be revised if demand statistics in the UNODC *World Drug Report* were to change. The estimates will be updated periodically as new drug abuse data become available from Member States.

Countries/regions were grouped into two categories: 1) primarily destination countries/regions, and 2) primarily transit countries/regions for heroin trafficking:

A- Heroin consumption and seizures in main destination countries/regions

1-Europe (excluding the Russian Federation and Turkey):

Russia is analyzed separately since heroin flows to Russia via Central Asian countries (northern route) and not via the Balkan route, which supplies most of the European market.

Turkey is also analyzed separately as it is the main gateway for heroin trafficking on the Balkan route.

A total of 1.6 million people are estimated to consume

Table 11: Share of heroin seized in West and Central Europe by departure country/region, 2000-2008

Departure country/region	Per cent of total
Africa	1.6%
Central Asia	0.3%
Eastern Europe	5.7%
Gulf area and Middle East	1.4%
India	0.8%
Pakistan	4.7%
South-East Europe	83.8%
South-East Asia	1.4%
South America	0.2%

Table 12: Share of heroin seized in South-Eastern Europe by departure country, 2000-2008

Departure country	Per cent of total
Islamic Republic of Iran	7.3%
Turkey	92.7%

Table 13: Share of heroin seized in Turkey by departure country, 2000-2008

Departure country	Per cent of total
Islamic Republic of Iran	98%
Syrian Arab Republic	2%

Table 14: Share of heroin seized in Eastern Europe by departure country/region, 2000-2008

Departure country/region	Per cent of total
Central Asia	2%
Islamic Republic of Iran	4%
Russian Federation	20%
Turkey	59%
South Caucasus	14%

some 90 tons of heroin per year in Western, Central and Eastern Europe. European law enforcement institutions seize around 10 tons of heroin per year. Additionally, heroin trafficking from Europe to North America (USA and Canada) could be around 5 tons per year. To meet this combined demand, traffickers need to ship approximately 105-110 tons of heroin into Europe every year.

According to seizure information from UNODC and WCO for the years 2000-2008, 84 per cent of the heroin seized in Europe – (85-90) tons – was shipped from South-Eastern European (Balkan) countries.

Seizure data show that some 93 per cent – (80-85) tons – of the heroin seized in West and Central Europe transited Turkey before reaching South-East European (Balkan) countries. The remaining 6 tons traveled directly from the Islamic Republic of Iran via the Afghanistan-Iran/Central Asia-Caspian Sea-Azerbaijan/Georgia-Black Sea-Bulgaria route.

Seizure statistics indicate that the vast majority (98 per cent) of the heroin seized in Turkey comes from the Islamic Republic of Iran while the remaining 2 per cent (2 tons) flows from the neighbouring Syrian Arab Republic.

As for the heroin trafficking to Western and Central Europe via Eastern Europe, seizure data show that around 6 per cent of the total heroin seized in Europe – roughly equivalent to five tons – travel to Western and Central Europe from Eastern Europe every year. Of that total, around one ton is trafficked via the Russian Federation (according to seizure statistics from Eastern European countries), and one ton via the Afghanistan-Iran/Central Asia-Caspian Sea-Azerbaijan-Georgia-Black Sea-Ukraine route. The remaining three tons reach East Europe via the Afghanistan-Iran-Turkey-Ukraine route.

Heroin trafficking from Eastern Europe to Western and Central Europe is limited, although this route has been seeing more activity since 2007.

Some 2-3 tons are estimated to be trafficked to Europe via the Afghanistan-Pakistan-Africa-route. So, around 2 per cent of the total heroin seized in Europe was trafficked from Africa. Nigeria, South Africa and Ghana are the main African states sourcing heroin to Europe.

Between 2000 and 2008, 5 per cent of heroin seizures in Europe originated from Pakistan. This means that almost 5 tons of heroin are trafficked from Pakistan to Europe (mainly the United Kingdom and the Netherlands) each year. UK authorities estimate that around 25 per cent of the heroin found on their market is shipped directly from Pakistan to the UK (by air or sea).

Map 3:   Main heroin flows to Europe after 2002 (excluding the Russian Federation)

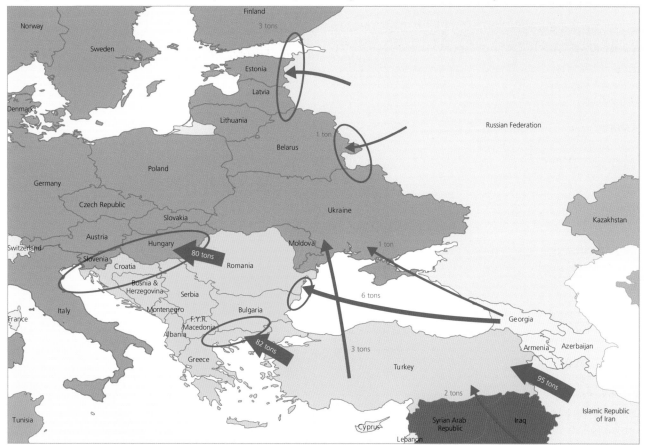

South and South-East Asia (except India and China) source an estimated one ton of heroin per year to Europe. Heroin trafficking from India is also reported in seizure statistics from both European countries and India. At least one ton of heroin is estimated to be trafficked from India to West and Central Europe each year.

Around one ton of heroin flows from the Gulf area and Middle Eastern countries (mainly the United Arab Emirates) to Europe every year.

The vast majority of the heroin trafficked from the Islamic Republic of Iran or Turkey toward Europe is transported by road or rail via the Bulgaria/Turkey and Greece/Turkey bor-

ders. In 2006 and 2007, around 100 kg of heroin were seized at Turkish airports,[10] representing only 1 per cent of the total heroin seized in that country. Negligible seizures are also made at Turkish seaports. In Europe, less than 5 per cent of the heroin seized coming from Turkey is intercepted at airports or seaports.

Heroin enters Bulgaria primarily by road from the Turkish border and leaves via Bulgaria's borders with Romania, Serbia and Greece. In 2007 and 2008, a number of cases of trafficking directly from Georgia to Bulgaria via maritime routes were reported. This route appears to be new and more time is needed to monitor and analyze its dynamics and further potential use.

Table 15:   Importance of heroin trafficking routes to Europe

Route	Size of heroin flow (tons)	Per cent
Balkan route (Afghanistan - I.R. of Iran - Turkey - S. Europe - Europe)	85	80.2%
Northern route (Afghanistan - C. Asia - Russia - Europe)	4	3.8%
Northern Balkan route (Afghanistan - I.R. of Iran - Caucasus - Europe)	7	6.6%
Directly from Pakistan	5	4.7%
Through Africa	2	1.8%
Directly from South and South-East Asia (except India)	1	0.9%
Through Middle East and Gulf area	1	0.9%
Directly from India	1	0.9%
Total	106	100%

10   Turkish Report on Drugs and Organized Crime (2006, 2007).

Table 16: Heroin seizures and consumption in Europe (excluding the Russian Federation and Turkey)

Country	Average heroin seizures between 2002 and 2006 (kg)	Per cent of total average heroin seizures in Europe	Number of heroin users	Heroin consumption (kg)	Per cent of total heroin consumption in Europe
United Kingdom	2,290	22%	321,440	18,610	21%
Italy	2,080	20%	305,360	17,680	20%
France	680	7%	165,290	9,570	11%
Germany	720	7%	117,940	6,830	8%
Ukraine	50	0%	131,370	4,370	5%
Spain	290	3%	74,320	4,300	5%
Poland	110	1%	55,000	3,180	4%
Portugal	120	1%	50,760	2,940	3%
Netherlands	940	9%	33,210	1,920	2%
Switzerland	230	2%	31,160	1,800	2%
Belgium	180	2%	28,950	1,680	2%
Austria	130	1%	25,650	1,490	2%
Hungary	210	2%	20,830	1,210	1%
Greece	280	3%	19,640	1,140	1%
Denmark	30	0%	19,480	1,130	1%
Ireland	50	0%	14,650	850	1%
Bulgaria	650	6%	26,450	810	1%
Estonia	0	0%	13,800	800	1%
Romania	180	2%	23,950	730	1%
Serbia and Montenegro	370	4%	22,420	690	1%
Slovakia	10	0%	11,670	680	1%
Norway	70	1%	10,240	590	1%
Czech Republic	30	0%	9,350	540	1%
Lithuania	0	0%	8,950	520	1%
Sweden	50	0%	8,370	480	1%
Slovenia	130	1%	7,450	430	0%
Latvia	0	0%	7,100	410	0%
Croatia	70	1%	10,000	310	0%
Albania	100	1%	9,680	300	0%
Bosnia and Herzegovina	30	0%	8,100	250	0%
Finland	10	0%	3,600	210	0%
Macedonia, FYR	130	1%	5,550	170	0%
Luxembourg	10	0%	2,930	170	0%
Malta	0	0%	1,610	90	0%
Belarus	10	0%	2,150	70	0%
Monaco	0	0%	1,940	60	0%
Cyprus	0	0%	950	50	0%
Iceland	0	0%	800	50	0%
Montenegro	0	0%	1,340	50	0%
Liechtenstein	0	0%	50	0	0%
Andorra	0	0%	N/A	N/A	N/A
Republic of Moldova	0	0%	N/A	N/A	N/A
Total	**10,250**		**1,613,500**	**87,160**	

Once heroin shipments are trafficked into Greece/Bulgaria from Turkey, some 20-25 tons of heroin travel to Italy and Switzerland via Albania (by sea) or via the former Yugoslav Republic of Macedonia-Serbia-Bosnia & Herzegovina-Slovenia/Croatia (by land). This amount is equivalent to the estimated heroin consumption in Italy and Switzerland. The rest (approximately 55-60 tons) goes to Germany/Netherlands via the Serbia/Romania-Hungary-Austria-Germany/Netherlands route. Once heroin reaches Germany/Netherlands, it is trafficked further to France, the UK and Spain.

In the consumer zone, seizure rates rise significantly. The total estimated heroin consumption in the UK is 18.6 tons, in Italy 17.6 tons, in France 9.5 tons and in Germany 6.8 tons per year. The correlation (correlation coefficient = 0.92) between heroin seizures and consumption indicates that most of the heroin seizures are proportionally larger in destination countries when compared to transit countries in South-East Europe.

Conversely, Bulgaria and to a lesser extent Greece seize only 1.5-2 per cent of the estimated quantity of heroin flowing through their territory. In Europe, major destination countries like the UK and Italy seize around 10 per cent of the heroin flowing (consumption + seizures) through their territory.

Fig. 11: Correlation between heroin seizures and heroin consumption in Europe (except the Russian Federation and Turkey)

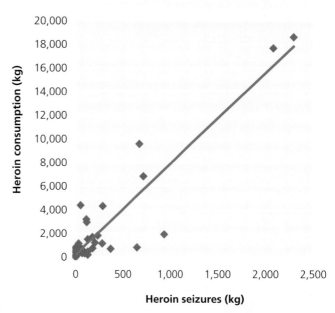

Map 4: Heroin seizures reported in Greece in 2003

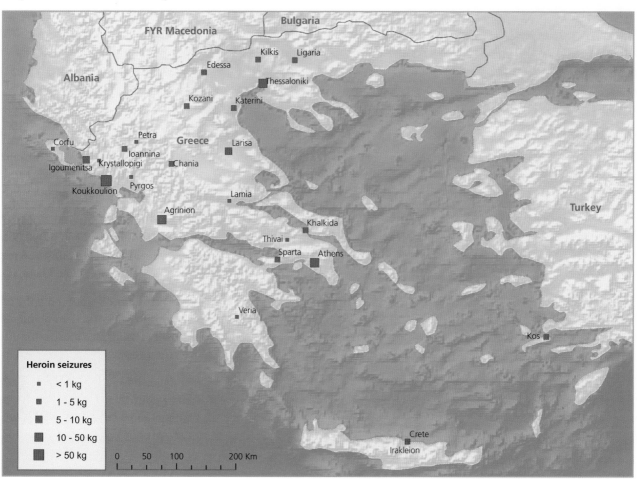

Source: UNODC/WCO. Note: The boundaries and names shown and the designations used on this map do not imply official endorsement or acceptance by the United Nations.

Map 5:   Heroin seizures reported in Bulgaria, 2002-2007

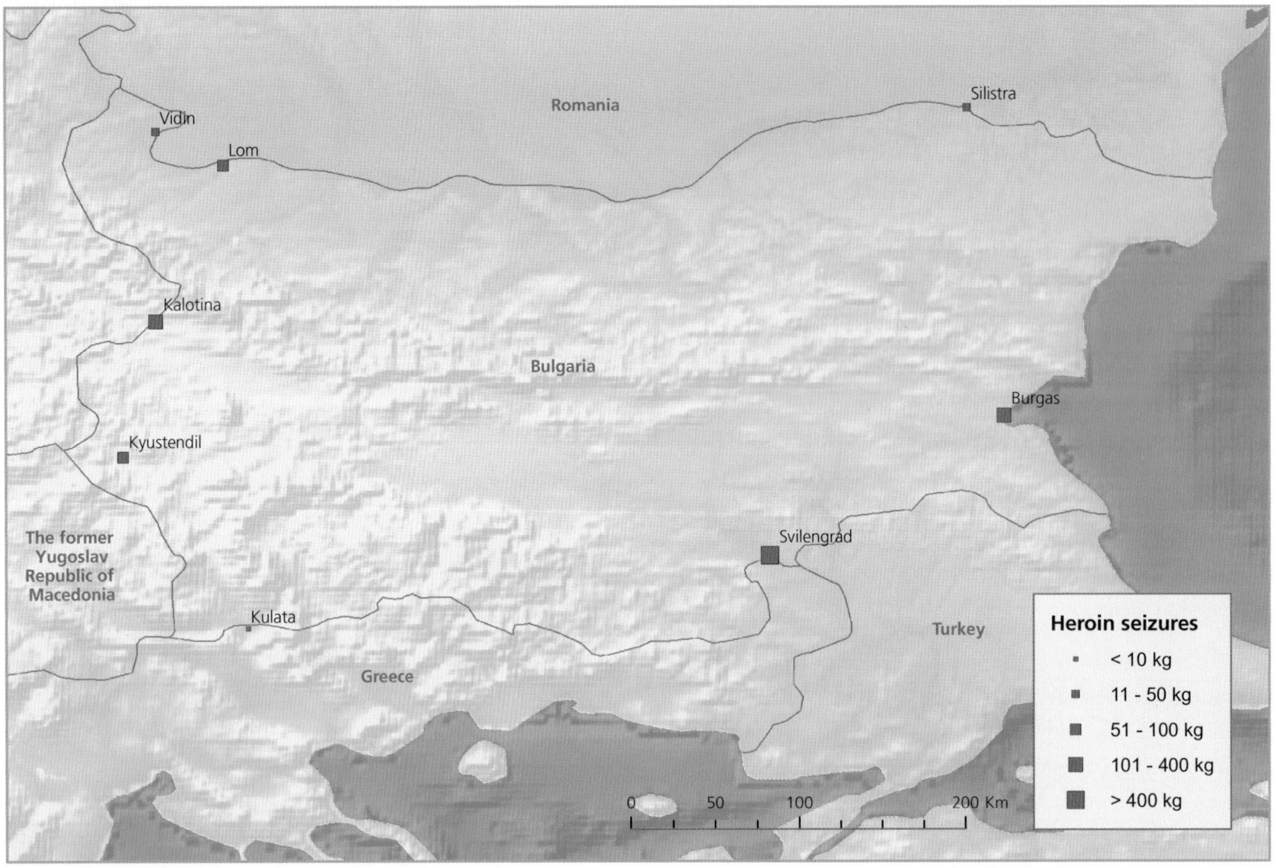

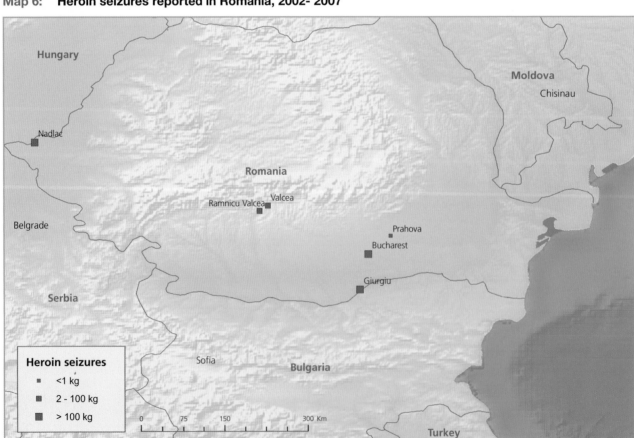

Source: UNODC/WCO. Note: The boundaries and names shown and the designations used on this map do not imply official endorsement or acceptance by the United Nations.

Map 6:   Heroin seizures reported in Romania, 2002- 2007

Source: UNODC/WCO. Note: The boundaries and names shown and the designations used on this map do not imply official endorsement or acceptance by the United Nations.

Map 7:   Heroin seizures reported in Germany, 2002-2007

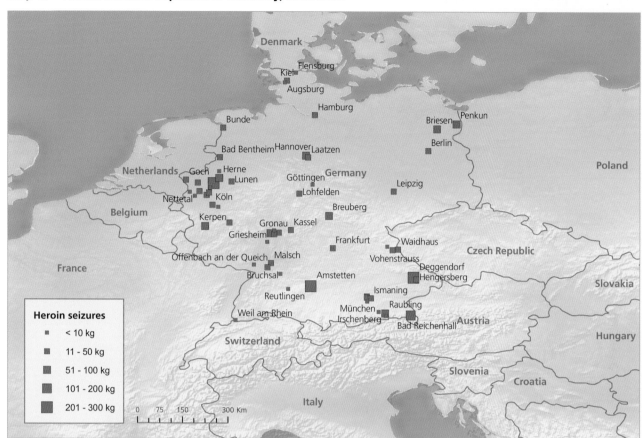

Source: UNODC/WCO. Note: The boundaries and names shown and the designations used on this map do not imply official endorsement or acceptance by the United Nations.

Map 8:   Heroin seizures reported in Europe, 2002-2008

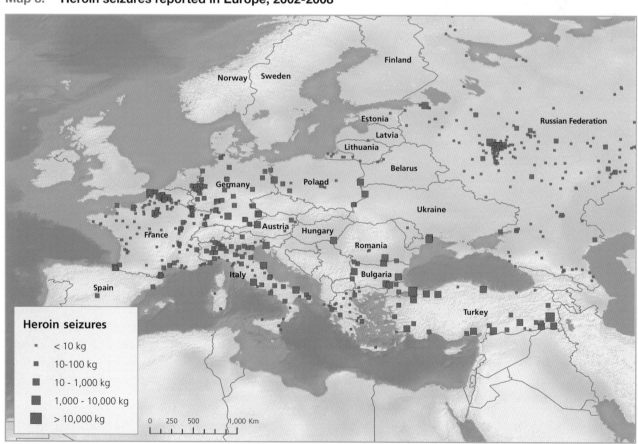

Source: UNODC/WCO. Note: The boundaries and names shown and the designations used on this map do not imply official endorsement or acceptance by the United Nations.

Map 9: Heroin flows from the Russian Federation, 2008

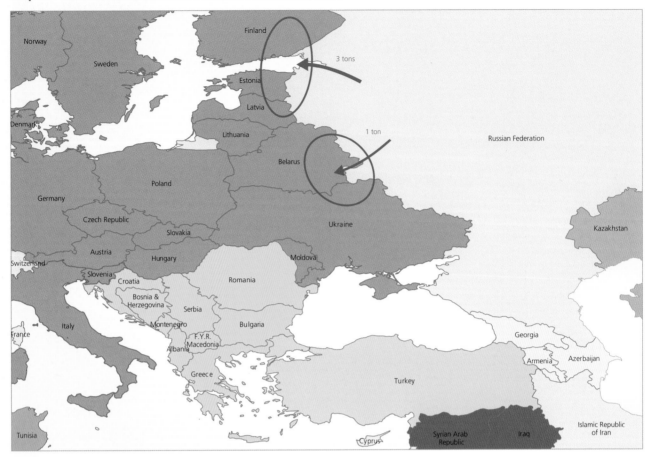

2-Russian Federation:

It is estimated that there are some 1.5 million heroin users in Russia according to the 2007 *World Drug Report*.

The number of drug addicts in Russia has increased sharply during the last decade. This trend correlates with the increase in heroin seizures seen across Russian territory.

The purity of the street level heroin used in Russia is estimated at 5 per cent, according to a study implemented by the National Research Center on Drug Addiction (NRC) of the Federal Agency on Health and Social Development and the UNODC Russia and Belarus Regional Office in 2009. According to the same study, a total of 70 tons of heroin (70 per cent purity; equal to the purity of heroin produced in Afghanistan) is estimated to be consumed by 1.5 million users in Russia per year.

Russian law enforcement agencies seize an average of 3 tons of heroin per year. According to ARQ data, Russia's near or immediate neighbours, such as Finland, Estonia, Belarus, Latvia, Lithuania, Poland and Ukraine, receive a portion of their heroin supply from Russia. The remainder comes via Iran-Caucasus and Turkey. Norway receives heroin from Russia as well as via the Balkan route.

The total estimated heroin consumption in Finland, Estonia, Belarus, Latvia, Lithuania, Ukraine, Poland, Sweden and Norway combined is around 10 tons per year. Of this,

the 2-3 tons that are consumed in Finland, Estonia, Belarus, Latvia, Lithuania and Poland are reported to be shipped from the Russian Federation.

In addition, some five tons of heroin are estimated to be trafficked from Eastern Europe to West and Central Europe. Of that total, one ton is estimated to be trafficked from the Russian Federation to Eastern Europe.

Consequently, around four tons of heroin are trafficked from the Russian Federation to Eastern and Northern European countries every year.

Altogether, some 75-80 tons of heroin – virtually all the heroin that reaches Russia - are estimated to be trafficked via the Afghanistan-Central Asia route (northern route).

3-China:

China borders two large opium producers: Afghanistan and Myanmar. 2.2 million Chinese heroin users are estimated to consume around 45 tons of heroin annually. Chinese law enforcement officials also seize 9 tons of heroin per year. In addition, according to heroin seizure data from Australia, half of the heroin consumed in Australia is shipped from China (around one ton). Thus, this market should receive at least 55 tons of heroin.

Opium production in Myanmar was sufficient to meet heroin demand in China until 2002. Following the sharp decrease in opium production in Myanmar, Afghan heroin

Map 10: Heroin seizures reported in the Russian Federation, 2000-2008

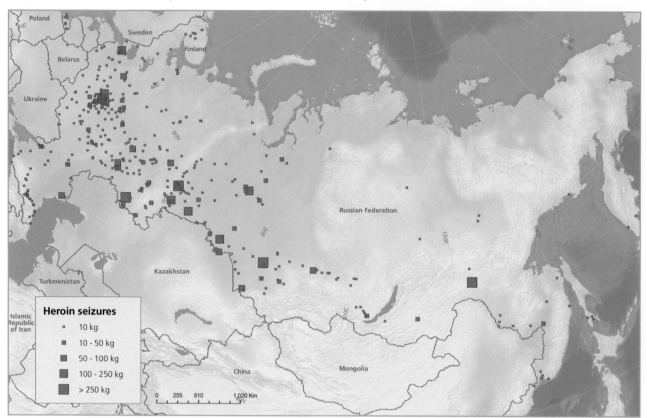

Source: UNODC/WCO. Note: The boundaries and names shown and the designations used on this map do not imply official endorsement or acceptance by the United Nations. Dotted line represents approximately the Line of Control in Jammu and Kashmir agreed upon by India and Pakistan. The final status of Jammu and Kashmir has not yet been agreed upon by the parties.

started being shipped to China. Despite the lack of detailed seizure information from China, data from Pakistan, Afghanistan, the United Arab Emirates, India and Thailand indicate trafficking of Afghan heroin from these countries to China.

Most heroin in China, however, continues to be produced in and trafficked from Myanmar and the Lao People's Democratic Republic, with which it shares 2,000 km of borders. According to the 2008 report of the National Narcotics Control Commission of China, Myanmar and Laos are the primary sources of foreign-produced drugs in China. WCO seizure data indicate that almost 70 per cent (38 tons) of the heroin seized in China comes from Myanmar. It appears that the remainder, some 25 per cent or about 15-17 tons, may be sourced in Afghanistan.

This estimate is supported by individual seizure data from Pakistan and the WCO which show that 11 per cent of the heroin seized in China comes from Pakistan. Thus, some 6-7 tons of heroin travel to China from Pakistan every year. Approximately one ton of heroin is also estimated to flow to China from countries of the Gulf and Middle East. Additionally, some four tons of heroin are trafficked to China from Africa every year. Seizure data from WCO and ARQ reports also indicate that between one and two tons of heroin are shipped to China from India, while an additional three to four tons are trafficked from other South-East Asian countries to China every year. Seizure statistics also show

Table 17: Share of heroin seized in China by departure country/region, 2000-2008

Departure country/region	Per cent of total
Africa	7.0%
Central Asia	0.8%
Gulf area and Middle East	1.3%
Hong Kong, China	0.2%
India	1.8%
Lao People's Democratic Republic	0.2%
Myanmar	68.6%
Pakistan	11.0%
Other South-East Asian countries	8.3%
Turkey	1.0%

Source: WCO.

limited heroin trafficking from Central Asian countries to China (one ton per year) bringing the total estimated Afghan heroin flow into China to around 18 tons per year.

According to some reports,[11] the level of heroin trafficking from Central Asia (especially from Tajikistan) to China may be higher than currently estimated. Given the paucity of information, it is currently difficult to estimate the importance and extent of this relatively new phenomenon.

11 *The Risk to China From Trafficking in Afghan Opiates*, The Program for Contemporary Silk Road Studies Narcotics, Organized Crime and Security in Eurasia, Uppsala University, Jacob Townsend.

Map 11: Heroin seizures reported in China, 2002-2008

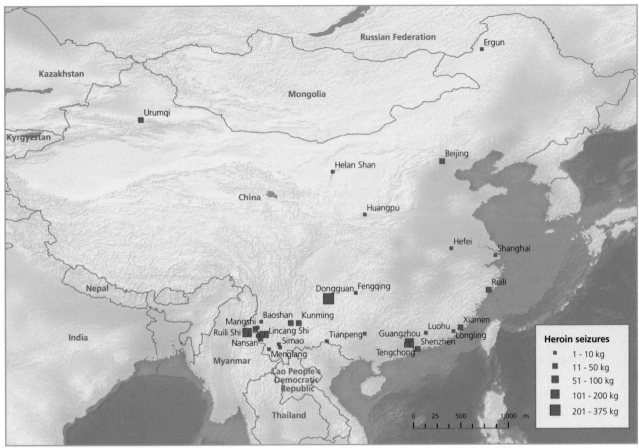

Source: UNODC/WCO. Note: The boundaries and names shown and the designations used on this map do not imply official endorsement or acceptance by the United Nations.

Similarly, undetermined quantities of heroin are also being moved from Afghanistan directly to China, mainly by air.

China is both a transit and destination country; it seizes around 16 per cent of the total estimated heroin trafficked across its borders.

4-India:

India is a significant heroin consumption market with 870,000 heroin users estimated to consume around 17.2 tons of heroin per year. Interviews at selected treatment centres in New Delhi revealed that the average user consumes 1 gram of heroin (at typical street purity of 5 per cent) per day, roughly equivalent to 0.05 grams of pure heroin per day. This means that individual users consume on average 20 grams of pure heroin annually.

Some seven tons of heroin are trafficked to North America from India, according to seizure data and ARQ responses from North American countries. Six tons of heroin are shipped to East and South-East Asia (mainly to Bangladesh, Nepal, Maldives and Sri Lanka), three tons to African countries and two tons to China. Additionally around one ton of heroin is estimated to be trafficked to West and Central Europe from India, bringing the total outflow of heroin to 19 tons. Lastly, Indian law enforcement officials seize around one ton of heroin per year. Thus, a total of 37

tons of heroin are needed to meet domestic demand and trafficking from India.

Some 13 tons of heroin are estimated to be trafficked to India from South-East Asia (excluding Myanmar) every year. Around three tons of heroin enter India directly from Afghanistan by air, and approximately one ton of heroin enters India from Myanmar. For the remaining 20 tons, the source is unknown. It might be sourced from Afghanistan via Pakistan and/or other routes and/or be produced in India (diverted from the licit to the illicit market).[12] In order to clarify this, an in-depth heroin consumption and trafficking study should be carried out in India.

5-South and South-East Asia – excluding India and China:

A total of 17 tons of heroin is needed every year to satisfy the demand of the estimated 850,000 heroin users in this region. Additionally, an average of two tons of heroin and morphine are seized annually in this region.

12 According to individual seizures and ARQ data from India, there is some diversion of licit opium, but the exact amount is unknown. Moreover, in 2007, the Central Bureau of Narcotics and West Bengal police destroyed 6,500 hectares of illicit opium cultivation in two districts of West Bengal. Although most of the illicit opium cultivation in this region was eradicated, the size of the area under cultivation raises questions about the level of illicit opium cultivation in India.

Map 12: Heroin seizures reported in India, 2002-2008

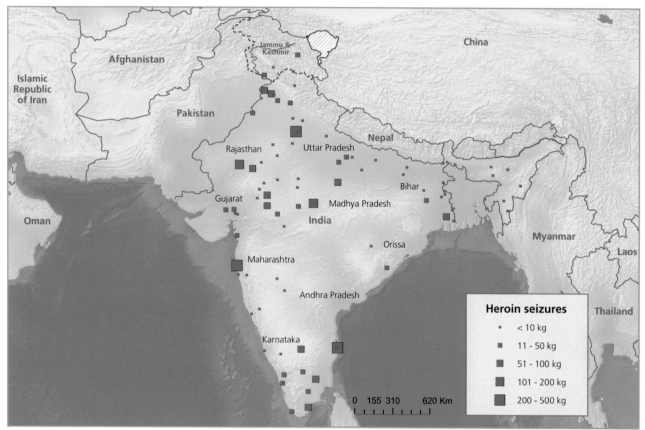

Heroin seizures
- < 10 kg
- 11 - 50 kg
- 51 - 100 kg
- 101 - 200 kg
- 200 - 500 kg

Source: UNODC/WCO. Note: The boundaries and names shown and the designations used on this map do not imply official endorsement or acceptance by the United Nations. Dotted line represents approximately the Line of Control in Jammu and Kashmir agreed upon by India and Pakistan. The final status of Jammu and Kashmir has not yet been agreed upon by the parties.

Moreover, an estimated 22 tons of heroin are trafficked from these two sub regions to China (3 tons), North America (3 tons), Europe (1 ton), India (13 ton), Oceania (1 ton) and Africa (1 ton).

Thus, a combined (consumption, seizures and trafficking) total of around 40 tons of heroin should flow to South and South-East Asia every year.

One fifth (9-10 tons) of the total average heroin production in Myanmar and the Lao People's Democratic Republic is transported to other South and South-East Asian countries every year.

An estimated 6 tons of heroin are shipped from India to meet demand in Bangladesh, Nepal, the Maldives and Sri Lanka per year.

Around 1 ton is imported via the Gulf area and Middle Eastern countries to South and South-East Asia every year.

The remaining 25 tons arrive from Pakistan.[13]

6-Oceania:

There are a total of 32,000 heroin users in Australia (28,000) and New Zealand (4,000), consuming around 1.8 tons of heroin per year. As total average heroin seizures hover at around 0.3 tons per year in both countries combined, a

total of around 2 tons of heroin flows into Australia (1.7 tons) and New Zealand (0.3 ton) every year.

Most of the heroin flowing into these countries is shipped from China (1 ton) and other South and South-East Asian countries.

7-North America (USA and Canada):

Based on opium production data provided to UNODC, the total estimated heroin consumption in the Americas is 26 tons per year. The majority is consumed in the USA (20-21 tons, by 1.2 million users), followed by Canada (about 1.3 tons, by 76,000 users). The average annual heroin seizure total in the USA is 2.1 tons, and around 50 kilograms in Canada. Combined, the total heroin flow to the USA and Canada is estimated at around 24-25 tons per year.

About 6 tons (30 per cent of the total estimated flow) of the heroin that reaches the USA and Canada via Latin America and Mexico is also produced there. The total heroin production of Latin America and Mexico is estimated at around 10 tons per year. Another 7 tons of heroin reaches the USA and Canada via South Asia (mainly India), and two tons come from Pakistan by air routes. 11 per cent (3 tons) of the heroin consumed in the USA and Canada could be traced back to Africa, whereas an average of 5 tons (20 per cent) flows from Europe every year.

13   According to WCO seizure data.

Map 13: Estimated regional heroin flows from Afghanistan, 2008

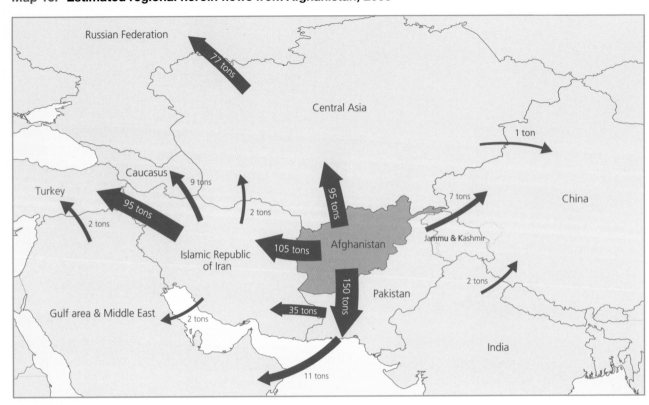

B- Heroin consumption and seizures in the main transit countries/regions

1-Pakistan

Between 2002 and 2005, an average of 375 tons of heroin was exported annually from Afghanistan to the rest of the world.

According to the UNODC Afghanistan opium survey reports, around 40 per cent - 150 tons - of Afghanistan's heroin production is trafficked to Pakistan. According to a drug use survey[14] implemented in 2006, there are approximately 547,000 heroin and 145,000 opium users in Pakistan. The heroin users are estimated to consume around 20 tons of pure heroin per year. Pakistani officials seize an average of 25-30 tons of heroin and morphine, or 18 per cent of the estimated yearly flow through the country. Thus the total volume of heroin consumed and seized in Pakistan is 45-50 tons per year, which leaves around 100-105 tons available to be trafficked to several destinations around the world.

As noted previously, heroin is smuggled from Pakistan to the Islamic Republic of Iran (35 tons), Africa (20 tons), South and South-East Asia (25 tons), the Middle East (11 tons – mainly UAE and except Iran), China (7 tons), Europe (6 tons – mainly to the UK) and North America (2 tons). Heroin from Pakistan bound for these various destinations is trafficked via air, land and sea routes.[15]

In the case of the United Arab Emirates, the high volumes of shipping and investment development opportunities there leave the country vulnerable to exploitation by narcotics traffickers and drug-related money-laundering.[16] The UAE, and Dubai in particular, is a major regional transportation, financial and shipping hub. Through this transhipment point, narcotics smuggled from Pakistan and to a lesser extent from the Islamic Republic of Iran, continue toward Africa, China and South-East Asia. Individual seizures data provided by the UAE indicates that at least 50 per cent of the heroin seized in the UAE was headed to Africa, and the rest to China.

Most of the 20 tons of heroin that flow from Pakistan to Africa every year have Ghana, Nigeria, South Africa and Tanzania as destinations.

Some 6 tons of Afghan heroin is trafficked from Pakistan via commercial flights to Europe every year, mainly to the United Kingdom, the Netherlands and Germany. Moreover, some 2 tons are estimated to be trafficked to North America every year.

Pakistan-based drug traffickers are thus exporting Afghan heroin to almost every region in the world.

14 *Problem Drug Use in Pakistan*, UNODC, 2006.

15 Heroin trafficking from Pakistan to India will be studied in detail in a forth-coming report (2010).

16 *International Narcotics Control Strategy Report (INCSR) 2009*, United States Department of State.

Map 14: Heroin seizures reported in Pakistan, 2002-2008

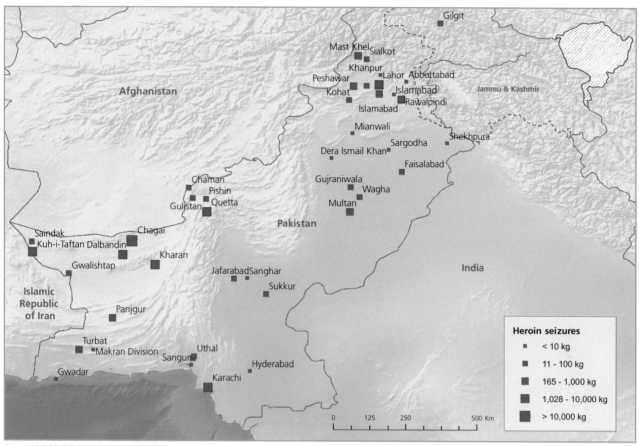

Source: UNODC/WCO. Note: The boundaries and names shown and the designations used on this map do not imply official endorsement or acceptance by the United Nations. Dotted line represents approximately the Line of Control in Jammu and Kashmir agreed upon by India and Pakistan. The final status of Jammu and Kashmir has not yet been agreed upon by the parties.

2-The Islamic Republic of Iran

According to the UNODC annual opium survey reports, approximately 105 tons (around 30 per cent) of Afghan heroin is trafficked directly into the Islamic Republic of Iran from Afghanistan. As explained previously, an additional 35 tons of heroin flow from Pakistan to Iran every year. The total amount of Afghan heroin entering Iran is thus around 140 tons per year.

Iran has an estimated heroin user population of around 400,000 individuals, consuming almost 14 tons of heroin per year. An average of 16 tons of heroin – 11 per cent of the total heroin flow to Iran – is seized in Iran annually.

In addition, some 95 tons of heroin flow from the Islamic Republic of Iran to Turkey to meet European demand. Turkish seizure data indicate that almost all heroin shipped to Turkey comes by way of Iran.

Some heroin is trafficked through Iran-Azerbaijan-Georgia-Black Sea to Bulgaria. Seizures statistics since 2007 indicate that 7 per cent of the heroin (approximately 6 tons) reaches South-East European countries via this route.

Since 2007, another emerging trafficking route has been observed, running from the Islamic Republic of Iran to Ukraine via the Caspian Sea or the Azerbaijan-Georgia route. The instability in the Caucasus[17] has facilitated the development of illicit drug trafficking and may further encourage traffickers to opt for this route rather than the traditional Iran-Turkey corridor. The Iran-Caucasus (Azerbaijan – Georgia) – Ukraine (via Black Sea) route gained importance after 2006. For example, a total of around one ton of heroin was seized in Azerbaijan and Ukraine with the help of intelligence from the Turkish narcotic police[18] in 2007 and 2008. It is cautiously estimated that around two tons of heroin are being trafficked via this route annually. Accurately estimating the size of the heroin flow on this route remains difficult due to the lack of data.

Additionally, an estimated two tons of heroin are trafficked from the Islamic Republic of Iran to other Middle Eastern countries, mainly the UAE.

To summarize, a total of 140 tons of heroin flow through Iran annually. Out of this, 105 tons come from Afghanistan. The remaining 35 tons are trafficked along the Afghanistan – Pakistan route into south-eastern Iran. Out of 140 tons, 110 tons leave the country.

---

17 Areas concerned include Abkhazia, South Ossetia, and Karabakh, as well as the semi-autonomous republic of Ajaria.

18 Reported by a Turkish delegate in Paris Pact meetings in 2007 and 2008.

Map 15: Heroin seizures reported in the Islamic Republic of Iran, 2002-2008

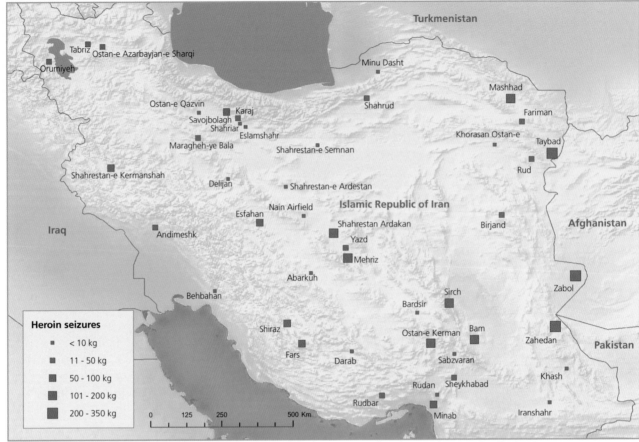

Source: UNODC/WCO. Note: The boundaries and names shown and the designations used on this map do not imply official endorsement or acceptance by the United Nations.

Individual drug seizure data from the Islamic Republic of Iran indicate a heroin flow from Pakistan to Iran and from Iran towards Turkey and, to a lesser extent, Turkmenistan. There are reports of heroin trafficking from Iran to Iraq, but information is sparse as a result of the security situation in this region. Traffickers may take advantage of that situation to establish new routes through Iraq. Over the past two years, 117 arrests related to drug trafficking were reported by Iraqis officials in northern Iraq (Sulaymaniyah province bordering Iran).[19]

3-Central Asian countries (Tajikistan, Uzbekistan, Turkmenistan, Kyrgyzstan and Kazakhstan):

Some 75-80 tons of heroin flow into the Russian Federation through the Afghanistan-Central Asia route. While Central Asian (CA) countries are the main trafficking route for Afghan heroin into the Russian Federation, they also have growing domestic markets. Around 12 tons of heroin is estimated to be consumed by 280,000 heroin users in CA countries annually. CA governments seize an average of 5 tons of heroin per year. All together, some 95 tons of heroin (25 per cent of Afghan heroin production) is estimated to be trafficked from Afghanistan to CA countries.

Heroin enters Central Asia (CA) through Afghanistan's borders with Tajikistan, Uzbekistan and Turkmenistan, the majority through the Afghanistan/Tajikistan borders, which are difficult to control due to their remoteness and challenging terrain. A quarter (25 tons) of the total flow is trafficked to the Russian Federation by rail and air from Tajikistan, Uzbekistan and Kyrgyzstan. The remaining 50-55 tons are trafficked toward the Russian Federation using overland routes, mainly via Kazakhstan. All highway and rail lines pass through Kazakhstan (with the exception of traffic through Turkmenistan's port on the Caspian Sea) as it is the only CA country which has land borders with the Russian Federation. Almost all the overland trafficking to Russia uses the following routes:

1. Afghanistan - Tajikistan/Kyrgyzstan - Kazakhstan,

2. Afghanistan - Uzbekistan - Kazakhstan,

3. Afghanistan - Turkmenistan - Kazakhstan,

4. Afghanistan - Uzbekistan - Kyrgyzstan - Kazakhstan.

The locations of heroin seizures in Central Asian countries and in the Russian Federation indicate the use of the above mentioned routes. An additional smaller route runs from Turkmenistan to the Russian Federation via the Caspian Sea.

19 *International Narcotics Control Strategy Report (INCSR) 2009*, United States Department of State.

Map 16: Heroin seizures reported in Tajikistan, 2002-2008

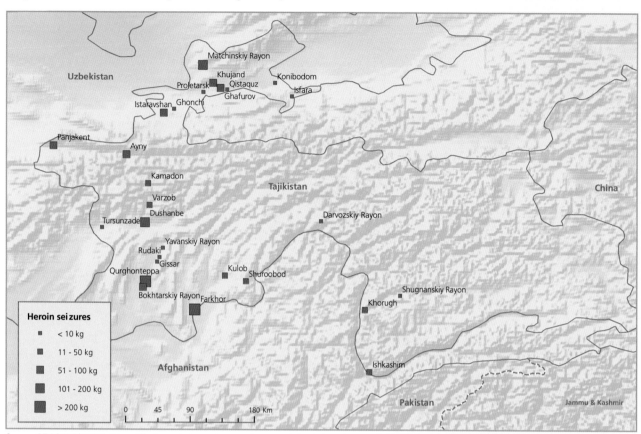

Source: UNODC/WCO. Note: The boundaries and names shown and the designations used on this map do not imply official endorsement or acceptance by the United Nations. Dotted line represents approximately the Line of Control in Jammu and Kashmir agreed upon by India and Pakistan. The final status of Jammu and Kashmir has not yet been agreed upon by the parties.

Map 17: Heroin seizures reported in Uzbekistan, 2002-2008

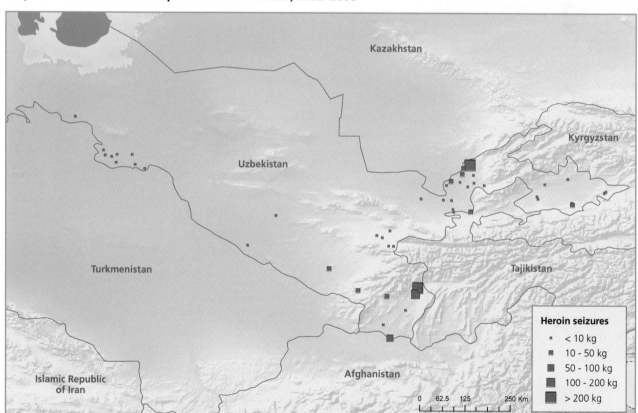

Source: UNODC/WCO. Note: The boundaries and names shown and the designations used on this map do not imply official endorsement or acceptance by the United Nations. Dotted line represents approximately the Line of Control in Jammu and Kashmir agreed upon by India and Pakistan. The final status of Jammu and Kashmir has not yet been agreed upon by the parties.

Map 18: Heroin seizures reported in Turkmenistan, 2002-2008

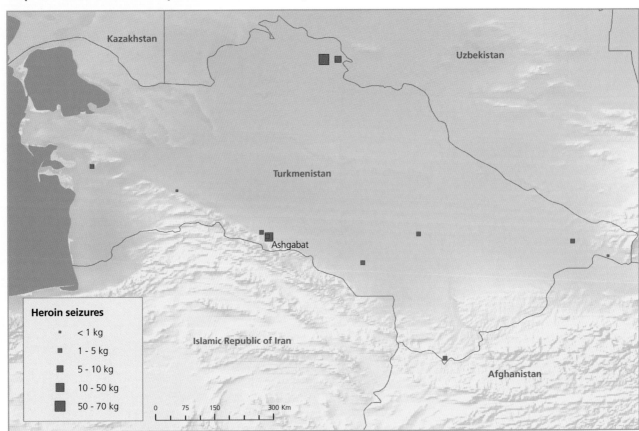

Source: UNODC/WCO. Note: The boundaries and names shown and the designations used on this map do not imply official endorsement or acceptance by the United Nations.

Map 19: Heroin seizures reported in Kyrgyzstan, 2002-2008

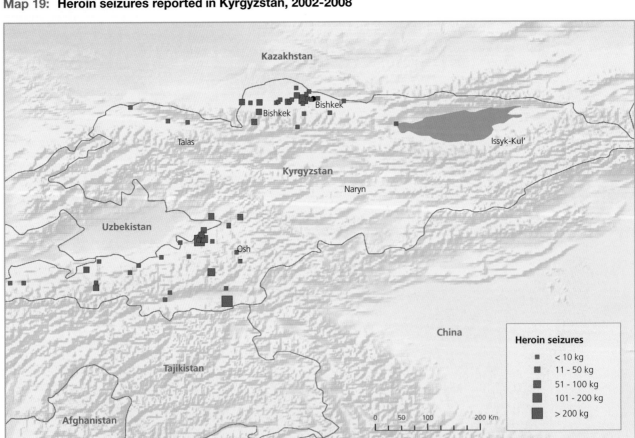

Source: UNODC/WCO. Note: The boundaries and names shown and the designations used on this map do not imply official endorsement or acceptance by the United Nations.

4-Caucasus countries (Azerbaijan, Armenia and Georgia):

Some 10 tons of heroin are estimated to be trafficked via the following routes:

1. Islamic Republic of Iran - Azerbaijan - Georgia - Black Sea - Ukraine and/or Bulgaria

2. Islamic Republic of Iran - Caspian Sea - Russia/ Georgia - Black Sea - Ukraine and/or Bulgaria.

3. Afghanistan - Turkmenistan - Caspian Sea - Azerbaijan

An increase in the level of trafficking has been observed along these routes, especially in the last two years (2007-2008). Unfortunately, there is a lack of information currently available to determine the significance of these routes and accurately estimate the level of trafficking. However, as reported by the Turkish narcotic police at several Paris Pact meetings in 2008, there were at least eight cases, accounting for the interception of 1 ton of heroin via the above-mentioned routes, in 2007-2008. In all these cases, Turkish narcotic police worked jointly with Ukrainian and Azeri counter-narcotic officials.

5-Turkey

Turkey's geographical location has made it a primary gateway for heroin trafficking to Europe. Annually, around an estimated 95 tons of heroin enter Turkey from the Islamic Republic of Iran and Iraq/Syrian Arab Republic (2 tons) on the way to Europe. Heroin is mainly smuggled into Turkey through its borders with Iran.

Turkish counter-narcotic officials seize annually around 10 tons of heroin, or 10 per cent of the estimated amount of heroin trafficked via Turkey. Total heroin consumption is estimated at one ton in Turkey. The remainder, 80-85 tons of heroin, is trafficked to Europe. Most of it is smuggled to Europe via the Turkey/Bulgaria and, to a lesser extent, the Turkey/Greece borders. A smaller volume of 2-3 tons is shipped by vessel to Ukraine via the Black Sea. There is also a small amount of heroin trafficked (by sea) directly from Turkey to Italy, Netherlands or Greece.

6-Africa

There are an estimated 1.2 million heroin users in Africa, who consume around 25 tons of heroin per year. Given the dearth of data on Africa (with regard to both prevalence and per capita consumption figures), this estimate may change once additional and more reliable data are made available from the countries in the region.

Map 20: Heroin flows to/from Turkey, 2008

Map 21: Heroin seizures reported in Turkey, 2002-2007

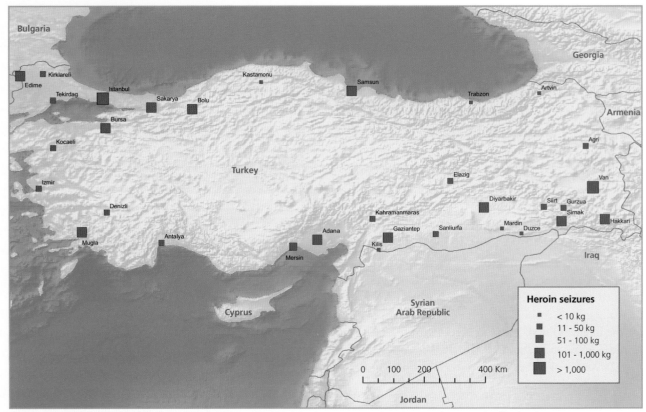

Heroin seizures
- ■ < 10 kg
- ■ 11 - 50 kg
- ■ 51 - 100 kg
- ■ 101 - 1,000 kg
- ■ > 1,000

Source: UNODC/WCO. Note: The boundaries and names shown and the designations used on this map do not imply official endorsement or acceptance by the United Nations.

African law enforcement officials seize around 0.3 tons of heroin per year. As previously explained, heroin is transshipped from Africa to North America (3 tons/year), China (4 tons/year) and Europe (2 tons/year). Consequently, around 30-33 tons of heroin need to be shipped to Africa to satisfy local and international markets.

Most heroin trafficked to Africa travels from Pakistan. Of the estimated 33-ton African heroin market, up to 20 tons may be sourced in Pakistan. The remainder is trafficked from the United Arab Emirates and the Middle East (5 tons), the Islamic Republic of Iran (4 tons), India (3 tons) and 1 ton from South and South-East Asian countries.

7-United Arab Emirates (UAE) and other Gulf area and Middle Eastern countries (excluding the Islamic Republic of Iran):

The total estimated heroin consumption of the 26,000 users in the Gulf area and the Middle East (excluding the Islamic Republic of Iran) is around 1.6 tons per year. These countries seize approximately 0.5 tons of heroin per year.

Around 10-12 tons of heroin is trafficked from Pakistan to the Gulf area and Middle Eastern countries each year. This is supplemented by an additional four tons trafficked from the Islamic Republic of Iran. This is in line with the seizure information from the UAE which estimates that 20 per cent of the heroin trafficked to the UAE is shipped from Iran.

Out of 12-13 tons of incoming heroin, 2 tons are consumed and seized in the Gulf area and Middle Eastern countries. The rest, some 10 tons, proceeds to China (one ton), Africa (five tons – mainly Ethiopia, Nigeria and Tanzania), Europe (one ton), Turkey (two tons), and South and South-East Asian countries (one ton), according to the combined seizure data from these countries and the UAE.

Map 22: Heroin seizures reported in the United Arab Emirates, 2007

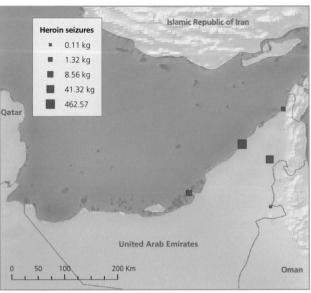

Heroin seizures
- ■ 0.11 kg
- ■ 1.32 kg
- ■ 8.56 kg
- ■ 41.32 kg
- ■ 462.57

Source: UNODC/WCO. Note: The boundaries and names shown and the designations used on this map do not imply official endorsement or acceptance by the United Nations.

Opium trafficking

A total of 4 million opium users worldwide consume 1,000-1,300 tons of raw opium annually. Half of all users live in South and South-East Asia and Oceania, regions that are supplied by opium from Myanmar. India is a major market with around 675,000 users estimated to consume around 70 tons of opium per year. The remaining users in these regions are estimated to consume approximately 100 tons of opium per year. Nearly all the opium consumed in these regions originates from Myanmar or is produced locally in the Lao People's Democratic Republic, Viet Nam, Thailand and some other South and South-East Asian countries, but to a very limited extent.

According to Government reports, opium is not being trafficked into India. Consequently, the 70 tons of opium estimated to be consumed in India annually should be produced locally.

A total of 900-950 tons of opium is consumed domestically in countries and regions to which Afghan opium is trafficked (the Islamic Republic of Iran, Pakistan, Central Asia, the Russian Federation, Turkey, Europe and Africa). There, the total annual average amount of opium seized is around 220 tons. It is thus cautiously estimated that a total of 1,100 -1,200 tons of opium is required to meet the demand, after seizures, in these regions annually.

Russian opium users are estimated to consume 55-60 tons per year, while those in Central Asia consume approximately 30-35 tons. Opium users in the Baltic and Eastern European countries consume around 35 tons per year. In these regions, total average opium seizures amount to

Table 18: Total opium seizures in Central Asia (kg), 1996-2007

Opium seizure (kg)	1996	1997	1998	1999	2000	2001	2002	2003	2004	2005	2006	2007	Average (1996-2007)
Kazakhstan	502	1,000	314	170	136	36	14	193	353	669	637	336	363
Kyrgyzstan	1,490	1,640	172	151	1,405	469	109	46	318	117	302	271	541
Tajikistan	3,405	3,456	1,190	1,269	4,778	3,664	1,624	2,371	2,316	1,104	1,387	2,542	2,426
Turkmenistan	1,750	1,410	1,412	4,600	2,419	267	1,200	138	666	749	2,656	2,284	1,629
Uzbekistan	1,866	2,364	1,935	3,292	2,008	241	76	151	385	108	759	731	1,160
Total	9,013	9,869	5,024	9,483	10,747	4,678	3,023	2,898	4,036	2,746	5,741	6,163	6,118

Map 23: Opium seizures reported in Central Asia, 2002-2008

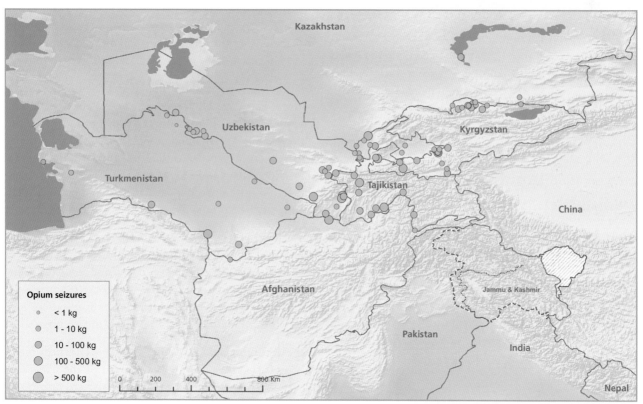

Source: UNODC/WCO. Note: The boundaries and names shown and the designations used on this map do not imply official endorsement or acceptance by the United Nations. Dotted line represents approximately the Line of Control in Jammu and Kashmir agreed upon by India and Pakistan. The final status of Jammu and Kashmir has not yet been agreed upon by the parties.

Map 24: Opium seizures reported in the Islamic Republic of Iran, 2002-2007

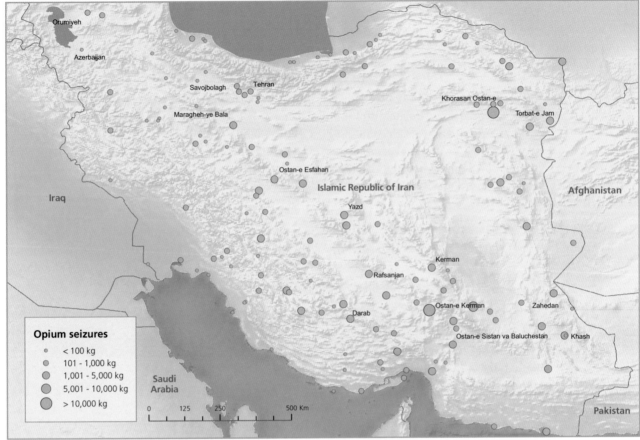

Source: UNODC/WCO. Note: The boundaries and names shown and the designations used on this map do not imply official endorsement or acceptance by the United Nations.

approximately 5 tons. This means that 120-130 tons of raw opium are trafficked from Afghanistan to Central Asia, and of this, 90-95 tons reach Russia.

Although opium consumption in the Russian Federation has been increasing since 1999, the amount of opium seized by the Central Asian countries (except Kazakhstan) decreased sharply after 2001. As shown in table 20, between 2001 and 2006 opium seizures in Central Asian countries were significantly below the 11-year average (6,118kg/year between 1996-2007). Exceptionally, in 2007, and especially in Turkmenistan and Tajikistan, the amount of opium seized was above the 11-year average.

1-Europe

A total of 95 tons of opium is estimated to be consumed in South-Eastern, Western and Central European countries per year. The average amount of opium seized in this region is around 740 kg per year. In Turkey, opium users consume nine tons, and an average of 200 kg is seized annually. This would indicate that 100 tons of opium are needed to meet demand, after seizures, in these countries every year. Most of this is trafficked via the Afghanistan-Iran-Turkey route.

2-The Islamic Republic of Iran

In Iran, 531,000 opium users are estimated to consume 450 tons of opium per year. Between 2002-2006, an average of

170-200 tons opium was seized each year. Thus, including the outbound opium trafficking from Iran, a total of 600-750 tons of raw opium is trafficked from Afghanistan to Iran every year. This calculation rests on the assumption[20] that there is no (or very limited) opium to heroin conversion being carried out in Iran, Turkey and Eastern Europe.

Opium mainly enters the Islamic Republic of Iran from the Nimroz, Farah and Hirat provinces in western Afghanistan. The locations of opium seizures in Iran and Pakistan also show possible Afghan opium trafficking from Pakistan into Iran's eastern Sistan-Balochistan province. Around 17 per cent of the total opium seized in Pakistan is intercepted in the Iran/Pakistan border area, which indicates Afghan opium trafficking from Western Pakistan into the Islamic Republic of Iran.

There were comparatively few opium interceptions close to the Iran/Iraq and Iran/Turkey borders, and along the coast-line. However, some opium seizures were carried out on the Iran/Turkmenistan border, which may indicate opium trafficking from Iran to Turkmenistan, and/or vice versa.

Generally, most opium seizures in Iran are carried out in July and August, following completion of the harvest in most Afghan provinces (especially the southern provinces).

---

20 This assumption is based on the absence of official data indicating that such conversion would be taking place in the countries concerned.

Map 25: Opium seizures reported in Pakistan, 2000-2008

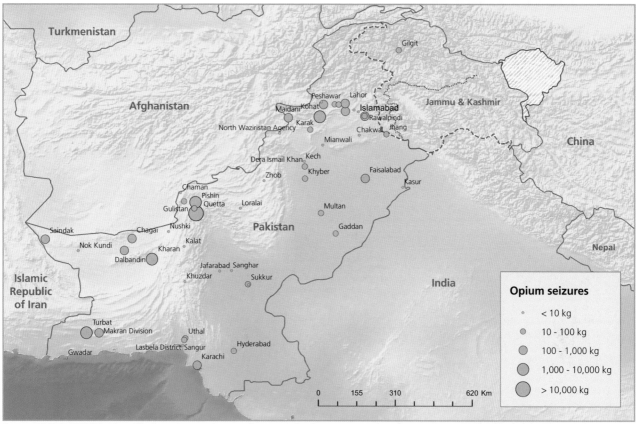

Source: UNODC/WCO. Note: The boundaries and names shown and the designations used on this map do not imply official endorsement or acceptance by the United Nations. Dotted line represents approximately the Line of Control in Jammu and Kashmir agreed upon by India and Pakistan. The final status of Jammu and Kashmir has not yet been agreed upon by the parties.

3-Africa

In Africa, opium use is reported only by Egypt. According to the *World Drug Report 2008*, 0.7 per cent of the adult population, or 343,000 people, are opiate users. Half are heroin users and the other half opium users. Opium users in Egypt are estimated to consume around 55-60 tons of opium per year (an average of almost one gram per day per user). However, no opium seizures from any country have Egypt as their purported destination. The government has reported a small amount of opium poppy cultivation, but in order to produce 60 tons of opium, at least 1,000 ha of poppy cultivation is needed. This indicates that either the figure for opiate/heroin users should be revised or the level of opium poppy cultivation in Egypt is higher than currently estimated.[21]

---

21 Egyptian authorities have questioned the national data, as reported in the 2005/06 household survey of Egypt (275 opiate users out of 40,083 persons interviewed, equivalent to a prevalence rate of 0.7 per cent, of which some three quarters used opium, that is, 0.5 per cent, according to a breakdown found in student surveys) accurately reflected the extent of opiate use in the country. The way the survey was conducted, it cannot be excluded that the positive responses included persons who used to experiment with opiates in the past, but no longer use opium. Out of the total number of drug users (all drugs), 75 per cent consumed drugs regularly or were dependent drug users and 25 per cent used them 'for trial and amusement' purposes. Applying the 75 per cent ratio, the prevalence of opium consumption could fall to 0.4 per cent. Extrapolating results from a national student survey in Egypt (lifetime use of opium by 48 students and of heroin by 15 students out of 18,349 students interviewed, that is, 0.3 per cent and 0.1 per cent, respectively) to the national level would result in far lower annual prevalence rates of opiate

4-Pakistan

Some 80 tons of opium are consumed annually in Pakistan (similar to Afghanistan).

Since 1996, the highest volumes of opium seizures in Pakistan were recorded in 1999 and 2007. Between 1996 and 2007, Pakistani law enforcement officers seized an average of 7,200 kg of opium per year, making Pakistan the second most important interception country in the world (after the Islamic Republic of Iran).

Between 2004 and 2007, 97 per cent of opium seizures in Pakistan were carried out in 17 cities. Eight of these are located in Balochistan province, which accounts for 72 per cent of total opium seizures in Pakistan. Punjab province accounts for 21 per cent.

Highlights on opiate flows

Heroin consumption in the world is estimated at around 340 tons per year. Europe consumes more than a quarter (26 per cent) of this amount (excluding the Russian Federation), followed by the Russian Federation with 21 per cent and China with 17 per cent. The average amount of

---

use among the general population (0.14 per cent, including 0.1 per cent using opium). Based on the latter results the necessary opium consumption would amount to some 12 tons, equivalent to areas under poppy cultivation between 400 and 1,000 ha.

Table 19: Distribution of opium seizures reported in Pakistan by location, 2002-2008

Region	Percentage of total opium seized in Pakistan	City
FATA	1%	Maidani
Punjab	1%	Rawalpindi
Balochistan	1%	Saindak
NWFP	1%	Peshawar
NWFP	1%	Attock
Sindh	1%	Karachi
Punjab	2%	Faisalabad
Balochistan	2%	Dalbandin
Balochistan	3%	Chagai
Balochistan	3%	Mekran
Balochistan	6%	Turbat
Balochistan	6%	Kharan
Balochistan	12%	Pishin
Punjab	18%	Kohat
Balochistan	39%	Quetta

Republic were the main heroin suppliers for markets in China, India and other countries in South, East and South-East Asia, and Oceania. But following the sharp decreases in opium production in Myanmar and Laos, Afghan heroin has started to be trafficked to all regions of the world.

Fig. 12: Global heroin consumption (340 tons)*

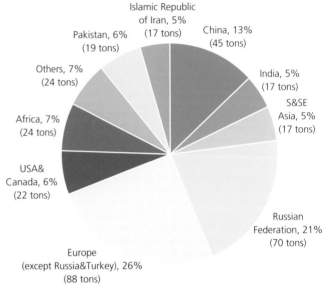

* 340 tons of heroin is equal to 2,600 tons of opium.
Source: UNODC.

heroin seized every year is around 90-95 tons. Thus, 430-440 tons of heroin are sufficient to meet annual global demand and seizures. Of this, 50 tons are supplied by heroin production in Myanmar. The rest is met by Afghan production.

Global annual opium consumption is estimated at 1,100 tons. Raw opium from Myanmar is consumed in South and East Asia, whereas opium from Afghanistan is consumed in South-East Asia, Central Asia, the Middle East and Europe. In addition to the opium production in these two countries, opium is produced in other regions like South America, Africa, South and East Asia.

Data from 1995-2005 indicate that the average opium production in the world amounted to 4,700 tons. Of this, around 3,300 tons (70 per cent) was processed into heroin and the rest was consumed (including seizures) as raw opium. According to currently available demand and seizure statistics, 4,700 tons of opium are sufficient for the heroin and opium consumption of the more than 15 million opiate users in the world, after deduction of 1,000 tons of seizures.

Since 2006, the average annual opium production in Afghanistan has been 7,300 tons (8,000 tons worldwide). There is no indication of a dramatic increase in global heroin consumption in recent years. This amount therefore far exceeds total global demand, to the extent that another 16 million drug users would be needed to consume it. It is estimated that around 12,000 tons of opium is stockpiled somewhere between Afghanistan and transit/destination countries.

Before 2002, Myanmar and the Lao People's Democratic

Between 2002 and 2006, around half of global heroin and morphine seizures were made by two of Afghanistan's neighbours: Pakistan (31 per cent) and the Islamic Republic of Iran (19 per cent). Moreover, the same two countries made more than 90 per cent of global morphine seizures: Pakistan (61 per cent) and Iran (30 per cent). Morphine is used either to produce heroin or consumed as is.

Whereas Colombia, the main cocaine producing country, seizes around a quarter of its cocaine production, Afghanistan (like Myanmar) seizes only about 1 per cent of the heroin produced on its territory.

Fig. 13: Heroin and morphine seizures worldwide, 2002-2006

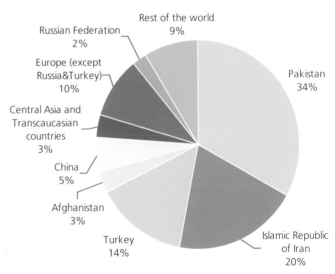

Table 21: Heroin flows worldwide (tons) after 2002

from \ to	Afghanistan	Myanmar	Europe	Turkey	Iran	Caucasus	Central Asia	Russia	Gulf area and Middle East	Pakistan	China	India	Africa	Oceania	USA and Canada	South and South-East Asia	Unknown	Total
Afghanistan	6		105				95			150	3						20	379
Myanmar	2										38	1					9	50
Europe															5			5
Turkey			85															85
Islamic Republic of Iran				95		9	2		2				4					112
Caucasus			7															7
Central Asia						2		77			1							80
Russia	4																	4
Gulf area and Middle East				1	2						1	5					1	10
Pakistan				5	35				11		6	20			2		25	104
China												1						1
India	1										2	3			7		6	19
Africa	2										4				3		3	12
Ocenia																		0
USA and Canada																		0
Rest of S & SE Asia	1										3	13	1	1	3			22
Unknown											20							20
Total	8	0	106	97	140	11	97	77	13	150	55	37	33	2	20	44		

Table 20: Annual heroin/morphine and all opiates flows and seizures in the world since 2002*

Country/Region	Heroin and morphine			All opiates (heroin, morphine and opium) in opium equivalent		
	Estimated flow (tons)	Average seizures* (tons)	Per cent of estimated flow intercepted	Estimated flow (tons)	Average seizures* (tons)	Per cent of estimated flow intercepted
Afghanistan	380	4	1%	3500	61	2%
Pakistan	150	26	18%	1135	189	17%
Islamic Republic of Iran	140	17	12%	1713	291	20%
Turkey	95	10	10%	768	69	9%
South East Europe**	90	1.5	2%	724	10.5	2%
Rest of Europe (except Russia)	105	9	9%	828	74	9%
Midde East& Gulf countries (except Iran)	14	0.5	4%	114	4	4%
Central Asia	95	5	5%	790	39	5%
Russian Federation	77	3	4%	627	23	4%
Africa	35	0.3	1%	305	2.3	7%
Myanmar	60	1	1%	920	12	2%
India	37	1	3%	328	11	3%
China	55	9	16%	398	73	18%
Rest of S & SE Asia	30	0.7	2%	285	16	6%
Oceania	2	0.3	13%	19	2.5	13%
USA and Canada	24	2	9%	168	17	10%

*Seizure averages for 2002-2006. **Bulgaria, Greece, Albania, Romania, Serbia, The former Yugoslav Republic of Macedonia, Bosnia, Croatia, Montenegro.

Map 26: Estimated heroin flows from Asia to the world (in tons)

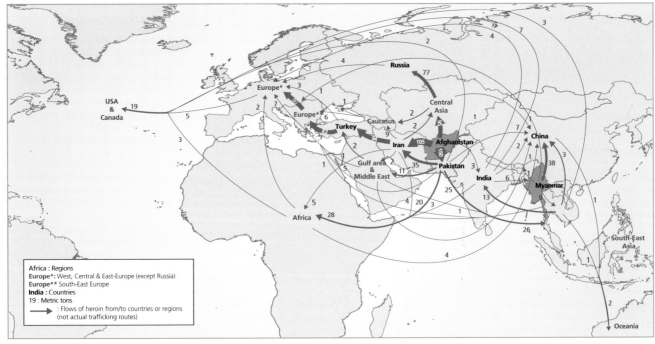

Source: UNODC.

The volume of heroin seizures declines as heroin gets closer to its main destination points. Moreover, while total heroin seizures in Europe account for 12 per cent of seizures worldwide, European users consume 27 per cent of the total heroin production.

Afghanistan's southern neighbour, Pakistan, seizes around 18 per cent of the total heroin and morphine flows from Afghanistan, whereas the Islamic Republic of Iran seizes 12 per cent. Afghanistan's northern neighbours, Tajikistan, Turkmenistan and Uzbekistan, seize another 5 per cent of the total Afghan heroin flow. The main destination country on the northern route, the Russian Federation, seizes 4 per cent of the estimated amount of incoming heroin.

On the Balkan route, Turkey seizes some 9 per cent of the heroin it receives from the Islamic Republic of Iran. Turkey's border countries, Greece and Bulgaria, seize only 2 per cent. The main destination countries on this route (the United Kingdom and Italy) each seize around 10 per cent of the heroin trafficked across their borders.

China, a significant destination country, seizes around 16 per cent of the heroin trafficked across its borders. Countries in Oceania seize around 13 per cent while the USA and Canada both seize 9 per cent of the heroin shipped into their territories.

The total estimated heroin flow to India is around 40 tons per year. Half of this is shipped from other South and South-East Asian countries and Afghanistan. The source of the remaining 20 tons is unknown. It may be sourced in Afghanistan and trafficked via Pakistan or through other routes, or be produced in India (diverted from licit to illicit). To shed light on this, a detailed heroin consumption and trafficking study should be carried out in India.

India only seizes around 2 per cent of the incoming heroin.

The lowest seizure rates are reported in Africa, Myanmar and Afghanistan with 1 per cent.

Looking at all opiates combined (opium, heroin and morphine), between 2002 and 2006, on average, 20 per cent of the estimated global opiate flow was seized in the world every year. Seizures as a proportion of the estimated opiate flow affecting Afghanistan, Africa, Myanmar and South-East Europe (except Turkey), East, South and South-East Asia (except China) and India are quite low (1-3 per cent), compared with the ratio for other countries, such as the Islamic Republic of Iran (20 per cent), China (18 per cent) and Pakistan (17 per cent).

All these calculations and estimations are based on the data available to UNODC. In order to more accurately estimate the heroin flows worldwide, consumption estimates are needed for each country. Unfortunately, this information is currently unavailable. In this report, regional average heroin consumption figures provided by a limited number of countries were used. In order to achieve greater accuracy, global mechanisms should be established to collect data on heroin consumption.

Despite several UN resolutions and/or conventions on sharing detailed drug seizure data with UNODC, some countries have yet to provide this data. As for the ARQ data, UNODC receives these from most countries. But many fields in these forms are not comprehensively filled in by Member States. There are also related challenges of data collection and storage capacity. Thus, there is scope to build up systems of data collection, processing, analysis and exchange at the national and international levels, as well as maintaining databases on drug trafficking and related forms of organized crime.

The findings in this report provide the best, first estimates given the data available. As the heroin flow model relies heavily on global demand statistics it will be updated regularly as these figures change.

Detailed individual seizure statistics provided by Member States are also necessary to acquire a better understanding of heroin and opium trafficking routes.

5. Opiate trafficking routes

Afghanistan

Opium and heroin are trafficked by road through the porous border between Afghanistan and the neighbouring countries of Pakistan, the Islamic Republic of Iran, Tajikistan, Uzbekistan and Turkmenistan. There are 14 official and at least 500 unofficial border crossing points between Afghanistan and its neighbours.

Since 2007, opium poppy cultivation has mainly been concentrated in southern and western Afghanistan. There remain, however, significant opiate trafficking routes from eastern Afghanistan to Pakistan and from northern Afghanistan to Tajikistan/Uzbekistan/Turkmenistan. Heroin and opium are trafficked within Afghanistan using overland routes from the south to the west, north and east. Traffickers use the main highways and some secondary roads for this purpose. In Afghanistan, there are checkpoints at the

entry and exit points of each province. Given that Afghan law enforcement officials seize only one per cent of the opium produced in Afghanistan, this raises the question of corruption and/or lack of capacity at these checkpoints.

Once heroin/opium reaches northern Afghanistan, especially the Badakshan and Takhar provinces, it becomes increasingly challenging to interdict trafficking to Tajikistan due to difficult geographical conditions (high rugged mountain terrain) along their borders with Central Asia. The Panj River at the borders between Afghanistan and Tajikistan/Uzbekistan helps traffickers to smuggle opiates undetected (including night crossings).

There are more than 100 active heroin labs in Afghanistan, but this is likely a low estimate.[22] Heroin labs are usually small in size and relatively easy to conceal. There are also some mobile labs hidden in the back of trucks in Afghanistan, according to surveyors from the Afghan Ministry of Counter Narcotics.

Although there is a high amount of trafficking from Hilmand province to Pakistan, there are no official border checkpoints at the Pakistan/Hilmand border, which leaves approximately 110 kilometres of border completely uncontrolled. According to seizure data from Pakistan, there is a high amount of opiate seizures close to the Dalbandin area

Map 27: Heroin and opium trafficking routes and unofficial border crossing points in Afghanistan, 2008

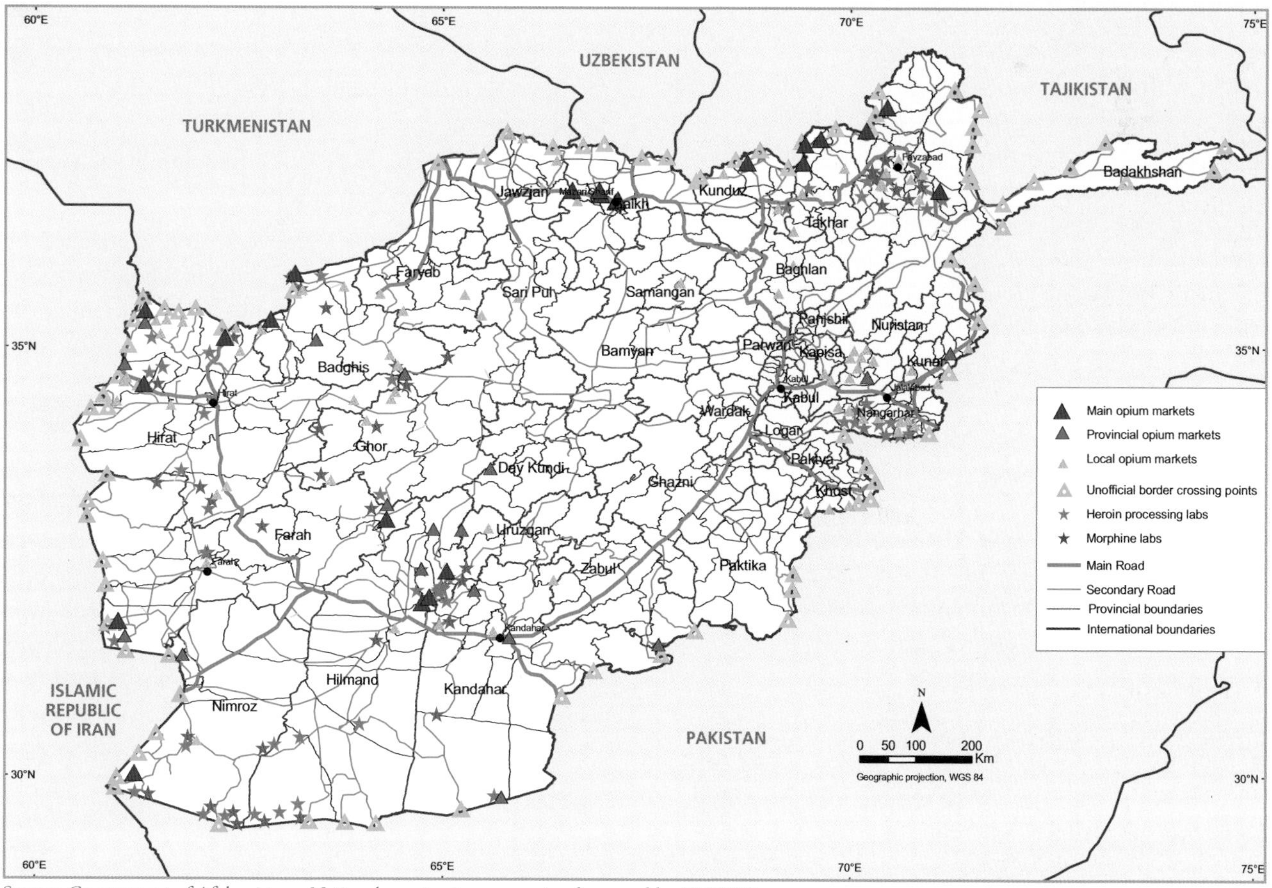

Source: Government of Afghanistan - National monitoring system implemented by UNODC.

22 Estimating and/or targeting processing laboratories is not an easy task, as they can function virtually anywhere, using a few metal drums and a press.

Map 28:   Official border crossing points between Afghanistan and its neighbours

Note: The boundaries and names shown and the designations used on this map do not imply official endorsement or acceptance by the United Nations. Dotted line represents approximately the Line of Control in Jammu and Kashmir agreed upon by India and Pakistan. The final status of Jammu and Kashmir has not yet been agreed upon by the parties.

in Chagai district (Balochistan province), near Hilmand's border with Pakistan. However, there is no official border crossing point between Afghanistan and Pakistan in this area (Chagai). There is also a lack of government presence in southern Nimroz, a major trafficking hub for smuggling into Iran and Pakistan. In addition, there are numerous heroin labs in Hilmand province, which indicates likely precursor trafficking from Dalbandin and other border cities of Pakistan into Hilmand province.

Pakistan

Heroin and opium enters Pakistan from Afghanistan's eastern and southern provinces.

From eastern Afghanistan, through Nangarhar, Kunar, Khost and Paktika provinces, heroin and opium are trafficked into the Federally Administered Tribal Areas (FATA) region of Pakistan where insurgent groups linked to the Taliban and Al-Qaeda increasingly hold sway.

Negligible opiate seizures have been reported in FATA over the last several years. Significant heroin seizures have been reported in the adjacent North Western Frontier Province (NWFP) region which, although similarly restive, is under the full control of the Pakistan Government.

Opiates are trafficked through FATA in three main directions:

a. Towards China via Gilgit (northern areas), by road

b. Towards India through the NWFP - Chakwai/ Rawalpindi - Sailkot - Wagha route

c. Towards Karachi via NWFP - Rawalpindi - Chawai-Faisaba - Mutan-Sukkur route

Opiate trafficking in this region is mainly controlled by Pakistani drug trafficking groups, most of whom have kinship ties across the border and some of whom enjoy the support and protection of insurgency groups. Moreover, Pakistani authorities have indicated increasing involvement of West African groups, particularly Nigerians, in the opiate trade in and out of Pakistan.

Opiates leave southern Afghanistan through Hilmand, Kandahar and Nimroz provinces, mainly into the cities of Quetta and Dalbandin in Balochistan. Some of these opiates then travel to Karachi to be hidden in cargo containers for shipment via air or sea or via commercial airlines. Another portion is trafficked to eastern Iran by road and rail. A third route is via the southern sea ports of Pakistan (Gwadar and Pasni) through Panjgour city in Pakistan.

From Pakistan, opiates are shipped to several destinations worldwide:

i.   China: by air or road

ii. India (only heroin): by road

iii. East and South-East Asia: by air and sea

Map 29: Drug trafficking routes in Pakistan

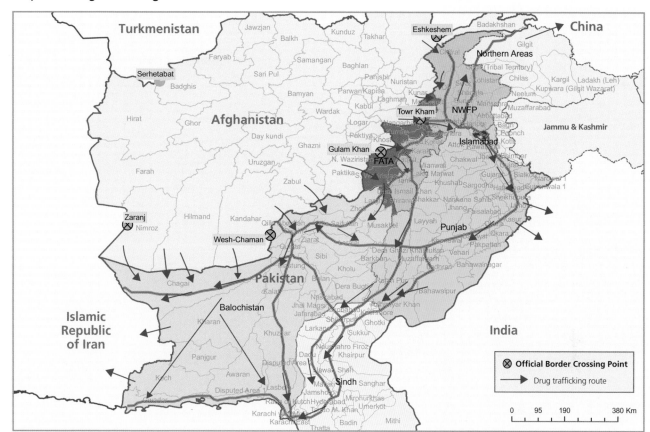

Note: The boundaries and names shown and the designations used on this map do not imply official endorsement or acceptance by the United Nations. Dotted line represents approximately the Line of Control in Jammu and Kashmir agreed upon by India and Pakistan. The final status of Jammu and Kashmir has not yet been agreed upon by the parties.

iv.   The Islamic Republic of Iran: by road

v.   Gulf area countries: by air and sea

vi.   North America: by air

vii.   Europe: by air

viii.   Africa: by air and sea

Balkan route

The Islamic Republic of Iran

Opiates are smuggled into Iran from the Afghan provinces of Hirat, Farah and Nimroz, and the Pakistani province of Balochistan. A third route proceeds from Turkmenistan, but is not as significant as the previous two.

There are three official border crossing points between Afghanistan and the Islamic Republic of Iran and many more unofficial ones on the 949-kilometer Iran-Afghanistan border.

Main opiate trafficking routes:

a.   Afghanistan (Hirat/Farah provinces) - Iran: Khorasan - Semnan - Tehran - Zanjan - Azarbaycan-e-khavari - Turkey.

b.   Afghanistan (Hirat province) - Iran: Khorasan - Turkmenistan - Caspian Sea - Azerbaijan - Georgia - Black Sea.

c.   Afghanistan (Hirat province) - Iran: Khorasan - Semnan - Mazandaran - Caspian Sea - Azerbaijan or Turkmenistan.

d.   Afghanistan (Nimroz province) or Pakistan (Balochistan province) - Iran: Sistan-Balochistan - Kerman - Yazd - Esfahan - Markazi - Tehran - Zanjan - Azarbaycan-e-khavari - Turkey.

e.   Afghanistan (Nimroz province) or Pakistan (Balochistan province) - Iran: Sistan - Balochistan - Kerman - Hormuzgan to UAE/Africa/other Middle Eastern countries by sea.

f.   Afghanistan (Nimroz province) or Pakistan (Balochistan province) - Iran: Sistan - Balochistan - Kerman - Fars - Bushehr (to other Middle Eastern countries) - Kohkiluyeh - Khuzestan to Kuwait and Iraq.

Between 2005 and 2007, many seizures were reported on railways along these routes in Iran. This is an indication that traffickers in Iran make ample use of the railway networks in addition to road transportation.

Turkey

The vast majority of opiates cross into Turkey from the Islamic Republic of Iran. Trafficking patterns indicate that the narcotics cross from the Azarbaycan-e-khavari province of Iran into Turkey, traverse Turkey's Hakkari and/or Van

Map 30: Major drug trafficking routes in the Islamic Republic of Iran

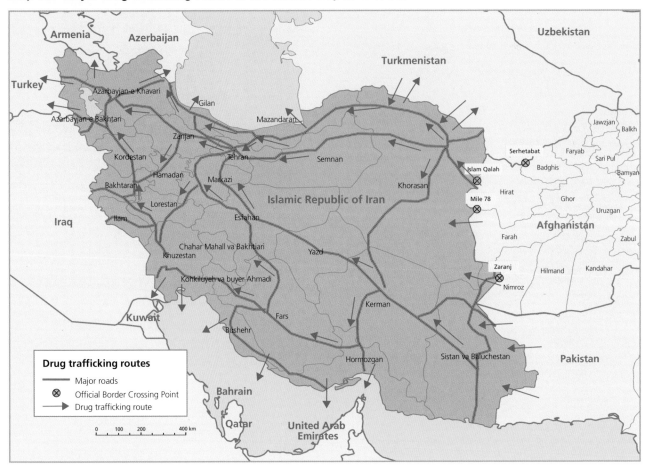

districts, and then mostly travel via the following routes:

a. Hakkari/Van - south-eastern cities - central Anatolia cities - Istanbul - Edirne to Bulgaria/Greece

b. Hakkari/Van - south-eastern cities - southern/western Anatolia cities to Greece/Cyprus with sea transportation

c. Hakkari/Van - south-eastern cities - central Anatolia cities - northern Anatolia cities - Ukraine (with smaller amounts to Georgia).

There is also opiate trafficking by air from Turkey to Europe. However, the Turkey/Europe land route has established infrastructure to support the vast majority of the trafficking which takes place via road or rail transport. On a monthly basis, the average number of vehicles entering or leaving Turkey is around 350,000. Almost half of this number is recorded at the Turkey/Bulgaria border (Kapikule) where around 5,000 vehicles cross every day. Each month, an average of 10,000-13,000 vehicles cross the Turkey - Greece border in both directions.

An average of 20,000 vehicles travel from the Gurbulak (Iran/Turkey) border each month. The Iraq - Turkey border crossing (Habur) processes significantly more vehicles (around 80,000 vehicles per month) than Gurbulak, however.

There is also a rail network connecting Turkey/Bulgaria, Turkey/Greece, Turkey/Iran and Turkey/Iraq.

Balkans

The vast majority of the heroin and opium that enters Bulgaria and Greece is trafficked via Turkey by road and rail transportation. These opiates are then trafficked to two main destinations: Germany/Netherlands and Italy.

a. Trafficking route to Germany/Netherlands: From Bulgaria, opiates are smuggled to Romania and Hungary, continue to Austria, and then to Germany/Netherlands. A smaller amount passes through the Bulgaria - Serbia - Austria route. Once heroin/opium reaches Germany, it travels further to the UK via the Netherlands and France.

b. Trafficking route to Italy: Most of the opiates smuggled into Italy come via Albania and to a lesser extent form Greece.

Another route to Italy is the Albania-Croatia-Slovakia corridor. A portion is also trafficked to Switzerland from Croatia/Italy.

This route is largely dominated by Albanian criminal groups using the Balkan region as a base for their drug smuggling activities.

Map 31: Opiate trafficking routes in Central Asia

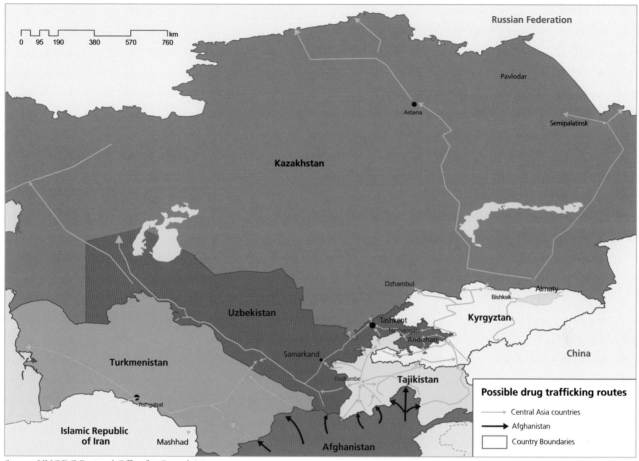

Source: UNODC Regional Office for Central Asia.

Northern route

Afghan opiates enter Central Asia via the borders of Tajikistan, Uzbekistan and Turkmenistan, and proceed to their destinations in the Russian Federation. Apart from air routes, Kazakhstan is an obligatory transit corridor to reach Russia.

Opiates enter Tajikistan from the provinces of Badakshan, Takhar and Kunduz in northern Afghanistan. The shipments are then transported by road across the country into Kyrgyzstan and Uzbekistan. There is also heroin trafficking by air and railway from Tajikistan to Russia.

Opiates enter Uzbekistan from a) Balkh and Kunduz provinces of Afghanistan, b) Tajikistan's border with Uzbekistan, and c) Kyrgyzstan's border with Uzbekistan.

From Uzbekistan, opiates travel further to Kazakhstan, but a small amount is trafficked to Turkmenistan and Kyrgyzstan. Opiates are also trafficked to Russia from Uzbekistan by air.

Kyrgyzstan does not have a border with Afghanistan, which means that the country sources Afghan opiates from Tajikistan (Pamir highway) and Uzbekistan (Ferghana valley). Once in Kyrgyzstan, flows converge towards the Kazakhstan border. There is an air and railway network from Kyrgyzstan through Kazakhstan to the Russian Federation which is also used for opiate trafficking.

Opiates enter Turkmenistan from Afghanistan (through Hirat, Badghis, Faryab and Jawzjan provinces) and the Islamic Republic of Iran. Once in Turkmenistan, the main opiate routes run through Kazakhstan (via the Caspian Sea and/or Uzbekistan). Another opiate route travels to Azerbaijan or Russia via the Caspian Sea.

Once opiates reach Kazakhstan, they are further smuggled through its north-western borders into the Russian Federation. Within Russia, opiates travel in almost every direction since Russia is a main destination country for Afghan opiates. Opiates not destined for the Russian market travel further into South-Eastern Europe via its borders with Latvia, Estonia and Ukraine by road, sea and railways. An additional opiate route runs through Russia into northern Europe via the border with Finland.

Other routes

Afghan heroin is trafficked to almost all regions worldwide. Trafficking on the northern and Balkan routes is undertaken primarily by road. With the additional use of air and sea transportation networks, Afghan heroin is shipped to the following destinations:

- North America: By commercial aircraft from Europe, Africa, Pakistan and India.

- China: By air, mainly from Pakistan and the United Arab Emirates.

- South Asian countries: By air or sea via Pakistan.

- Australia: From China (heroin from Myanmar) and South-East Asian countries (Afghan heroin).

- Europe: Mainly by air and sea from Africa and Pakistan.

- Ukraine: Since 2007, heroin trafficking to Ukraine via the Iran-Azerbaijan-Georgia-Black Sea route has been increasing.

- In 2008, heroin trafficking cases from Georgia to Bulgaria via the Black Sea were reported.

6. Value of the opiate trade

The opiate market (like all illicit drug markets) is controlled by well-established trafficking organizations of various sizes in cooperation with corrupt officials. In some regions, the trade is facilitated by insurgent groups. The total value of the opiate market is estimated at US$ 65 billion, or 20 per cent of the US$ 320 billion[23] global illicit drug trade.

An estimated 11.3 million heroin users pay around US$ 56 billion to drug dealers per year. The size of the opium market is estimated at around US$ 7 billion. Consequently, the combined total heroin/opium market is worth upwards of US$ 60-65 billion per year. This amount is higher than the GDP of 120 countries in the world and comparable to the GDP of Viet Nam (US$ 71 billion).

One kilogram of pure brown heroin at the Afghanistan/Pakistan border costs US$ 3,200, while in Europe, the same heroin fetches US$ 150,000-170,000 per kilogram, a markup of 30-50 times the original price.

Estimating the value is difficult because of the substantial price increases that occur as goods move along trafficking routes, as well as the number of times a shipment may change hands. One kilogram of high quality heroin at the Iran/Afghanistan or Iran/Pakistan border is around US$ 5,000/kg. When the same heroin reaches the Iran/Turkey border its price per kilogram increases to approximately US$ 8,000, a 60 per cent increase. Based on the estimated flows through this route, organized crime groups or individuals organizing the heroin trafficking from the Afghanistan/Iran border to the Turkey/Iran border stand to pocket some US$ 450-600 million per year.

The estimated worth of opiates trafficked through the Afghanistan/Iran border is US$ 1 billion. Iranian opiate users spend around US$ 1.4 billion a year. European opiate users spend more than ten times that amount on Afghan heroin and opium, an average of US$ 20 billion/year.

As heroin gets closer to its main destinations, the profit level increases and organized crime groups realize higher profit margins. The wholesale price of high quality heroin at Turkey's borders with Bulgaria and Greece is around US$ 20,000. That price more than doubles (to US$ 45,000) once it reaches Germany. The estimated annual profit of organized crime groups managing heroin trafficking between Iran/Turkey and further to the Turkey/Bulgaria and/or Turkey/Greece borders is around US$ 8,000 per kilogram, totalling US$ 600-700 million. Groups organizing the heroin trafficking from Turkey/Bulgaria to Germany generate profits of US$ 25,000 per kg.

The total estimated value of opiate trafficking in Pakistan is around US$ 1 billion per year. In addition to supporting independent drug traffickers and organized groups, the drug trade may also serve as a significant source of funding for some of the insurgent groups active in the border areas of Pakistan and Afghanistan.

Fig. 14: Global opiate market value (US$ 65 billion/year)

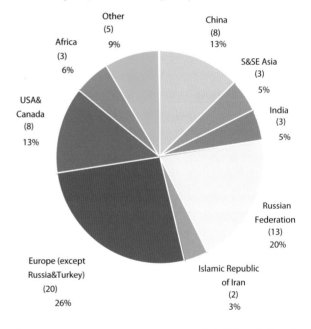

Chinese opiate users pay approximately US$ 10 billion/year to domestic drug dealers. Chinese heroin wholesalers pay around US$ 98,000 to Chinese/Myanmar traffickers for a kilogram of heroin at the China/Myanmar border and sell it to retailers in China for around US$ 130,000 per kg.

In North and South America, the total size of the opiate market is estimated at US$ 21 billion/year. In the USA alone, the market is worth an estimated US$ 7.8 billion/year to drug dealers (US$ 2.5 billion for opiates from Latin America/Mexico and US$ 5.3 billion for Afghan opiates).

Central Asia is a major transit route for Afghan heroin/opium. Around 25 per cent of all the Afghan heroin flows through Central Asia into the Russian Federation. The estimated value of opiates trafficked through the Afghanistan/Central Asia border area is around US$ 350-400 million. This amount increases several times on the way to

Russia. Kazakhstan is the main hub in Central Asia before the Afghan opiates reach the Russian Federation. It is estimated that at least 50 tons of Afghan heroin flow to Russia (Russian opiate users pay around US$ 13 billion/year to drug dealers) via Kazakhstan. This means that a considerable amount of drug money is circulating in Central Asia. Central Asian economies are highly cash-based and there are always differences between official and informal exchange rates. This provides a potential money-laundering mechanism for drug traffickers.

7. Afghan opiates in new markets

Until 2002, the main destination for Afghan opiates was Europe (and to a lesser extent the USA and Canada). In parallel with the decrease in opium production in Myanmar, the availability of Afghan opiates increased in these traditional markets and in a number of other markets across the world. In the year 2000, opium production in South and South-East Asia (mainly Myanmar and the Lao People's Democratic Republic) was 1,260 tons, but by 2002 it had decreased to 950 tons and in 2007, 469 tons. Conversely, as of 2000 (except in 2001), opium production in Afghanistan began to increase.

As there was no proportional decrease in heroin consumption in East, South and South-East Asia and the Pacific, the heroin gap in these markets was filled by Afghan heroin. Seizures of Afghan heroin have been reported in almost all countries in this region. With a large population of heroin users, China became an especially attractive market for Afghan heroin after 2002.

Africa is an emerging destination for Afghan heroin. One of the indicators is the rise in the number of heroin users, which increased by an estimated 54 per cent between 2004 and 2008. Perhaps due to improved security along traditional trafficking routes, some African countries are increasingly used as transit points for Afghan heroin trafficking, especially to Europe and North America.

As of the year 2000, the Russian Federation became another important destination for Afghan heroin, due to the increase in the number of heroin users in that country.

8. Precursor trafficking

Without precursor chemicals there can be no heroin processing, but precursor control has lagged behind other drug control initiatives. Afghanistan's neighbours have tended to develop border security and counter-narcotics policies in isolation, while limited capacity within Afghanistan has inhibited effective cooperation in areas such as backtracking investigations. The bulk of Afghan law enforcement resources and manpower is directed toward interdicting opiate exports. While the Government is publicly committed to precursor control, recent donor interest

in this area is starting from a low base. Only a handful of agencies include precursor modules in their law enforcement training curricula, and relevant equipment is not widely held, even among otherwise well-equipped forces.

The chemicals used in heroin processing range from unrestricted, common chemicals to internationally monitored and more exotic substances. UNODC estimates that approximately two thirds of Afghan opium production is transformed into heroin in-country.[24] Around 10,000 tons of precursor chemicals are required, including acetic anhydride, ammonium chloride, hydrochloric acid, acetone, lime and sodium bicarbonate.[25]

This section begins with a discussion of the chemicals of major concern for heroin precursor control. With a focus on acetic anhydride, price data is considered, which shows significant increases in procurement costs. Mapping seizures in Afghanistan, source and transit countries demonstrates that only a tiny proportion of flows has been interdicted. Precursor trafficking for Afghan heroin production is multi-directional and multi-modal.

Targets for heroin precursor control

Acetic anhydride is the most common chemical used to convert morphine to heroin. However, it does have potential substitutes. The most likely of these is acetyl chloride, a chemical that is more difficult to handle but which is not internationally controlled. UNODC noted in India that "[o]ne recent trend detected during certain investigations has been the use of acetyl chloride as a substitute chemical for acetic anhydride".[26] The United States Drug Enforcement Administration has also observed that acetyl chloride can be used to convert opium into heroin.[27]

Small quantities of acetyl chloride have been found in heroin laboratories outside Afghanistan, although acetic anhydride was also present. The acetyl chloride appeared to be used as a 'kick-starter' before the application of acetic anhydride. A sizeable seizure of acetyl chloride occurred in Iran in 2008 (see further discussion below). Overall, however, it appears that acetyl chloride remains much less commonly used than acetic anhydride. If some laboratories have found ways to bypass acetic anhydride in heroin synthesis, there is a general consensus that such chemicals would be of the acetyl family, a common group that includes acetic acid. Theoretically, acetic anhydride may be manufactured on-site in Afghanistan from acetic acid (or any other sub-

---

24 UNODC, "Precursors used in heroin manufacture: strengthening operational activities in Eurasia", 2006.

25 Not included in the 10,000 tons and often forgotten, wood and water are two inputs required in large quantities for heroin production. Around 500 litres of water are needed for each kilogram of heroin, a constraint on the location of laboratories. Significant stocks of firewood are also needed to heat cooking barrels.

26 UNODC, "South Asia Regional Profile", 2005.

27 U.S. Department of Justice Drug Enforcement Administration, "Opium Poppy Cultivation and Heroin Processing in Southeast Asia", March 2001.

stance containing the active acetyl group). The Director General of the Pakistani Anti Narcotic Force (ANF) reported to UNODC that a number of non-restricted chemicals were being smuggled to Afghanistan, including acetic acid and acetyl chloride.[28] Significant movements and seizures of acetic acid have been noted, such as:

- From 1998 to 2001, Customs in Urumchi (Xinjiang, China) reported confiscating 69 tons of acetic acid (no other details are available).[29]
- In 2001, a drug trafficking network attempted to deliver 50 tons of acetic acid, disguised as fabric products, via South Korea to the Islamic Republic of Iran.[30]
- Two consignments of acetic acid (17.7 tons and 16.2 tons) were stopped in the Islamic Republic of Iran in July 2005.
- A seizure of 1,200 litres of acetic acid in May 2008 during Operation TARCET at the Hayraton checkpoint on the Uzbek-Afghan border.

Most chemists currently believe that on-site manufacturing of a chemical to effectively acetylize morphine in Afghanistan would be exceedingly difficult with limited expertise and in the rudimentary facilities used for heroin processing. Among others, the head of Counter Narcotics Police of Afghanistan's (CNPA) intelligence and analysis section agreed.[31] Conversely, UNODC sources in the south reported that each fixed laboratory has one foreigner (Pakistani and Turkish were two nationalities mentioned) who could likely provide sufficient expertise.

UNODC is aware of only one seizure confirmed as acetic acid within Afghanistan, in August 2005 (120 litres). However, precursor seizure information is sparse in Afghanistan and it is common to refer to all liquid suspected precursors as 'acid'. It is therefore possible that acetic acid has been seized but not identified.[32] A high-ranking CNPA officer also reported to UNODC that acetic acid had been seized during lab interdictions but provided no further details.[33]

Sizeable seizures of sulphuric acid, particularly in Central Asia, have led some to speculate that it may be used in some step of heroin processing. It is commonly thought to be used solely in cocaine manufacturing,[34] although a 2002 DEA[35] report described one heroin recipe in Afghanistan as involving "3 ½ litres of methanol, 5 litres of sulphuric acid, 0.5 litres of ammonium hydroxide and 3 cups of charcoal."[36]

In March 2008, the Drug Control Agency (DCA) of the Kyrgyz Republic reported two seizures of sulphuric acid totalling 5,493 kilograms. During the second stage of the Collective Security Treaty Organization (CSTO) Channel-2007 operation, the Tajik DCA reported seizing 1,856 kilograms of the substance. The same report claimed the acid was used to produce heroin from opium.[37] Furthermore, Afghanistan's Drug Regulation Committee (DRC) and the Uzbek authorities have dealt with a complex but ultimately unsuccessful attempt by an Afghan company to import tons of sulphuric acid.

Prices

Throughout 2008 and into 2009, UNODC received acetic anhydride price reports in Afghanistan that clustered quite consistently in the range of US$300-400 per litre. Prices up to US$750 per litre were also reported several times, most of these coming from Badakshan.[38] To put this price in perspective, licit purchases of acetic anhydride cost less than US$1 per litre. As recently as 2005, processors in Afghanistan were paying around US$65 per litre. Earlier, 1998 prices ranged from US$13 - 34.[39] Overall, there appears to have been a large and quite rapid increase in the price of illicit acetic anhydride.

A similar trend has been observed in China, which reported an increase in illicit acetic anhydride prices of nearly 50 per cent between 2004 and 2007, from approximately US$10,300 per ton to US$17,500 per ton.[40] Taken together, these developments suggest that the trade in heroin precursors may be experiencing disruption, presumably as a result of better international cooperation and improved interdiction of acetic anhydride in particular.

At these prices, acetic anhydride makes up a significant proportion of the costs of processing heroin. For example, in February 2009 in Nangarhar, acetic anhydride costed around US$350 per liter. A kilogram of dry opium was US$108. On the understanding that 2 litres of acetic anhydride and 7 kg of dry opium are required for 1 kg of white heroin hydrochloride, the cost of these inputs is US$1,456. In the same month, the highest purity heroin found by UNODC's price monitoring in Nangarhar was selling for US$1,902 per kilogram. On face value, that leaves a margin of only US$446 per kilogram, excluding all other input costs, such as other precursor chemicals and labour.

The most likely explanation is that between lab and sale there is significant cutting of the heroin, which means that

28 UNODC mission to Pakistan, 2007.

29 Xinjiang Ribao, Urumqi, in Chinese, 3 April 2002.

30 Yonhap news agency, 25 September 2005.

31 Interview with CNPA official, June 2008.

32 In illicit heroin production, acetic acid can also be used in place of ammonium chloride or ammonia solutions as a reagent to adjust alkalinity in the precipitation of morphine from an opium solution.

33 Interview, November 2008.

34 One kilogram of cocaine base requires the use of 3 litres of concentrated sulphuric acid, 10 kilograms of lime, 60 to 80 liters of kerosene, 200 grams of potassium permanganate, and one litre of concentrated ammonia.

35 Drug Enforcement Administration, USA.

36 DEA, *Heroin Laboratories in Afghanistan*, April 2002, p. 40. See also

UNODC, opium poppy survey 2006 p.129.

37 Sulphuric acid can also be used to make Hydrochloric acid in illicit laboratories by mixing it with common sodium chloride (table salt, rock salt or iodized salt); (source: US Department of Justice DEA, "Chemicals used in the clandestine production of drugs", p.50, September 2000).

38 It is likely that these were generated by laboratories in Badakshan seeking acetic anhydride quickly to fulfil an immediate order for heroin.

39 UNODC, "The opium economy in Afghanistan: an international problem", 2003.

40 "China's Drug Control Efforts", *Office of China National Narcotics Control Commission*, June 25, 2008.

Fig. 15: Acetic anhydride prices in Afghanistan, 2006-2008 (US$)

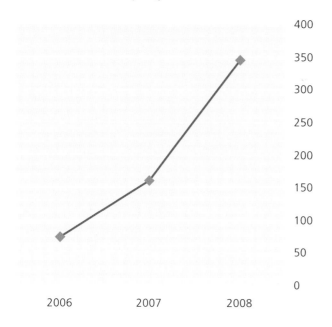

Source: Counter Narcotic Police of Afghanistan (CNPA)

The case of Nangarhar – February 2009

Acetic anhydride = $350 / L
x 2 =   **$700**

Dry opium = $108 / kg
x 7 =   **$756**

Two inputs – total cost: **$1,456**

White heroin hydrochloride: **$1,902 / kg**

Margin =   **$446 / kg**

EXCLUDES other precursors, lab set-up, transport, bribes, labour

1 kg from the lab becomes 1.5, 2 or 3 kg when sold. Nevertheless, the comparison between US$700 of acetic anhydride and US$756 of opium indicates the relative importance of precursors in the cost structure of heroin processing, even in a province such as Nangarhar, where the opium price is at least 30 per cent higher than in the south.

Seizures in Afghanistan

If two thirds of Afghan opium is converted to heroin within Afghanistan, this requires approximately 1,300 tons of acetic anhydride. As Afghanistan has no licit use of acetic anhydride at present, the country does not produce it and has not issued any licences for its importation. In other words, all acetic anhydride used in heroin processing has been smuggled into Afghanistan and any acetic anhydride in the country is illegally possessed. Moreover, none of Afghanistan's neighbours (Central Asian countries, Pakistan, the Islamic Republic of Iran) officially produce acetic anhydride and few shipments of licitly traded acetic anhydride were reported to the International Narcotics Control Board by Afghanistan's immediate neighbours.

It is difficult to obtain comprehensive seizure information in Afghanistan. In 2008, UNODC's seizure database registered the quantities shown on the following page. The fact that the largest seizures were of 'other precursors' indicates the limited capacity for chemical testing in Afghanistan at present. With an estimated 1,300 tons of acetic anhydride required for heroin production, the seizure statistics suggest that only 1.09 per cent of illegal imports were seized.[41]

41 There is a thriving 'secondary trade' in precursor chemicals, that is, interdicted shipments which are then sold on by seizing officers/agencies. UNODC's seizure database attempts to exclude these, the quantities of which are still flowing into the drug trade.

Significantly, more than half of the quantity seized occurred in just two incidents (in Kandahar and Paktya).

Two major caveats are relevant. First, it is quite possible that 'other precursors' include acetic anhydride that was never positively identified prior to destruction. This can be considered acetic anhydride removed from the drug trade, although the deterrent and punitive effect is obviously smaller without associated criminal justice responses. Second, there are huge quantities of chemicals stored near Afghan border crossing points, where they have been placed by border authorities, generally because their attempted importation had no accompanying paperwork. Again, it's possible that these include acetic anhydride, although those attempting to import it would have a strong financial incentive to salvage these chemicals through bribery or unauthorized removal from the haphazard storage sites.

The following figures summarize UNODC's data on precursor seizures in Afghanistan in 2008. In assessing the seizures by agency, it should be noted that the 2008 database did not capture multi-agency seizures, but only permitted the identification of a lead agency. In particular, this may underestimate the activities of the International Security Assistance Force (ISAF), who provided security support to several raids on heroin processing facilities and drug/precursor storage sites.

The significant quantity of precursors seized by the ABP is related to the large border stockpiles mentioned above – particularly at Kandahar's crossings – but also suggests little overlap between lab destructions and precursor seizures. Even stripping out ABP seizures on the grounds that very few were positively identified as precursors relevant to heroin production (most were 'other precursors'), it remains

Table 22: Precursor seizures in Afghanistan in 2008, by province

Province	Ammonium chloride (kg)	Sodium bicarbonate (kg)	Ammonia (L)	Acetic anhydride (L)	Acetone (L)	Lime (kg)	Carbon (kg)	Hydroch. acid (L)	Other precursors (kg)
Wardak	0	0	0	100	0	0	0	0	172
Zabul	60	0	0	0	0	0	0	0	0
Kapisa	0	0	0	0	0	0	0	0	32
Baghlan	0	0	0	0	0	0	0	0	2,281
Nimroz	0	0	0	0	0	0	0	0	748
Paktya	2,382	0	0	2,310	0	0	0	0	0
Takhar	20	0	0	40	0	0	0	0	184
Kabul	5,489	737	0	880	0	0	174	0	773
Badakhshan	474	0	10	40	0	0	126	0	209
Kandahar	55	278	0	7,500	0	0	0	0	22,375
Balkh	0	0	0	0	0	0	0	0	2
Hirat	0	0	0	0	0	0	0	0	16
Hilmand	8,270	370	0	82	0	0	480	0	2,564
Nangarhar	2,664	280	0	3,282	30	718	750	890	4,572
Total	19,414	1,665	10	14,234	30	718	1,530	890	33,927

Source: UNODC Afghanistan Office.

true that most lab raids do not result in large quantities of precursors being seized. This is indicative of the logistical arrangements involved in precursor distribution (see below). It also suggests that the highest-value targeting would involve identifying large volumes in transit near the borders or in illicit stockpiles before distribution to labs. The three provinces that witnessed more than 10,000 kg of seizures in 2008 – Nangarhar, Hilmand and Kandahar – all host significant numbers of heroin processing laboratories.

The relatively small seizures in Hirat, Farah and Nimroz are a concern, given what is known and suspected about the large quantities of chemical imports over the western borders, as well as the proliferation of processing facilities in these areas.

There have been three notable precursor seizures in Afghanistan in 2009:

1. Interception at Kabul airport of 220 litres of acetic anhydride on a flight arriving from Delhi. It appears that the chemicals were diverted after purchase from France. Strangely, the cargo wrapping placed on the containers did not match the airline by which the chemicals were smuggled.

2. Around 4 tons of ammonium chloride[42] in Kunduz province, where there were no precursor seizures recorded in 2008. Details on the intended destination(s) were not available.

3. A raid of several days' duration in Marja district of Hilmand, infamous as a hub for drug traffick-

Fig. 16: Seizures of all precursors by agency in Afghanistan (kg equivalents), 2008

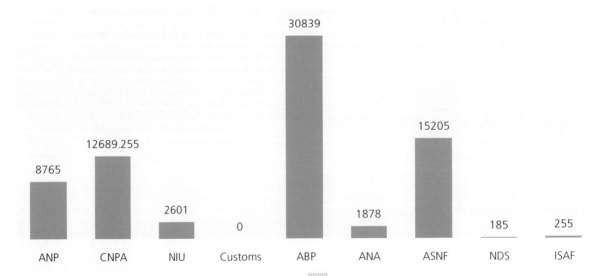

Source: UNODC Afghanistan Office.

42 Ammonium chloride is a non-controlled chemical used to precipitate opium into morphine base.

Map 32: Location of precursor seizures in 2008, by province

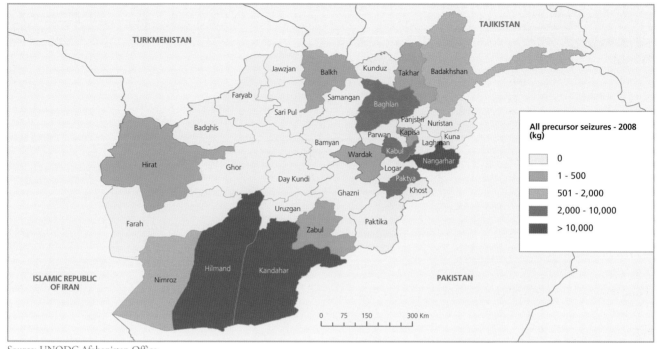

Source: UNODC Afghanistan Office.

ing and an area held tightly by the insurgency. As a result, nearly 2 tons of acetic anhydride were seized along with 24 tons of ammonium chloride and other chemicals.

Seizures in source and transit countries

Pakistan

The manufacturing of acetic anhydride was discontinued in Pakistan in 1995, but the country borders two major chemical producers, China and India. Based on seizure data, Pakistan appears to be a major source of precursors entering Afghanistan. "Traditional routes", such as precursor smuggling across the Indo-Pakistan border, seem to have fallen in disuse. The largest precursor flows arrive at Karachi or other seaports on Balochistan's coast, in recent years often from or via the Republic of Korea. The majority then crosses Pakistan's borders with the southern Afghan provinces of Nimroz, Hilmand and Kandahar. A primary hub appears to be the Baramcha bazaar[43] (Dishu district of Hilmand), a village that straddles the border. Former Afghan Border Police (ABP) officers also asserted that the Gardi Jangle refugee camp[44] south of Baramcha was a major precursor supply route for southern labs.[45]

Seizure data and field research in eastern Afghanistan indicate that significant precursor trafficking occurs along the eastern belt of Paktya and Nangarhar, which border the Khyber and Kurram Agencies of Pakistan's Federally Administered Tribal Areas (FATA). The major legal crossing point in the area is Torkham, which processes hundreds of vehicles a day.

While eastern Afghanistan requires significant quantities of precursor chemicals for its processing facilities, there have been no seizures of acetic anhydride reported from Karachi, the main seaport. One confirmed route crosses into Pakistan's Kurram agency through the town of Sada and into Paktya province, although it is unknown how the chemicals reached Pakistan. It remains likely that acetic anhydride entering eastern Afghanistan arrived in Pakistan by sea, but smaller amounts may also come by air into Islamabad (or Peshawar). Backtracking investigations related to precursors in eastern Afghanistan are needed to determine whether they have branched off the Karachi/Baluchistan trunk routes or are fed by other means.

The Islamic Republic of Iran

Iran shares a 949 kilometre long border with the Afghan provinces of Hirat, Farah and Nimroz.[46] Iran's road and rail infrastructure is useful for smugglers and there are numerous entry points into Afghanistan that are used by various networks to smuggle goods, weapons and narcotics. The continued development of trade links with Iran will provide further opportunities for precursor traffickers to blend in with licit trade flows, while numerous smuggling routes on the Afghan-Iranian border (particularly in Farah and Nimroz) have good potential for precursor traffickers.

One established route through Iran runs from Busan

---

43 Phone interview with Nimroz border official, 14 September 2008

44 Gardi Jangle is an old Afghan refugee camp. It is located in the Dalbandin area of Chagai district. In 2007, there were reportedly some 43,000 residents still inhabiting the camp. Source: Thomas H. Johnson, On the Edge of the Big Muddy: The Taliban Resurgence in Afghanistan, China and Eurasia Forum Quarterly, Volume 5, No. 2 (2007) p. 93-129, http://www.silkroadstudies.org/new/docs/CEF/Quarterly/May_2007/Johnson.pdf

45 UNODC Mission to Afghanistan Mazar-Sharif and Hairatan, (25-27 March 2008).

46 Iran also shares a 976 km border with Pakistan's Balochistan province.

Map 33: Precursor seizures reported in and around Afghanistan, 2000-2008

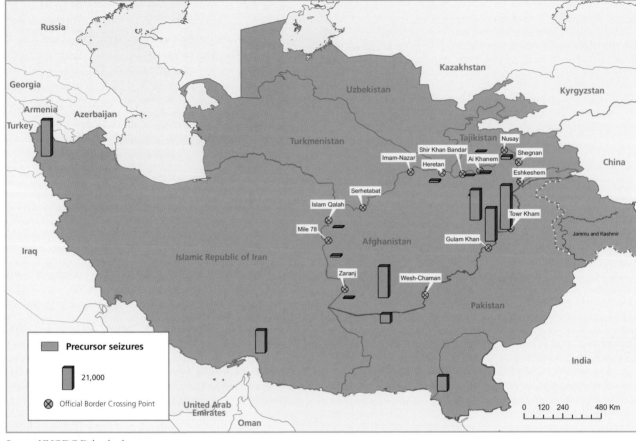

Source: UNODC Delta database.

port in South Korea to Afghanistan via Bandar Abbas port (Iran), using commercial containers. Bandar Abbas remains the likeliest entry point for large shipments of acetic anhydride and other chemicals and most of Iran's reported precursor seizures in the past fifteen years have occurred there.[47] In 2001, two shipments of acetic anhydride (38 tons concealed in textile shipments) from South Korea destined for Afghanistan were intercepted at Bandar Abbas.[48] Perhaps the most telling suggestion that precursor smuggling from Iran still takes place came from an April 2008 seizure during Operation TARCET,[49] uncovering a shipment of 5 tons of acetic anhydride at Bandar Abbas, also destined for Afghanistan. Earlier that year, Iranian customs had seized nearly 16 tons of acetyl chloride, a chemical which can also be used in heroin production. Assuming that precursor shipments follow transportation corridors, those shipped through Bandar Abbas likely head for Nimroz province in Afghanistan along the 950 km Bandar Abbas-Milak/Zaranj road.[50]

There is also evidence that shipments of precursors transit Iran by road, including two large acetic acid[51] consignments (17,700 kilograms and 16,173 kilograms) from Turkey stopped at Bazargan Customs on the Iran-Turkey border (July 2005).[52] Such shipments would likely head east towards the Islam Qala crossing point in Hirat province.

Central Asia

Afghanistan's borders with the Central Asian countries of Tajikistan, Uzbekistan and Turkmenistan are 2,600 kilometres long. The Uzbek and Tajik borders are marked by the Amu Darya River, while the area around the Turkmen border is for the most part undulating desert gradually ceding to the Amu Darya River in the north near Afghanistan's Jawzjan province. This blue border is punctured by three river ports, Keleft (Jawzjan province-Turkmenistan), Hayraton (Balkh province-Uzbekistan) and Sher Khan Bandar (Kunduz-Tajikistan). Most cross-border trade is conducted through Hayraton and Sher Khan Bandar. Beyond bilateral trade, Afghanistan provides an important link between Central and South Asia, especially in giving Central Asian countries access to the seaports of Pakistan and Iran. Despite this, trade between Central Asia and Afghanistan is far below its potential, according a recent

---

47 Summary of the Turkish Drug Report 2001, http://candidates2003.emcdda. europa.eu/download/tr/turkey-nr-2001-en.doc.

48 Ibid.

49 TARCET is an international operation coordinated by the INCB Precursors Unit, the objectives of Operation Tarcet are twofold: (a) to educate key law enforcement officers on methods used to identify and intercept smuggled consignments of chemicals; and (b) to intercept consignments of smuggled chemicals using modern methodologies.

50 Iran Daily, February 24 2005, www.iran-daily.com/1383/2221/pdf/i5.pdf.

51 In illicit heroin production, acetic acid can also be used in place of ammonium chloride or ammonia solutions as a reagent to adjust alkalinity in the precipitation of morphine from an opium solution.

52 The acetic acid was transiting from Iran toward Uzbekistan using TIR Carnet.

assessment by ADB experts,[53] and presenting fewer opportunities for precursor smugglers than the eastern or southern borders, which see larger trade volumes.

Central Asia was a major transit region for acetic anhydride during the 1990s. From 1996-2000, Turkmenistan reported seizing nearly 150 tons and Uzbekistan approximately 72 tons of this chemical.[54] Since then, very few seizures of acetic anhydride have been reported in Central Asia. One exception was a 2002 seizure of 200 litres of unidentified precursors in Termez (on the Uzbek-Afghan border close to Hayraton), travelling in a humanitarian cargo vehicle.[55] In addition, in June 2008, a seizure of 156 litres of acetic anhydride was reported in the Tajik capital Dushanbe.

The region's proximity to major acetic anhydride producers – China and Russia – still puts it at risk of being a transit zone for chemicals destined to Afghanistan. Of note, Uzbekistan and Kazakhstan both reportedly manufacture, import and export controlled chemicals, including acetic anhydride, for the needs of chemical, mining, pharmaceutical and other industries.[56]

Russian Federation

According to the International Narcotics Control Board, Russia was identified as the source of a number of acetic anhydride seizures in Turkey from 2004-2006. A more recent example concerns a seizure in November 2007 of 10 tons of acetic anhydride destined for Afghanistan, occurring in Dzerzhinsk[57] and involving a Russian citizen of Afghan origin.[58] According to Russian law enforcement the seized chemicals[59] were to be shipped in a truck to Afghanistan via Tajikistan.[60] The substance was reportedly a smaller portion of a much larger delivery to Afghanistan.[61]

China

Precursors may also be sourced east of Central Asia, in China, which is a major licit producer of precursors including acetic anhydride. Available Chinese statistics on seizures do not usually include disaggregated data on type of chemical and place of apprehension. China reported seizing 15 tons of acetic anhydride in 2003,[62] but no further details were available. Nevertheless, there were large seizures of chemicals in Xinjiang province (bordering Pakistan, Central Asia and a remote area of Afghanistan). More recently, a 2006 Chinese media report quoting Urumchi Customs at Korgas (Kazakh-Chinese border) and Irkeshtam (Kyrgyzstan-Chinese border) which reported seizing more than 75 tons of acetic anhydride (along with 4 tons of potassium permanganate) in "recent years".[63] Although the destination was not specified, it is possible that some of these precursors were destined for Afghanistan. Indeed, it is possible that Chinese-produced precursor chemicals will be increasingly exported to Afghanistan due to the decline of Myanmar as a heroin producer.

More recent cases of illicit precursor export attempts from China include a 2007 shipment of 80 tons of acetic anhydride to Afghanistan stopped by Chinese authorities.[64] In Afghanistan itself, fragmentary evidence suggests that some precursor chemicals have Chinese origins, such as an 11-ton seizure of acetic anhydride in Nangarhar province in January 2003.[65]

China has a 76 km manned border with Afghanistan, and there are plans to establish a customs post of the Afghan side.[66] There are, however, few reasons to imagine much precursor trafficking across these two remote borders since easier alternatives exist. There are small but well established opiate trafficking routes from China's South-east to its western borders. Many analysts believe that these routes continue into Central Asia. Other forms of smuggling – such as in metals or household goods – across Central Asian-Chinese borders have been observed.[67] It is also possible that precursors are shipped by sea to Pakistan from China, taking advantage of the bilateral trade flows.

India

India is a licit manufacturer of precursor chemicals, including acetic anhydride. Precursors are also trafficked from India, but seizure data seems to mostly confine this to air routes. This included the abovementioned 200 litres of acetic anhydride in 2009, arriving from Delhi after diversion from a company in France. More recently, India's Directorate of Revenue Intelligence quoted by media sources reported seizing 110 litres of acetic anhydride in

53   Asian Development Bank, *Afghanistan's Trade with CAREC Neighbors: Evidence from Surveys of Border Crossing Points in Hairatan and Sher Khan Bandar,* October 29, 2008.

54   No seizures were reported in Tajikistan during this period.

55   Economic Cooperation Organization Drug Control Coordination Unit (ECO DCCU), Uzbekistan Country Profile 2003.

56   Minutes of the UNODC/DEA seminar, 8-12 December 2003, Tashkent, Uzbekistan.

57   The chemicals were produced in Dzerzhinsk, a town approximately 250 miles east of Moscow.

58   "Russian police seize large batch of heroin precursor destined for Afghanistan", ITAR-TASS news agency, 7 November 2007.

59   Some other seizures include 1,500 litres of acetic anhydride in Voronezh (February 2005) which were sold wholesale at 293 dollars per litre. Source: Police seize large stockpile of drug components in central Russia, BBC monitoring, 8 February 2005.

60   The chemicals were to be disguised as mosquito repellent and solvent used in plastic production.

61   International Narcotics Control Strategy Report, 2008.

62   Information provided by the UNODC Regional Centre for Asia and the Pacific, Bangkok, 2006.

63   http://news.xinhuanet.com/newscenter/2006-04/11/content_4409290.htm (In Chinese).

64   http://www.incb.org/pdf/precursors-report/2007/en/chapter-iii.pdf.

65   According to the INCB, barrels of hydrogen peroxide "purportedly" from the Republic of South Korea were hidden in larger drums labeled as petroleum jelly - apparently shipped from China.

66   http://www.adb.org/Documents/Events/2008/CAREC-Tariff-Collection-Supervision/Afghanistan-Country-Report.pdf.

67   UNODC, "Precursor control on Central Asia's borders with China", 2006.

Amristar (India-Pakistan border) which was to be smuggled into Pakistan.

The logistics of precursor trafficking

Some precursor chemicals have licit uses in Afghanistan, and those intended for heroin production have been able to camouflage themselves easily within trade flows. Movements of acetic anhydride with no licit use, however, have relied on low awareness, lack of testing equipment, corruption, unregulated crossing points, fraudulent declaration and concealment. In all cases, the large volume of trade and traffic between Afghanistan and its neighbours, including the widespread use of 'semi-official' border crossing points, provides useful cover.

A recurring theme in interviews with Afghan law enforcement officials was that chemicals were being smuggled into Afghanistan disguised as motor oil. This is logical since liquids are the easiest way to conceal or falsely declare chemicals like acetic anhydride. UNODC found the same in its 2007 drug flow survey and one recent seizure of 12 tons of acetic anhydride in Korea was to be disguised as motor oil.[68] Similarly, one CNPA officer argued that some traffickers were involved in the car oil business, which would be a useful cover for precursor trafficking. Other false declarations of liquids have included hydrogen peroxide, with one network using this disguise to send over 50 tons of acetic anhydride to southern Afghanistan between April 2007 and March 2008[69].

The conventional view of precursor trafficking holds that, unlike opiates trafficking, it is generally confined to serviceable roads and railways, mostly using container trucks. This is partly due to the hazardous nature of some chemicals and the large quantities required. It is also because precursor smuggling has faced a lower risk of interdiction than drug smuggling and has enjoyed a lower profit margin in the past. Combined with the direction of trade flows mentioned above, this view encourages a focus on four major transport routes into Afghanistan, that is, the major road crossings of Islam Qala, Torkham and Spin Boldak, plus the railway across Hayraton into Balkh.

As an example of the importance of cross-border trade to the Afghan economy, commercial cargo makes up more than half of Afghanistan's operational budget through duties at Islam Qala (Iran-Pakistan) and Torkham on the Afghan-Pakistan border.[70] Other important crossings include Zaranj (Nimroz province-Iran), Torghundi (Hirat province-Turkmenistan), Aquina (Faryab Province-Turkmenistan) Sher Khan Bandar (Kunduz province-Turkmenistan) and Ghulam Khan (Khost province-Pakistan).

Fieldwork and seizures in neighbouring countries suggest that smugglers use heavy transport and railways to approach the Afghan border. However, the four routes mentioned above are not the only methods used to deliver into Afghanistan. All manners of land-based conveyances have been noted, including pack animals, human carriers and private vehicles.[71]

Once across the border, there is again a great range of onward logistics. Some ventures have involved disaggregating shipments to cross the border, then consolidating them to move in bulk throughout Afghanistan. This was apparently the case with a truck intercepted in Paktya in 2006. At the same time, small consignments are also seized in transit in Afghanistan, most likely from internal hubs to specific labs.

The recent price rises of acetic anhydride may be expected to cause changes in the logistics of precursor trafficking, although the distribution of risk makes it unclear what these changes will be. Whereas the traditional view suggested that it would be a high-volume, low-margin business, theoretically it would now be quite profitable to smuggle even minor amounts of acetic anhydride. This could encourage a greater use of irregular crossings and small-scale shipments.

However, as mentioned earlier, it appears that price rises have been driven primarily by better control mechanisms in source countries. If the risk of diversion is greater than the risk of interception near or in Afghanistan – a reasonable hypothesis given low seizure rates in Afghanistan – then it is likely that profit margins are high at the start of the trafficking chain, that is, immediately after diversion. Given that licit acetic anhydride is mostly used in bulk industrial processes, the somewhat counter-intuitive fact is that attempting to divert quantities less than a few hundred litres is more suspicious than large purchases.

The profit margin for moving acetic anhydride across the Afghan border may therefore not be very attractive. Small cross-border shipments would only make sense if they were integrated into a drug processing network so that the risk and labour could be internalized into the network's costs of production. Alternatively, they would make sense for a group specialized in and contracted to divert and deliver into Afghanistan. Again, the relatively small additional margin to cross the Afghan border would be compensated by reaping the entire wedge between licit prices and prices in Afghanistan.

In light of this, the absence of seizures at Afghanistan's major crossing points may be interpreted in two ways. First, it may indicate that precursor smuggling already carries risks so high that smugglers rely primarily on irregular crossings (note that this does not necessarily mean *small-*

---

68 "South Korean police arrest Taliban-linked drug ring", *Taipei Times*, July 5 2008, http://www.taipeitimes.com/News/world/archives/2008/07/05/2003416563.

69 CARICC information bulletin 29, August 4, 2008.

70 Interview with Afghanistan General Directorate for Customs, July 25 2008.

71 Of note, extensive cross-border smuggling of other goods takes place using pack mules, including opiates (often accompanied by armed guard escort).

Fig. 17: **Truck movements at key border points of Afghanistan, 2007-2008**

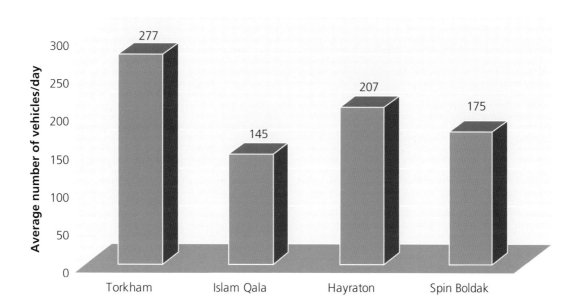

Source: Afghan Directorate for Customs, Ministry of Finance, Asian Development Bank

scale shipments). Second, it may indicate an effective combination of corruption and little technical capacity at official crossings, so that risks remain low of using transport corridors.

Opiates and precursors – do routes overlap?

In a general sense, major opiate and precursor routes use the same transport infrastructure across Afghanistan's borders. For example, drugs are trafficked along the Islam Qala/Bandar-Abbas or Zaranj/Bandar Abbas corridors, which also double as precursors transport routes into Afghanistan. Similarly, the Karachi-Kandahar precursor route is an important route for opiates trafficking in the reverse direction, onwards to Europe (via Gulf-area states).[72] The Iran-Turkey-SEE Balkan route has also historically been a major precursor trafficking route in the reverse direction.[73] Further afield, major acetic anhydride sources for Afghanistan – such as Europe, China and the Russian Federation – are also big consumers of Afghan opiates, which creates the possibility that long-range networks exporting opiates from Afghanistan make contacts to obtain precursors for importation.

Once at the Afghan border and given 1) the number of entry points and 2) the seeming ease by which some networks operate, there is at least some degree of overlap if only because of the convergence on provinces such as Hilmand or Nangarhar. Regarding the latter, opiate seizures indicate that Nangarhar doubles as a major trafficking and exit point for narcotics. Some smaller opiate trails lead to drug bazaars in Pakistan's FATA and are reportedly used for precursor trafficking in the opposite direction. Some sources suggest that vehicles carrying precursors unload in Afghanistan, re-load with opiates and reverse course into Pakistan,[74] a practice common for other contraband exchanges in Pakistan.[75]

Opiates and precursors – do actors overlap?

Successful economic networks in Afghanistan tend to combine licit and illicit activities, at least because petty corruption is needed to expedite business. Thus, even if the logistics of moving large amounts of chemicals are somewhat different to those involved in transporting opiates, the same contacts can be used to avoid detection – and shipments of more than a ton of opiates are quite common. Additionally, the apparent pressure on precursor supplies may have led to a consolidation of this market, which would tend to favour a few larger networks capable of funding and concealing major diversions.

CNPA officials have assessed that many smugglers are involved in both opiate and precursor trafficking, but provided no further specifics. There is some evidence of network overlap since a number of in-country seizures (not including lab interdictions) have included both drugs and precursor chemicals. A prominent example was the recent operation in Marja (Nad Ali district – Hilmand province),

72   UNODC, *Illicit drugs situation in the regions neighboring Afghanistan and the response of ODCCP*, October 12 2002, p.13.

73   INCB, 2001, *Report on the Implementation of Article 12 of the United Nations Convention against Illicit Traffic in Narcotic Drugs and Psychotropic Substances of 1988*, www.incb.org/pdf/e/tr/pre/2002/precursors_2002_3b_2.pdf.

74   Interview with CNPA Nangarhar, Kabul, 2008.

75   Most goods smuggled into Pakistan are in fact returning goods. Under a long-standing agreement, goods destined for Afghanistan enter the port of Karachi duty free, The merchandise is ferried north across the border and then routinely smuggled back and sold in Pakistan at higher prices. See: Irfanullah, Akberzai, *Mini Subsector Assessment: Edible Oil Subsector -Eastern Region of Afghanistan*, ALP-ER, September 2005.

which found opium, heroin and precursor chemicals all under the protection of the Taliban in a major illicit bazaar. Similarly, seizure data in-country indicates that trafficking takes place along or close to the main ring road. This indicates that the logistics used in other forms of trafficking seem to apply as demonstrated by a 2007 UNODC study on opiate flows which concludes that approximately 70 per cent of drug trafficking takes place along the main roads, sustained by the strong support and involvement of the local governmental authorities.[76]

The direct exchange of heroin for precursors has been reported only in Badakshan. Given the high quality opium in Nangarhar and current prices of acetic anhydride, one litre of acetic anhydride could potentially fetch 5-6 kg of opium. Outside Afghanistan, the INCB 2004 report described a seizure of 370 litres of acetic anhydride from Albania being smuggled to Turkey for a similar exchange.[77]

Laboratories

The ultimate destination for all precursor chemicals are the hundreds of heroin labs puncturing the Afghan landscape, which are for the most part makeshift. Some recent developments illustrate the constantly changing nature of the Afghan drug trade. Laboratories are increasingly mobile[78] and many are using fuel instead of wood.

Heroin processing laboratories have proliferated in recent years. They are concentrated in Nangarhar (east) and Badakhshan (north-east), and in the south and west of the country. The emerging pattern has been a continuous shift in favour of southern provinces where widespread cultivation and low or no government control make labs attractive targets for both processors and traffickers. [79]

While southern pre-eminence is clearly evident in the high numbers of heroin and morphine labs, the western region compares well with a near equal amount of total labs but more morphine labs. One observation is that many laboratories are situated close to the border such as in Nangarhar (Aichin district) and Hilmand (Baramcha bazaar), which limits cross-country transportation. Proximity to the border is one factor for the concentrations of labs, but so is instability. Security issues in both regions undermines interdiction efforts against laboratories and proximity to the border facilitates smuggling logistics for processors and precursor chemicals. Conversely, the fact that illicit precursor shipments will need to move towards only these few final destination points should lead to greater vulnerability in the supply chains.

Precursor control

Given current knowledge of heroin processing and the logistics of precursor trafficking, a focus on acetic anhydride and on the major transport routes into Afghanistan is warranted. In Afghanistan, precursor control is at an embryonic stage and although it might seem a modest aim, forcing precursor trafficking to be more like drug trafficking – smaller-scale with more reliance on irregular crossings – would be a good first step in increasing its intelligence footprint and the inconvenience involved in supplying labs. Targeting Islam Qala, Torkham and Chaman-Spin Boldak for increased precursor awareness plus (basic) procedures and equipment to raise the risks of trafficking through these arteries would be a good start. A watching brief on the Hayraton railway is also justified.

Beyond this, the two highest-value targets for mobile precursor detection are the Kandahar/Hilmand southern border and the Farah/Nimroz western border. Large-scale use of irregular crossings for precursor trafficking across these borders is probably common. Afghan Border Police (ABP) capacity is necessary, but law enforcement agencies would also likely require Afghan National Army (ANA)/ISAF support to deal with the security situation in these areas.

---

76   UNODC, *Monitoring of drug flows in Afghanistan*, October 2007.

77   INCB, 2003, *Report on the Implementation of Article 12 of the United Nations Convention against Illicit Traffic in Narcotic Drugs and Psychotropic Substances of 1988*, http://www.incb.org/pdf/e/tr/pre/2004/precursors_3.pdf.

78   Interview with CNPA intelligence and interdiction unit, Kabul, June 2008; interview with ISAF analysts, Kabul, July 2009.

79   An example of this is the 2007 relocation of a dozen laboratories from Badakhshan to Hilmand province where the highest concentrations of labs is observed.

B. THE SOURCE OF THE TRADE

1. Opium poppy cultivation patterns: 2002-2009[80]

Opium poppy cultivation has been a staple of Afghanistan's economy for over two decades with the last five years producing bumper crop upon bumper crop. The opium economy is now deeply entrenched in Afghanistan and its reach extends far beyond its borders. Opium leaves no one untouched - including the law enforcement agencies tasked with curbing the drug trade - and increasingly fuels domestic consumption, which affects the most disadvantaged segments of Afghan society. The problems associated with drug use have worsened steadily over the past two decades in Afghanistan.

Opium is the country's biggest export and one in seven Afghans is reportedly involved in some aspect of the trade. UNODC estimates that 6.5[81] per cent of the Afghan population is involved in growing poppy. In areas such as Hilmand, where cultivation is concentrated, this share rises to a staggering 80 per cent. Criminal revenues thus continue to comprise a significant component of the national economy.

The pattern in Afghanistan in recent years has been concentration of the area under opium poppy cultivation. As such, reductions in cultivation in the northern, eastern and central regions are offset and even supplanted by a parallel expansion in opium production in the south.

Cultivation mirrors the shifting of routes in response to interdiction and law enforcement presence. Based on UNODC's observations of recent opium poppy planting, southern pre-eminence has once again intensified. In 2009,

the southern province of Hilmand accounted for 60 per cent of Afghanistan's opium production. To the east of Hilmand, Kandahar province produced 17 per cent. 99 per cent of Afghanistan's opium economy is based on production in southern and western provinces. Western provinces accounted for 12 per cent of the total opium production in 2009. Opium production in the rest of Afghanistan was negligible.

Opium poppy cultivation is not a new phenomenon in Afghanistan, but the country's global pre-eminence as an exporter is relatively recent. Opium poppy was traditionally cultivated in some parts of Afghanistan as far back as the eighteenth century.[82] The first significant increases in cultivation levels were reported in the 1980s as Turkish, Pakistani and Iranian anti-narcotics policies were being successfully enforced. This gradual shift further solidified towards the end of the Soviet period (1987) and during the "warlord period" when opium became a surrogate currency to fund various factions at war with one another. There was no let up during the Taliban period as cultivation continued to expand, reaching 91,000 ha in 1999, which was then the highest level of cultivation ever recorded in the country. During the Taliban regime (1996-2001) a 10 per cent "agricultural tax" was levied on opium farmers. In 2001, the Taliban regime announced an opium poppy ban and cultivation decreased to 8,000 ha. The Taliban successfully appealed to religious sentiments to justify the ban in the south, but also made use of more robust methods in the more resistant east (such as Nangarhar province).[83] It should be noted that while the opium ban concerned opium poppy cultivation, no policy toward opium trading and heroin manufacture was enunciated and the Taliban continued to levy taxes on these activities.

Fig. 18: Opium poppy cultivation in Afghanistan, 1994-2009

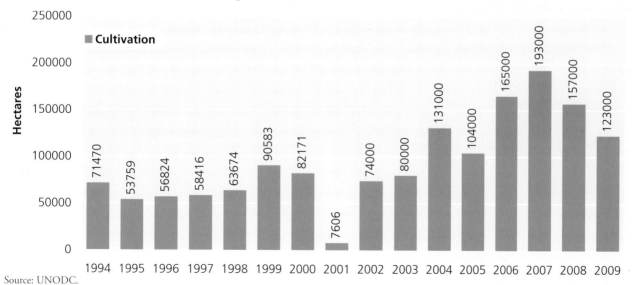

Source: UNODC.

---

80 At the time of the preparation of this report, 2009 Afghanistan opium cultivation/production figures were only available at the provincial and national levels. The analysis of district patterns and trends thus refers to the period 2002-2008.

81 UNODC, *Afghanistan opium survey 2009.*

82 UNODC, *The opium economy in Afghanistan: An international problem,* 2003.

83 UNODC, *The Impact of the Taliban Prohibition on Opium Poppy Cultivation in Afghanistan,* 25 May 2001.

Fig. 19: Opium production in Afghanistan, 1994-2009

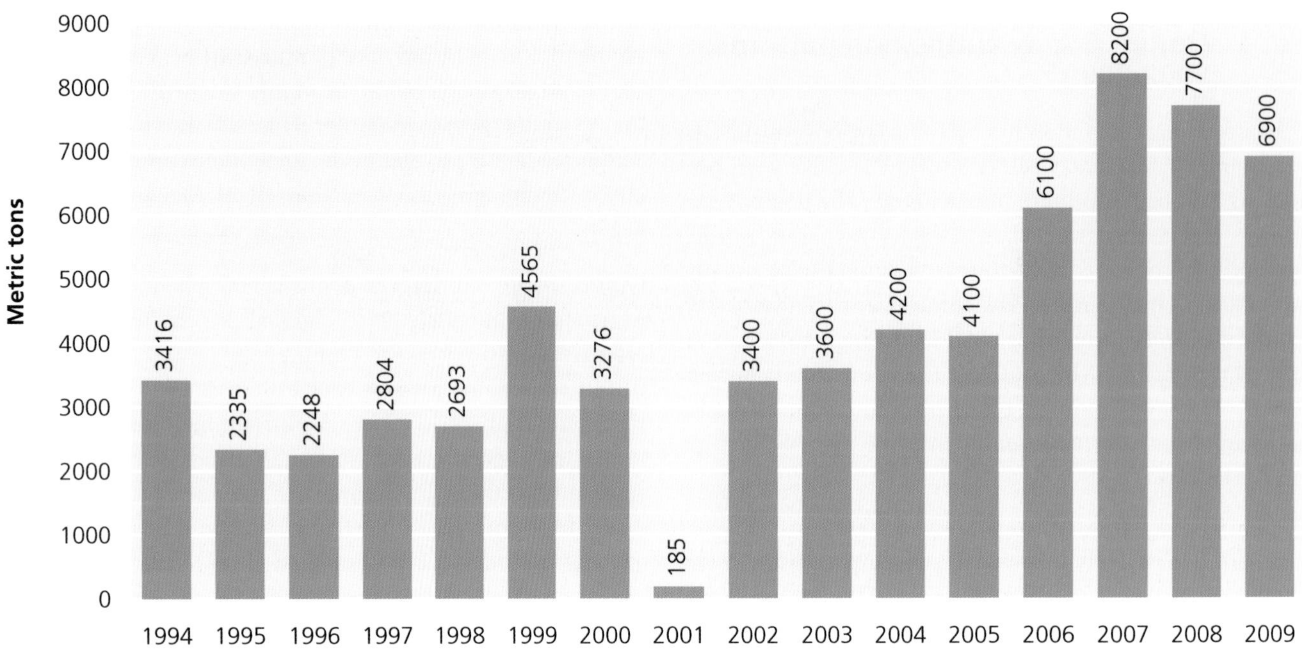

Source: UNODC.

Following the Taliban's ouster, large-scale opium production resumed, amounting to 6,900 tons in 2009. Between 1995 and 2005, the average annual opium production was around 3,300 tons. This stable trend came to an end in 2006 as production increased sharply, reaching 6,100 tons in 2006, 8,200 tons in 2007, 7,700 tons in 2008 and decreased to 6,900 tons in 2009. The average dry opium yield per hectare was 56 kg/ha in 2009 in Afghanistan, an increase from the previous year when it stood at 49 kg/ha. According to UNODC opium poppy surveys, this is the highest average yield ever recorded for Afghanistan.

Between 2002 and 2009, a total of 44,200 tons of opium were produced in Afghanistan, an amount roughly equivalent to 6,314 tons of heroin. Afghanistan became the principal illicit opiate exporter in the world, especially after the sharp decrease in opium production in Myanmar in 2002, which increased the relative importance of Afghan opium production even further.

During the same period (2002-2009), 80 per cent of the opium was produced in six Afghan provinces (Hilmand, Nangarhar, Kandahar, Badakshan, Uruzgan and Farah). Badakshan and Nangarhar aside, the bulk of the production took place in four provinces in southern Afghanistan. Almost half of all opium was produced in Hilmand province (44 per cent). The next provinces in order of importance were Kandahar (9 per cent) and Nangarhar (9 per cent).

During the period 2003 and 2009, the total farm-gate value of the total opium produced in Afghanistan was US$ 5.9 billion. Out of US$ 5.9 billion, 2.2 billion (38 per cent) went to Hilmand farmers and 874 million (15 per cent) to Nangarhar farmers.

Table 23: Opium production (2002-2009) and farm-gate income (2003*-2009)

Province	Total opium production for the period 2002-2009 (tons)	Per cent of total	Total farm-gate income (billion of US$) for the period (2003-2009)	Per cent of total
Hilmand	19,620	44%	2,262	38%
Nangarhar	4,035	9%	874	15%
Kandahar	4,007	9%	475	8%
Badakshan	2,581	6%	505	9%
Uruzgan	2,520	6%	356	6%
Farah	2,297	5%	263	4%
Other	9,141	21%	1,165	20%
Total	**44,200**	**100%**	**5,865**	**100%**

* No income data available for 2002.

Map 34: Opium poppy cultivation trends in Afghanistan, 2002-2009

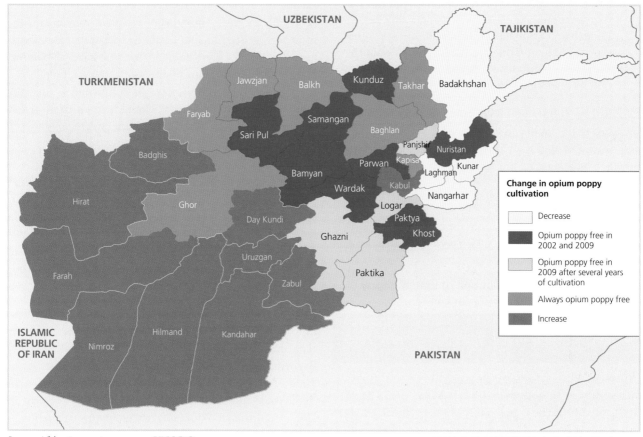

Source: Afghanistan opium surveys, UNODC.

Expansion of opium poppy cultivation in Afghanistan

In 2002, total opium poppy cultivation covered 74,000 ha, spread across 17 provinces (the total number of provinces in Afghanistan is 34) and production reached 3,400 tons. In 2009, opium poppy cultivation was observed in 14 provinces, but cultivation increased by 66 per cent (123,000 ha) and production by 129 per cent (6,900 tons) compared to 2002. Following a chronological order from 2002 and 2009, Afghan provinces can be categorized into five groups on the basis of their opium poppy cultivation status:

a. *Consistently poppy-free provinces:* Ghazni, Logar, Paktika and Panjshir. All four provinces maintained a poppy-free status between 2002 and 2009.

b. *Reclaimed provinces:* Bamyan, Khost, Kunduz, Nuristan, Paktya, Parwan, Saripul and Wardak. These eight provinces regained their original opium poppy-free status in 2008 (and continued to be poppy free in 2009) after five years of continuous cultivation between 2003 and 2007.

c. *Gained provinces:* Baghlan, Balkh, Faryab, Ghor, Jawzjan, Kapisa, Takhar and Samangan. These provinces were cultivating opium poppy in 2002 and between 2007 and 2009 had all become poppy-free.

d. *Progressive provinces:* In four provinces (Badakshan, Kunar, Laghman and Nangarhar), the total opium poppy cultivated area was 30,000 ha in 2002 but by 2009 it had decreased to 1,100 ha

Fig. 20: Share of opium production by province, Afghanistan (2002-2009)

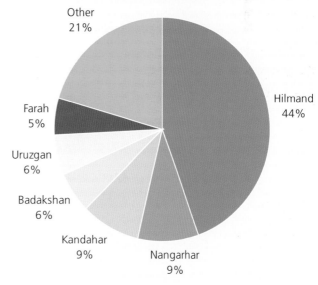

Source: Afghanistan opium surveys, UNODC.

e. *Relapsed provinces:* In 10 provinces (Hilmand, Hirat, Kabul, Kandahar, Badghis, Day Kundi, Farah, Nimroz, Uruzgan and Zabul), opium poppy cultivation has shown a marked increase in 2009 compared to 2002. In 2002, the total area under cultivation in these provinces was 40,500 ha but in 2009, it had increased threefold reaching 122,000 ha. The most dramatic increase in terms of magnitude and on a percentage basis was in Hilmand province (39,990 ha). During the same period, opium poppy cultivation also sharply increased in Farah (11,905 ha), Kandahar (15,840 ha), Nimroz (430 ha) and Uruzgan (4,120 ha). In other provinces (Hirat, Kabul, Badghis, Day Kundi and Zabul), increases in cultivation were comparatively modest.

Comparing 2002 and 2009, opium poppy cultivation increased in the south and west, decreased in the east, north and north-east and remained mostly stable in the central provinces of Afghanistan.

Cultivation trends in "relapsed provinces"

Total opium poppy cultivation appears to be essentially confined to these provinces, which account for 99 per cent

Table 24: Regional distribution of opium poppy cultivation in 2002 and 2009

Region	2002 (ha)	2009 (ha)	Change 2002-2009 (ha)
Central	96	132	+36
East	21,909	593	-21,316
North	691	0	-691
North-east	9,054	557	-8,497
South	39,220	103,014	+63,794
West	3,076	18,800	+15,724
Total	**74,046**	**123,096**	**+49,050**

of total opium poppy cultivation in Afghanistan in 2009, leaving the remaining provinces (24) either poppy-free or nearly poppy-free. Among the "relapsed provinces", the most critical are Hilmand, Farah, Kandahar, Badgish, Uruzgan, Zabul and Day Kundi. In the provinces of Nimroz, Hirat and Kabul opium poppy cultivation is limited to a few districts, and the increase in cultivation is not very high, relative to 2009 figures. The security situation is also comparatively better than in the seven critical provinces.

Hilmand:

Hilmand has long been one of the most important opium producing provinces in Afghanistan, with a history of production dating back to before the 1950s. Production increased from the 1990s onward,[84] and between the years 1990 and 2000, Hilmand accounted for 40-55 per cent of the total area under opium poppy cultivation in Afghanistan.

In 2002, Hilmand's share was 41 per cent of total cultivation. From 2002-2005, it annually ranged from 19-26 per cent, due to increases in Kandahar, Farah, Hirat, Badghis, Baghlan, Day Kundi, Faryab, Zabul and Nimroz. As of 2006, Hilmand's share of total opium production in Afghanistan increased sharply, climbing to 57 per cent in 2009. Compared to 2002, total opium poppy cultivation in Hilmand increased by 131 per cent in 2006, nearly doubling to 243 per cent in 2007, 245 per cent in 2008 and 133 per cent in 2009. These figures are a clear indication that opium poppy cultivation patterns changed dramatically in Hilmand especially after 2005. Otherwise, from

Table 25: Opium poppy cultivation trends in "relapsed provinces", 2002-2009

Province	2002	2003	2004	2005	2006	2007	2008	2009	Change 2002-2009 (ha)	Change 2002-2009 (per cent)
Badgish	26	170	614	2,967	3,205	4,219	587	5,411	+5,385	+20,712%
Day Kundi	0	2,445	3,715	2,581	7,044	3,346	2,273	3,002	+3,002	+100%
Farah	500	1,700	2,288	10,240	7,694	14,865	15,010	12,405	+11,905	+2,381%
Hilmand	29,950	15,371	29,353	26,500	69,324	102,770	103,590	69,883	+39,933	+133%
Hirat	50	134	2,531	1,924	2,287	1,525	266	556	+506	+1,012%
Kabul	58	237	282	-	80	500	310	132	+74	+128%
Kandahar	3,970	3,055	4,959	12,989	12,619	16,615	14,623	19,811	+15,841	+399%
Nimroz	300	26	115	1,690	1,955	6,507	6,203	428	+128	+43%
Uruzgan	5,100	4,698	7,365	2,024	9,703	9,204	9,939	9,224	+4,124	+81%
Zabul	200	2,541	2,977	2,053	3,210	1,611	2,335	1,144	+944	+472%
Other provinces	33,459	47,934	70,586	35,689	41,815	27,466	915	1,004	-32,455	-97%
Total	**74,000**	**80,000**	**131,000**	**104,000**	**165,000**	**193,000**	**157,253**	**123,000**	**+49,000**	**+66%**

84 *Afghanistan's Drug Industry*, World Bank and UNODC, p 95.

Table 26: Distribution of opium poppy cultivation in Afghanistan by province, 2002-2009

Province	2002	2003	2004	2005	2006	2007	2008	2009
Badgish	0.0%	0.2%	0.5%	2.9%	1.9%	2.2%	0.4%	4.4%
Day Kundi	0.0%	3.1%	2.8%	2.5%	4.3%	1.7%	1.4%	2.4%
Farah	0.7%	2.1%	1.7%	9.8%	4.7%	7.7%	9.5%	10.1%
Hilmand	40.5%	19.2%	22.4%	25.5%	42.0%	53.2%	65.9%	56.8%
Hirat	0.1%	0.2%	1.9%	1.9%	1.4%	0.8%	0.2%	0.5%
Kabul	0.1%	0.3%	0.2%	0.0%	0.0%	0.3%	0.2%	0.1%
Kandahar	5.4%	3.8%	3.8%	12.5%	7.6%	8.6%	9.3%	16.1%
Nimroz	0.4%	0.0%	0.1%	1.6%	1.2%	3.4%	3.9%	0.3%
Uruzgan	6.9%	5.9%	5.6%	1.9%	5.9%	4.8%	6.3%	7.5%
Zabul	0.3%	3.2%	2.3%	2.0%	1.9%	0.8%	1.5%	0.9%
Other provinces	45.2%	59.9%	53.9%	34.3%	25.3%	14.2%	0.6%	0.8%
Total	100%	100%	100%	100 %	100%	100%	100%	100%

1994 to 2005 (except 2001), the amount of opium poppy cultivation was in the range of 15,000-45,000 ha. The crucial 2006-2009 period should therefore be carefully analyzed in order to understand the motivations behind opium poppy cultivation in Hilmand province.

In 2007 and 2008, opium cultivation in Hilmand covered slightly more than 100,000 ha which is nearly 3.5 times higher than the 2002 level, and the highest amount of cultivation ever reported at the national level in Afghanistan. But in 2009, cultivation dropped to 69,883 ha, almost the level of 2006 (69,324 ha). The total arable land in Hilmand covers 316,400 ha[85] and 22 per cent of it was under poppy cultivation in 2009, compared to 18 per cent in 2002. These figures are much higher than in other Afghan provinces. As an example, in 2009, opium poppy was cultivated on 7 per cent of total arable land in Kandahar and 8 per cent in Farah province.

The population of Hilmand is around 782,000, according to the Central Statistics office of Afghanistan. Around 95 per cent of Hilmand's population (or 739,000 people) live in rural areas. According to UNODC reports, the vast majority of the farmers in Hilmand province (approximately 114,000 families) grow opium poppy. In Afghanistan, the average opium cultivated land per farmer was 0.43 ha, while in Hilmand it stood at 0.9 ha per farmer in 2008. The average poppy cultivated area per farmer in rural areas is highest in Naway-Barakzayi (2.1 ha) and Musa Qala (1.7 ha) districts. Musa Qala district was under intermittent Taliban control after 2005.

Opium poppy is cultivated in all of Hilmand's districts but

the crop coverage is denser and more concentrated in the districts of Nad-e-ali, Nahri Sarraj, Musa Qala and Naway-i-Barakzayi. In 2008, these four districts accounted for 57 per cent of the total opium poppy cultivation in Hilmand province.

In most poppy growing provinces in Afghanistan, the crop is not generally cultivated close to provincial centres. But in Hilmand, poppy cultivation is much denser in the provin-

Table 27: Average opium poppy cultivation per family in Hilmand* by district, 2008

District	Total rural population (1,000)	Total number of families	Average poppy area per family (ha)
Baghran	68.4	10,523	0.4
Dishu (Registan)	17.2	2,646	0.3
Garmser (Hazarjuft)	73.8	11,354	0.7
Kajaki	59.9	9,215	0.7
Lashkar Gah	50.5	7,769	1.0
Musa Qala	49.7	7,646	1.7
Nad Ali	99.2	15,262	1.4
Nahri Sarraj	90.1	13,862	1.0
Naw Zad	78.0	12,000	0.3
Naway-i Barakzayi	42.7	6,569	2.1
Reg (Khan Nishin)	22.1	3,400	1.4
Sangin	50.3	7,738	0.7
Washer	13.0	2,000	0.8
Province	**714.9**	**109,985**	**0.9**

85   *Afghanistan opium survey 2008*, UNODC.

*District estimations for 2009 were not available at the time of writing.

Fig. 21: Distribution of opium poppy cultivation in Hilmand by district, 2008

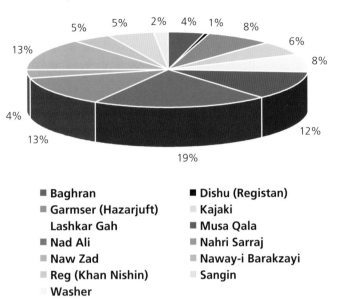

- Baghran
- Garmser (Hazarjuft)
- Lashkar Gah
- Nad Ali
- Naw Zad
- Reg (Khan Nishin)
- Washer
- Dishu (Registan)
- Kajaki
- Musa Qala
- Nahri Sarraj
- Naway-i Barakzayi
- Sangin

Map 35: Extent of opium poppy cultivation in the districts of Hilmand, 2008

Source: Afghanistan opium survey, 2008, UNODC.

cial centre, Lashkar Gah, and adjacent districts. One reason is the availability of efficient irrigation systems in these districts. Another is the lack of Government control even in the district centre. Residents of Hilmand thus have little to fear from eradication or government actions against poppy cultivation.

Between 1996 and 2005, the amount of opium poppy cultivation was largely stable in all Hilmand districts. Thereafter, sharp increases were observed, especially in Nad Ali

(784 per cent), Musa Qala (663 per cent), Lashkar Gah (490 per cent) and Naway-I Barakzayi (448 per cent).

Kandahar:

Similar to Hilmand province, opium poppy cultivation in Kandahar was stable between 1996 and 2004 (except 2001). In 2005, cultivation increased threefold compared to 2004. Since then, the rate has hovered between 12,000 and 17,000 ha.

Table 28: Opium poppy cultivation in the districts of Hilmand, 1996-2008*

District	1996	1997	1998	1999	2000	2001	2002	2003	2004	2005	2006	2007	2008	Change between 2005-2008 (%)
Baghran	1,267	2,754	2,910	2,794	2,653		1,800	2,309	2,232	2,507	2,890	4,287	4,279	+71%
Dishu (Registan)							-		369	911	851	1,160	688	-24%
Garmser (Hazarjuft)	942	1,993	1,205	2,643	2,765		2,020	462	1,922	1,912	6,168	6,523	8,000	+318%
Kajaki	2,814	3,904	3,959	5,746	4,625		2,640	1,392	1,676	1,639	6,760	5,807	6,240	+281%
Lashkar Gah	1,054	1,325	1,869	2,528	3,145		1,140	605	1,380	1,332	4,008	6,320	7,857	+490%
Musa Qala	3,924	4,360	5,574	7,013	5,686		3,690	2,455	2,404	1,664	6,371	8,854	12,687	+663%
Nad Ali	4,035	5,102	5,156	8,667	8,323		5,880	870	4,177	2,356	11,652	20,045	20,824	+784%
Nahri Sarraj	4,309	4,807	2,426	4,041	4,378		1,850	1,575	6,486	3,548	10,386	22,769	13,270	+274%
Naw Zad	3,596	1,585	3,605	4,424	5,085		2,650	3,096	1,051	3,737	2,707	6,192	3,863	+3%
Naway-i Barakzayi	505	722	1,150	2,581	3,246		2,730	1,240	3,506	2,552	10,168	6,314	13,978	+448%
Reg (Khan Nishin)				222			1,940		1,893	2,772	3,765	8,484	4,720	+70%
Sangin	1,909	1,971	1,734	2,646	1,711		2,810	777	1,365	1,184	2,862	5,150	5,532	+367%
Washer	555	877	1,084	1,469	1,014		800	590	892	386	735	865	1,653	+328%
Total	24,910	29,400	30,672	44,552	42,853	0	29,950	15,371	29,353	26,500	69,323	102,770	103,590	+291%

*District estimations for 2009 were not available at the time of writing.

Table 29: Opium poppy cultivation in the district of Kandahar province, 1996-2008*

District	1994	1995	1996	1997	1998	1999	2000	2001	2002	2003	2004	2005	2006	2007	2008
Arghandab	211	87	331	561	399	750	459		330	139	261	287	735	1,016	57
Arghistan						38	13		80	14	651	2,449	784	310	28
Daman						110	50		190	357	895	775	183	375	19
Ghorak	347	803	692	1,503	1,126	1,109	574		380	166	241	233	336	1,445	232
Kandahar (Dand)	320	53	234	21	73	227	156		640	293		0	1,367	1,220	590
Khakrez	362	274	627	286	518	632	320		560	312	145	185	217	132	1,224
Maruf	30	16	1		3	5	17	-		63	117	150	464	914	182
Maywand	256	333	618	1,278	2,497	2,022	995		1,090	353	514	1,281	1,362	2,878	3,375
Miya Nishin														322	1,603
Nesh														432	3,284
Panjwayi**	250	357	266	255	134	132	184		150	482	864	4,687	4,714		
Reg											0	327		4	0
Shah Wali Kot	678	97	94	127	162	236	238		260	489	923	2,379	1,593	1,258	560
Shorabak										111	45	19	409	308	4
Spin Boldak	1,170	107	194	91	317	261	26		290	277	303	218	454	768	541
Zhari														5,232	2,923
Total	3,624	2,127	3,057	4,122	5,229	5,522	3,034	0	3,970	3,055	4,959	12,990	12,618	16,615	14,623

*District estimations for 2009 were not available at the time of writing.
** As of 2007, Panjwayi district ceased to exist and was replaced by the districts of Miya Nishin and Zhari.

Map 36: Extent of opium poppy cultivation in the district of Kandahar province, 2008

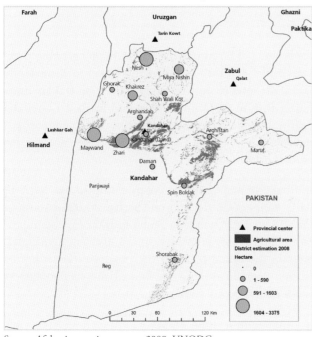

Source: Afghanistan opium survey, 2008, UNODC.

Table 30: Average opium poppy cultivation per family in Kandahar by district, 2008*

District	Total rural population (1,000)	Total number of families	Average poppy area per family (ha)
Arghandab	51.6	7,938	0.01
Arghistan	28.9	4,446	0.01
Daman	24.8	3,815	0.00
Ghorak	8.0	1,231	0.19
Kandahar (Dand)	144.3	22,200	0.03
Khakrez	19.2	2,954	0.41
Maruf	27.7	4,262	0.04
Maywand	40.7	6,262	0.54
Miya Nishin	12.6	1,938	0.83
Nesh	11.3	1,738	1.89
Reg	1.6	246	0.00
Shah Wali Kot	36.4	5,600	0.10
Shorabak	9.6	1,477	0.00
Spin Boldak	41.0	6,308	0.09
Zhari	49.5	7,615	0.38
Province	**507.2**	**78,031**	**0.19**

*District estimations for 2009 were not available at the time of writing.

In Kandahar province, Ghorak and Maywand were two important opium cultivating districts before 2001. After 2001, cultivation decreased in Ghorak, while it remained stable or increased slightly in Maywand. As of 2004, Shah Wali Kot (which is far from the provincial centre) and Panjwayi (including Zhari district) joined Maywand as important cultivation districts. In 2008, the majority of cultivation took place in districts far from the provincial centre like Zhari, Nesh, Miya Nishin, Maywand and Khakrez. Districts near the centre like Arghandab, Arghistan, Daman and Dand were nearly poppy-free, unlike in neighbouring

Hilmand province. This indicates better government control (in terms of opium poppy cultivation) in the central part of the province. The districts of Maywand (Kandahar), Lashkar Gah and Naway-i-Barakzayi (Hilmand) have been under intensive poppy cultivation since 2005. They are on the main road from Kandahar to Hilmand, between Dand (Kandahar) and Nad Ali (Hilmand).

An estimated 672,000 people (103,000 families) live in Kandahar's rural areas.[86] The average opium poppy cultivation area per family was 0.16 ha, which is 7 times less than Hilmand in 2008. This indicates that most families in Kandahar were not involved in opium poppy cultivation or that they cultivate smaller amounts than farmers in Hilmand. The average area per family is highest in Kandahar's Nesh district (1.89 ha).

The total arable land in Kandahar is 299,000 ha. In 2009, 7 per cent of the arable land was under opium poppy cultivation.

Nimroz

Until 2005, opium poppy cultivation always stood at less than 1,000 ha in Nimroz. However, as of 2005, cultivation started to increase very sharply, and amounted to 6,507 ha in 2007 and 6,200 ha in 2008. In 2009, cultivation dropped to 428 ha as the part of the main poppy cultivating district Khash Rod is now administrated under Farah province. The main opium poppy growing districts in Nimroz are Khash Rod (border district with Farah and Hilmand provinces) and Charburja. Since 2006, farmers in Khash Rod district (especially in the north-western part of the district) have been irrigating new agricultural areas in the desert through the use of deep wells. These newly created fields are 100 per cent covered with opium poppies.

Khash Rod district is at the border of Nimroz/Farah province where anti-government elements are very active. The increase in opium poppy cultivation in Nimroz seems to be at least partly insurgency-driven. In other districts of Nimroz, there is negligible opium poppy cultivation due to a lack of water and land. The total estimated rural population of Nimroz province is 139,000. Around 19,000 people (2,900 families) live in the rural areas of Khash Rod district. The total estimated amount of cultivated opium poppy in the district was 6,197 ha in 2008. The average opium poppy land per family is 2.1 ha in Khash Rod, much higher than the average in Hilmand (0.9 ha).

Total arable land in Nimroz is 66,000 ha. In 2008, 9.3 per cent of this was under opium poppy cultivation.

Map 37: Extent of opium poppy cultivation in the districts of Nimroz province, 2008

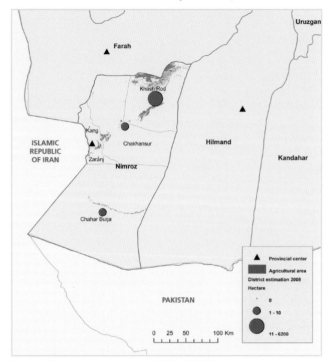

Source: Afghanistan opium survey, 2008, UNODC.

Farah

Farah was not an important opium poppy growing province before 2003 when cultivation began to increase. By 2005, the level of opium poppy cultivation was six times higher than in 2003. In 2009, it had reached 12,400 ha, nearly a 25-fold increase over 2002 levels. Opium poppy is mainly cultivated in the Bala Buluk and Bakwa districts, the latter of which borders Nimroz.

In Farah, the average opium poppy cultivated area was 1.32 ha in Gulistan district and one hectare in Bakwa district. Pusht Rod, Farah and Bala Buluk districts are also important opium poppy growing districts. Available agricultural areas in the western part of the province (bordering the Islamic Republic of Iran) are limited and cannot support much opium poppy cultivation.

Table 31: Opium poppy cultivation in districts of Nimroz province (ha), 1996-2008*

District	1996	1997	1998	1999	2000	2001	2002	2003	2004	2005	2006	2007	2008
Chahar Burja									65	526	1,119	87	4
Chakhansur									0		0	0	1
Kang	1	107	5	2					0		40	0	0
Khash Rod	135	535	6	201	219			26	50	1,164	661	6,421	6,197
Zaranj											135	0	0
Total	**136**	**642**	**11**	**203**	**219**	**0**	**300**	**26**	**115**	**1,690**	**1,955**	**6,507**	**6,203**

*District estimations for 2009 were not available at the time of writing.

86 Central Statistics Office of Afghanistan.

Table 32: Opium poppy cultivation in districts of Farah province, 1996-2008*

District	1996	1997	1998	1999	2000	2001	2002	2003	2004	2005	2006	2007	2008
Anar Dara									91	1,828	143	16	239
Bakwa	13	129	31	129	259				39	390	1,093	3,458	3,090
Bala Buluk	19	169	36	186	183			513	336	1,665	1,669	5,312	1,509
Farah	18	18	10	44	73				87	729	905	1,328	1,013
Gulistan	581	252	94	428	849			1,187	447	163	202	1,132	4,756
Khaki Safed									84	432	537	99	609
Lash Wa Juwayn									41	1,568	215	233	109
Pur Chaman									409	293	363	1,549	1,046
Pusht Rod									554	2,482	1,709	1,314	1,588
Qalay-I-Kah									189	407	506	337	888
Shib Koh									12	283	352	87	163
Total	**631**	**568**	**171**	**787**	**1,364**	**0**	**500**	**1,700**	**2,289**	**10,240**	**7,694**	**14,865**	**15,010**

*District estimations for 2009 were not available at the time of writing.

Table 33: Average opium poppy cultivation per family in Farah by district, 2008

District	Total rural population (1,000)	Total number of families	Average poppy area per family (ha)
Anar Dara	22.3	3,431	0.07
Bakwa	20.1	3,092	1.00
Bala Buluk	48.4	7,446	0.20
Farah	46.4	7,138	0.14
Gulistan	23.4	3,600	1.32
Khaki Safed	17.0	2,615	0.23
Lash Wa Juwayn	26.8	4,123	0.03
Pur Chaman	38.8	5,969	0.18
Pusht Rod	32.7	5,031	0.32
Qalay-I-Kah	21.6	3,323	0.27
Shib Koh	16.7	2,569	0.06
Province	**314.2**	**48,338**	**0.31**

Map 38: Extent of opium poppy cultivation in the districts of Farah province, 2008

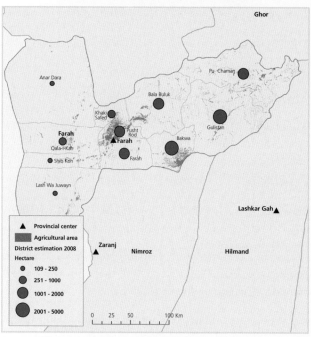

Source: Afghanistan opium survey, 2008, UNODC.

The total arable land in the province is 136,200 ha. In 2009, 9 per cent of this was under opium poppy cultivation.

Badghis

Opium poppy cultivation in Badghis was first reported in 2000. The following year, the province was again poppy-free, but as of 2002, cultivation picked up again. In 2005, cultivation dramatically increased, rising to 2,967 ha. It increased further in 2006, reaching 3,205 ha, and 4,219 ha in 2007. Due to severe drought problems, cultivation sharply decreased in 2008 (to 587 ha), but again increased to 5,400 ha in 2009.

Opium poppy is cultivated mainly in the Ghormach, Murghab and Qadis districts. Farmers mainly use rain-fed areas for opium poppy cultivation.

Increases in opium poppy cultivation ran parallel with increases in insecurity in Badghis province after 2003. After 2006, a few heroin labs were also reported close to the Turkmenistan border in the Ghomarch and Murghab districts. Although cultivation increased sharply, it still only accounted for 0.7 per cent of the total arable land in 2007.

Table 34:   Opium poppy cultivation in the districts of Badghis province, 1996-2008*

District	1996	1997	1998	1999	2000	2001	2002	2003	2004	2005	2006	2007	2008
Ab Kamari											127	0	11
Ghormach					20		4	101		944	624	250	328
Jawand									226	134	431	66	13
Muqur											220	149	7
Murghab					21		22	69	345	1,889	1,034	3,557	81
Qadis											391	198	146
Qala-i-Naw									43		378	0	0
Total	**0**	**0**	**0**	**0**	**41**	**0**	**26**	**170**	**614**	**2,967**	**3,205**	**4,219**	**587**

*District estimations for 2009 were not available at the time of writing.

Table 35:   Average opium poppy cultivation per family in Badghis by district, 2008

District	Total rural population (1,000)	Total number of families	Average poppy area per family (ha)
Ab Kamari	39.7	6108	0.00
Ghormach	39.5	6077	0.04
Jawand	53.8	8277	0.01
Muqur	19.3	2969	0.05
Murghab	51.0	7846	0.45
Qadis	63.6	9785	0.02
Qala-i-Naw	30.4	4677	0.00
Province	**297.3**	**45738**	**0.09**

Map 39:   Extent of opium poppy cultivation in the districts of Badghis province, 2008

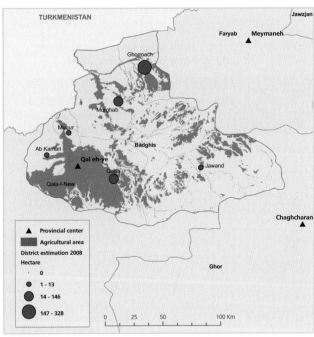

Source: Afghanistan opium survey, 2008, UNODC.

In the same year, the average opium poppy cultivated land per household in Badghis was 0.09 ha, with the highest amount in Murghab district (0.45 ha).

Badghis farmers are not very skilled in opium poppy cultivation and opium is not a major source of income for the province. Farmers are thus less likely to grow the plant and should government control increase, cultivation is likely to continue to decrease until the province is once again poppy-free.

Uruzgan

Between 1996 and 2005, the level of opium poppy cultivation in Uruzgan consistently ranged between 4,500 and 7,800 ha. In 2005, due to severe drought and disease, cultivation fell sharply in the province. This was short-lived, however, as it increased dramatically in 2006, reaching 9,703 ha. Cultivation levels remained more or less stable for

the next three years. Cultivation in Uruzgan is mainly concentrated in the Dihrawud, Shahidi Hassas and Tirin Kot districts..

A total of 251,400 people (38,677 families) live in the rural areas of Uruzgan. In 2008, the average opium poppy cultivated land area per household was 0.26 ha in this province. Dihrawud and Tirinkot are the traditional opium poppy growing districts. In Shadi Hassas, cultivation started to increase in 2006, reaching 4,403 ha in 2008 which is seven times higher than the level recorded in 2005.

The total arable land in Uruzgan province is 63,400 ha. In 2009, 15 per cent of this was under opium poppy cultivation.

Table 36: Opium poppy cultivation in the districts of Uruzgan province, 1996-2008*

District	1996	1997	1998	1999	2000	2001	2002	2003	2004	2005	2006	2007	2008
Chora	1,574	233	652	932	1,179	0	1,330	975	1,402	259	2,024	71	316
Dihrawud	2,923	1,870	1,033	1,243	726	0	1,340	1,282	2,523	209	1,704	3,538	2,849
Khas Uruzgan	0	0	0	0	130	0	-	580	358	338	886	173	304
Shahidi Hassas	0	0	1,158	1,110	802	0	1,190	1,333	782	646	1,127	3,109	4,403
Tirin Kot	3,271	2,484	1,445	1,194	1,494	0	750	469	1,874	221	3,348	2,312	2,067
Total	**7,872**	**4,986**	**4,661**	**4,989**	**4,725**	**0**	**5,100**	**4,698**	**7,365**	**2,025**	**9,703**	**9,203**	**9,939**

*District estimations for 2009 were not available at the time of writing.

Table 37: Average opium poppy cultivation per family in Uruzgan by district, 2008

District	Total rural population (1,000)	Total number of families	Average poppy area per family (ha)
Chora	35.0	5,385	0.06
Dihrawud	49.5	7,615	0.37
Khas Uruzgan	57.5	8,846	0.03
Shahidi Hassas	51.0	7,846	0.56
Tirin Kot	58.4	8,985	0.23
Province	**251.4**	**38,677**	**0.26**

Map 40: Extent of opium poppy cultivation in the districts of Uruzgan province, 2008

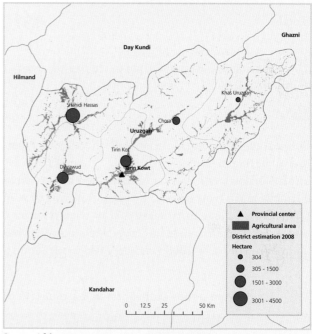

Source: Afghanistan opium survey, 2008, UNODC.

Zabul

Opium poppy cultivation was negligible in Zabul province before 2003. Since 2003, it has ranged between 1,500 and 3,000 ha in total. Limited cultivation has been observed in all districts of the province. Although the security situation seems to favour opium poppy cultivation, poor weather conditions do not, and the crop potential ratio remains negative in the province.

Table 38: Opium poppy cultivation in the districts of Zabul province, 1996-2008*

District	1996	1997	1998	1999	2000	2001	2002	2003	2004	2005	2006	2007	2008
Arghandab	0	0	0	74	139	0		302	526	205	346	79	55
Atghar								188	32	86	36	16	3
Daychopan	0	0	0	41	114	0		646	431	1,016	742	389	422
Kakar (Khak-e Afghan)												104	110
Mizan	255	154	160	373	383	0		309	251	56	123	129	289
Qalat	0	0	1	46	40	0		689	317	188	657	78	310
Shahjoy							0	178	679	240	538	320	237
Shamulzayi								65	44	16	35	159	153
Shinkay								164	287	102	228	139	105
Tarnak wa Jaldak	0	0	0	77	48	1			410	145	506	136	608
Total	**255**	**154**	**161**	**537**	**585**	**1**	**200**	**2,541**	**2,977**	**2,053**	**3,211**	**1,549**	**2,291**

*District estimations for 2009 are not available.

Table 39: Average opium poppy cultivation per family in Zabul by district, 2008

District	Total rural population (1,000)	Total number of families	Average poppy area per family (ha)
Arghandab	27.4	4,215	0.01
Atghar	7.3	1,123	0.00
Daychopan	33.1	5,092	0.08
Kakar (Khak-e Afghan)	20.2	3,108	0.04
Mizan	11.4	1,754	0.16
Qalat	19.8	3,046	0.10
Shahjoy	49.1	7,554	0.03
Shamulzayi	37.5	5,769	0.03
Shinkay	19.7	3,031	0.03
Tarnak wa Jaldak	14.4	2,215	0.27
Total	**239.9**	**36,908**	**0.06**

The estimated average opium poppy cultivated area per household is 0.06 ha in Zabul province.

Kabul

In Kabul province, opium poppy cultivation has been limited to the Surobi district since 1999. The rest of the province has maintained a poppy-free status. Security in Surobi district is much more precarious than in other districts in Kabul province and government control there is limited. Only 7,500 families reside in Surobi and cultivation was limited to 310 ha in 2008 (average 0.04 ha per family).

This indicates that only a limited number of households are relying on opium poppy cultivation and the district can become poppy-free with stronger law enforcement.

Hirat

Opium poppy cultivation (above 100 ha) was first reported in Hirat in the year 2000. In 2001 and 2002, cultivation amounted to less than 100 ha (poppy-free status). In 2003, cultivation rose slightly above this threshold but in 2004, a sharp increase brought it to a total of 2,531 ha. Between 2004 and 2007, opium poppy cultivation was largely stable

Table 40: Opium poppy cultivation in the districts of Kabul province (ha), 1996-2008*

District	1996	1997	1998	1999	2000	2001	2002	2003	2004	2005	2006	2007	2008
Bagrami											0	0	0
Chahar Asyab											0	0	0
Dih Sabz											0	0	0
Farza												0	0
Guldara											0	0	0
Istalif											0	0	0
Kabul											0	0	0
Kalakan											0	0	0
Khaki Jabbar											0	0	0
Mir Bacha Kot											0	0	0
Musayi											0	0	0
Paghman											0	0	0
Qarabagh											0	0	0
Shakar Dara											0	0	0
Surobi				132	340	29	58	237	282		80	500	310
Total	**0**	**0**	**0**	**132**	**340**	**29**	**58**	**237**	**282**	**0**	**80**	**500**	**310**

*District estimations for 2009 were not available at the time of writing.

Table 41: Opium poppy cultivation in districts of Hirat province (hectares), 1996-2008*

District	1996	1997	1998	1999	2000	2001	2002	2003	2004	2005	2006	2007	2008
Adraskan									133	9	99	196	22
Chishti Sharif									166	42	42	0	0
Farsi								134	28	110	111	0	0
Ghoryan									60	238	204	302	0
Gulran									240	33	32	0	0
Guzara									88	231	233	0	0
Hirat									0	16	16	0	0
Injil									41	394	382	0	0
Karukh									265	124	121	0	0
Kohsan									4	72	73	146	0
Kushk									73	64	50	367	43
Kushki Kuhna									3	15	15	0	0
Obe									842	144	131	0	0
Pashtun Zarghun		38			38				154	249	242	0	0
Shindand					146				427	54	408	516	201
Zinda Jan									7	128	129	0	0
Total	**0**	**38**	**0**	**0**	**184**	**0**	**50**	**134**	**2,531**	**1,924**	**2,288**	**1,526**	**266**

*District estimations for 2009 were not available at the time of writing.

at 2,000 ha. In 2008, cultivation decreased dramatically and was restricted to only three districts of Hirat province. Most of the opium production takes place in Shindand district where insurgent groups are very active.

In 2008, the average opium poppy cultivated land per family was 0.008 ha in the Adraskan, Kushk and Shindad districts of Hirat.

2. Opium poppy-free provinces

A region is defined as "opium poppy-free" when it is estimated to have less than 100 ha of poppy cultivation. Figure 22 represents the number of opium producing and poppy-free provinces in Afghanistan between 2002 and 2009. The years 2002 and 2008 are nearly identical in the numerical breakdown of poppy growing and opium free provinces. But in 2009, the number of opium poppy free provinces increased to the highest level since 2002. Between 2003 and 2006, the number of cultivating provinces increased before declining in 2006. The opposite trend is observed for the number of poppy-free provinces.

In 2006, UNODC presented a report which outlined a strategy to gradually increase the number of poppy-free provinces in Afghanistan and reduce cultivation in opium producing provinces. That same year, the main stakeholders (the USA and the United Kingdom) on counter narcotics in Afghanistan jointly with the Afghan Government announced the Good Performers Initiative (GPI)[87] under

Fig. 22: Number of opium growing and opium poppy-free provinces in Afghanistan, 2002-2009

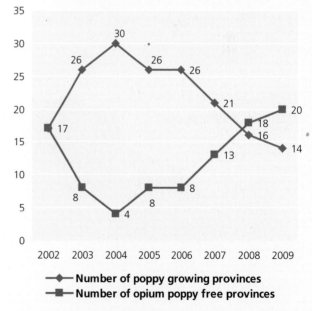

Source: Afghanistan opium surveys, UNODC.

the Counter Narcotics Trust Fund (CNTF)[88] in Afghanistan. The objective of the GPI is to support provinces which achieve sustained progress towards opium poppy elimination or remain poppy-free by providing financial support for their priority development projects.

---

87 http://www.undp.org.af/WhoWeAre/UNDPinAfghanistan/Projects/sbgs/prj_cntf.htm.

88 Counter Narcotics Trust Fund (CNTF), officially established on 29 October 2005, aims to mobilize additional resources needed by the Afghan Government to implement the National Drug Control Strategy (NDCS).

Map 41: Opium poppy cultivation in Afghanistan, 2002

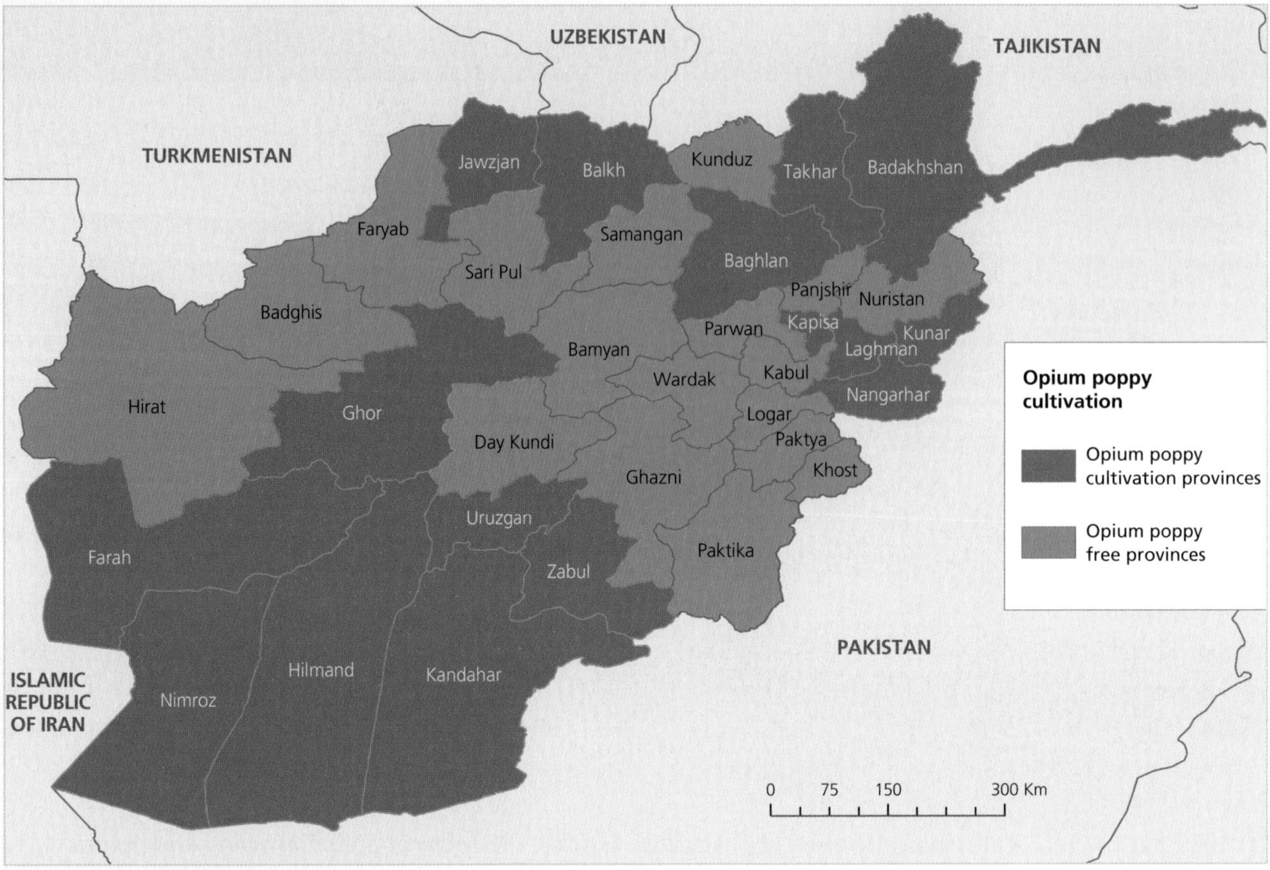

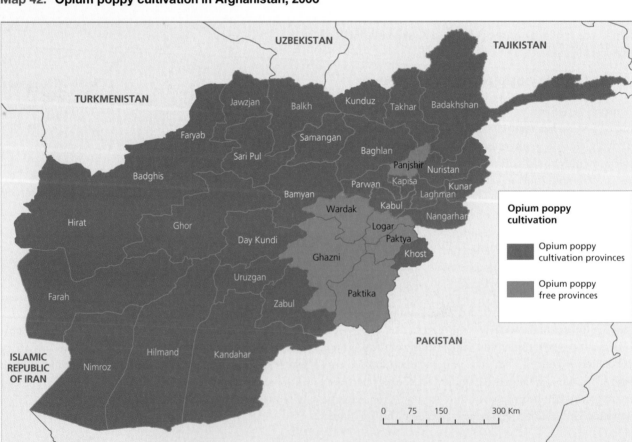

Source: Afghanistan opium survey 2002, UNODC.

Map 42: Opium poppy cultivation in Afghanistan, 2006

Source: Afghanistan opium survey 2006, UNODC.

Map 43: Opium poppy cultivation in Afghanistan, 2007

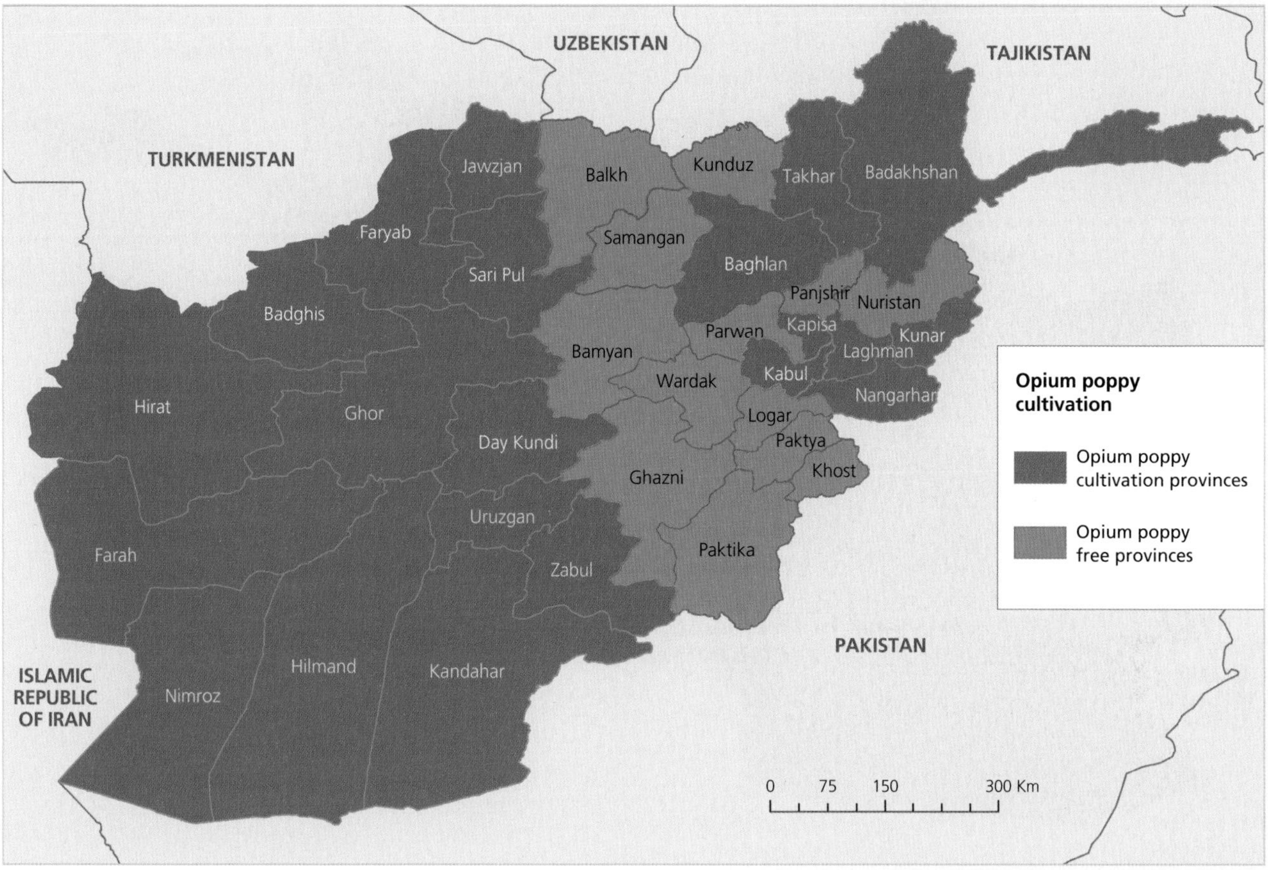

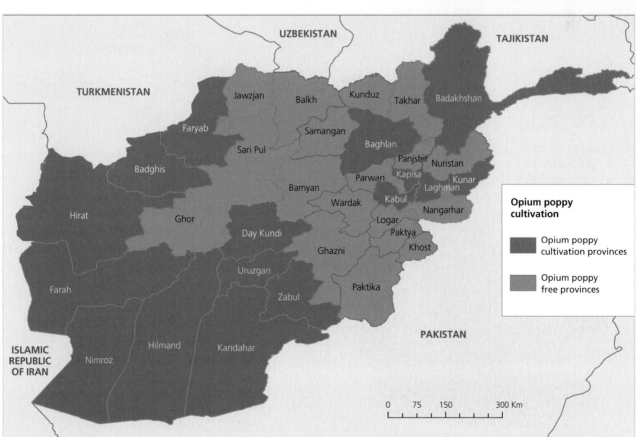

Source: Afghanistan opium survey 2007, UNODC.

Map 44: Opium poppy cultivation in Afghanistan, 2008

Source: Afghanistan opium survey 2008, UNODC.

Map 45: Opium poppy cultivation in Afghanistan, 2009

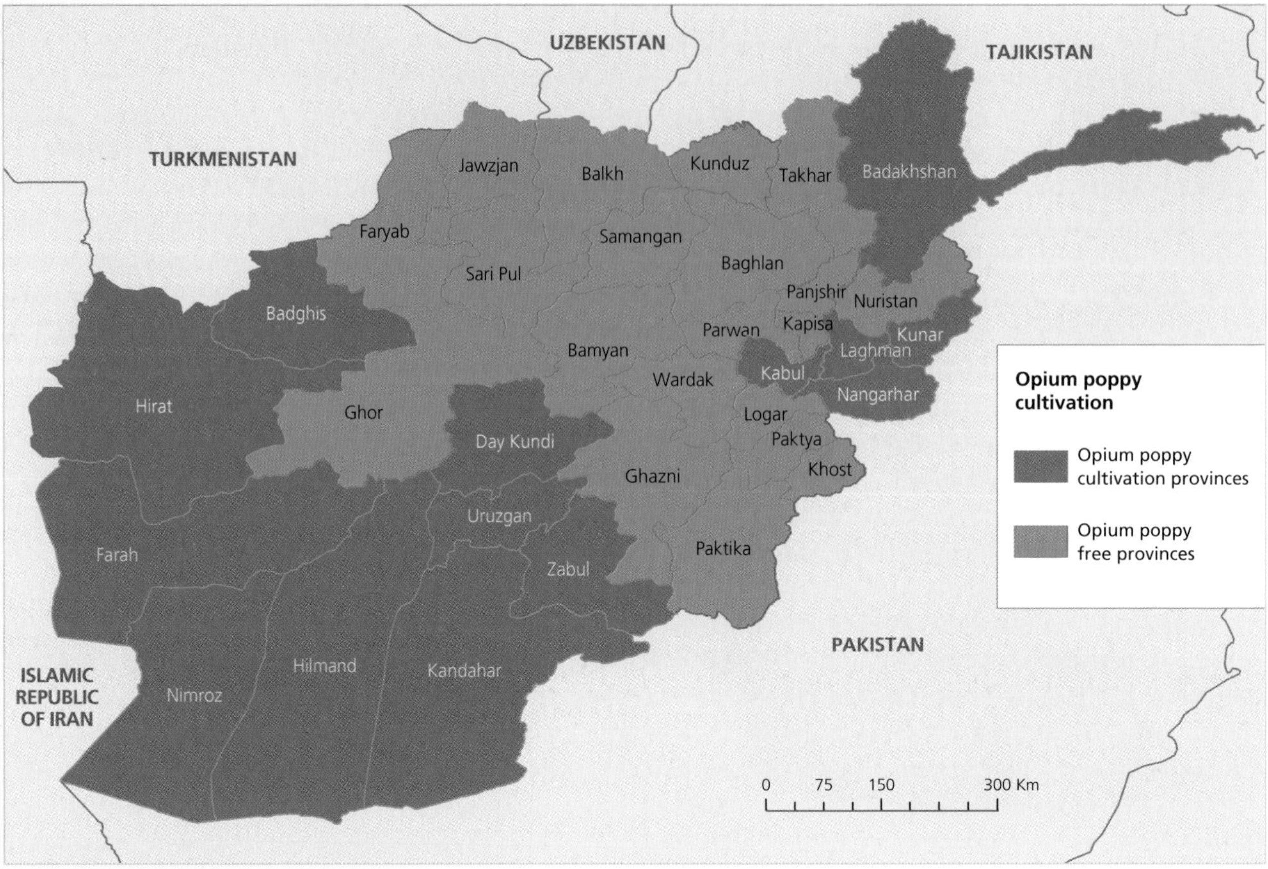

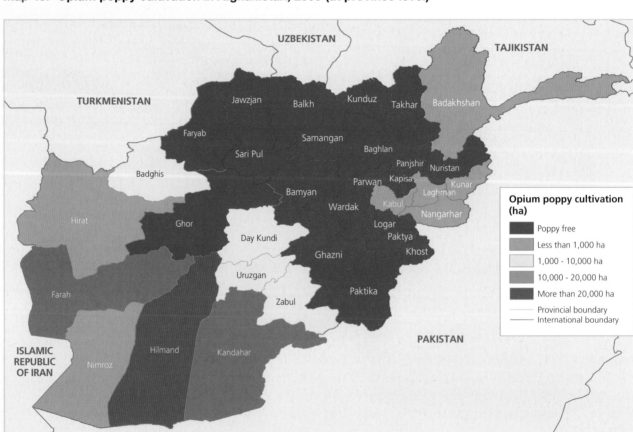

Source: Afghanistan opium survey 2009, UNODC.

Map 46: Opium poppy cultivation in Afghanistan, 2009 (at province level)

Source: Afghanistan opium survey 2009, UNODC.

Table 42: Opium poppy cultivation in the "reclaimed" provinces (ha), 1996-2009

Province	1996	1997	1998	1999	2000	2001	2002	2003	2004	2005	2006	2007	2008	2009
Bamyan				0	0	0	0	610	803	126	17	0	0	0
Faryab	0	0	0	0	36	0	28	766	3,249	2,665	3,040	2,866	291	0
Kunduz				38	489	0	16	49	224	275	102	0	0	0
Nuristan	0	0	4	0	0	0	0	648	765	1,554	1,516	0	0	0
Paktya	0	0	0	29	46	1	38	721	1,200	0	0	0	0	0
Parwan	0	0	0	0	0	0	0	0	1,310	0	124	0	0	0
Samangan				0	54	614	100	101	1,151	3,874	1,960	0	0	0
Sari Pul				0	146	0	57	1,428	1,974	3,227	2,251	260	0	0
Wardak	0	0	0	0	0	0	0	2,735	1,017	106	0	0	0	0
Total	**0**	**0**	**4**	**67**	**771**	**616**	**239**	**7,058**	**11,693**	**11,827**	**9,010**	**3,126**	**291**	**0**

In 2006 each of the six poppy-free provinces were awarded US$ 1,000,000 and eight provinces were awarded US$ 500,000 for having less than 1,000 hectares of opium poppy cultivation.

Seven more poppy-free provinces were announced in August 2007 bringing the total number of poppy-free provinces to 13. This figure reached 18 in 2008. In 2009, 20 provinces were declared opium poppy-free.

Consistently poppy-free provinces: Ghazni, Logar, Paktika and Panjshir provinces have maintained their poppy-free status irrespective of the security in the province or the financial status of the farmers. The people of Panjshir have tradition-ally been averse to drugs as evidenced by the prohibition of even tobacco under the late Commander Masood. Weather conditions in Ghazni and Logar are not favourable to opium poppy cultivation, and the farmers in these prov-inces have not shown any interest in opium poppy cultiva-tion in the past. Although suitable weather conditions and an extremely volatile security situation would seem to favour opium poppy cultivation, the people of Paktika seem to prefer cannabis cultivation instead.

Reclaimed provinces: a total of ten provinces, namely Bamyan, Faryab, Khost, Kunduz, Nuristan, Paktya, Parwan, Saripul, Samangan and Wardak were opium poppy-free in 2002. After five years of intermittent cultivation between 2003 and 2007, they regained opium poppy-free status in 2008 and in 2009.

The highest combined total opium cultivation for the nine provinces was 11,827 ha in 2005. In these provinces, opium poppy cultivation mainly started in the year 2000 and increased after 2002. The residents of these provinces gen-erally respect and follow the government's decisions. Only a very limited number of households tried opium poppy cultivation in these provinces but later stopped it. Addi-tionally, in some of these provinces, like Wardak and Nuris-tan, weather conditions are not favourable to opium poppy cultivation.

"Gained provinces": Balkh, Baghlan, Ghor, Jawzjan, Kapisa,

Takhar and Samangan provinces were not opium poppy-free in 2002, when the total area under cultivation was 3,800 ha. In 2008 and 2009, all became opium poppy-free. Within these provinces the most important one is Balkh since opium poppy cultivation reached up to 11,000 ha in 2005. Having this province achieve poppy-free status can be seen as an important milestone for the Afghan Government and the international community.

Balkh

Balkh province did not have high levels of poppy cultivation until 2005 when the total area under opium poppy cultiva-tion increased sharply to 10,837 ha. The following year, the area under cultivation progressively decreased again and the province was opium poppy-free in 2007, 2008 and 2009.

Balkh province has around 640,000 ha of arable land. Water is available throughout most of the province and farmers are mainly involved in wheat, vegetable and fruit cultivation. In the past, Balkh was the main cotton producing centre of Afghanistan, a sector heavily damaged after the Soviet inva-sion.

Fig. 23: Opium poppy cultivation in Balkh, 1996-2009

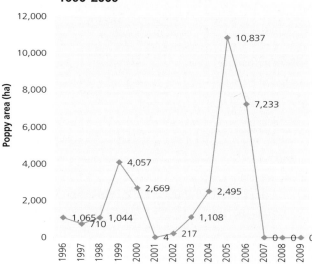

In 2005, only 1.5 per cent of the total arable land in the province was used for opium poppy cultivation. This indicates that opium has not been a major source of income in the province. Cultivation was mainly concentrated in three districts, Charbolak, Balkh and Chimtal. These districts are located in the centre of the province. Successfully maintaining the province poppy-free for two consecutive years is a testament to the strong commitment of the Governor, central government and the international community.

Between 2002 and 2007, a total of US$ 166 million[89] of alternative livelihood investment was provided to the province by international stakeholders. The amount of alternative livelihood investments to the province was increased following record levels of opium poppy cultivation in 2005. These encouraging results show that a commitment to rural development combined with strong law enforcement measures are essential to achieving poppy-free status.

Of course, significant problems remain, particularly affecting the poorest of Balkh residents. Most of Balkh's residents have accumulated debt.[90] The looming financial problems may leave them unable to feed their families, and some have started cannabis cultivation as a coping strategy, signalling a shift in agricultural livelihood strategies (also witnessed in Nangarhar).

3. Profile of opium poppy growing farmers and non-growing farmers

Although Afghanistan's gross domestic production (GDP) has increased sharply since 2002, it remains one of the poorest countries in the world.

Table 43: Afghanistan GDP, 2002-2008

Year	GDP, current prices (US$)	Change (per cent)
2002	4,009	
2003	4,435	+11%
2004	5,402	+22%
2005	6,483	+20%
2006	7,048	+9%
2007	8,842	+25%
2008	11,238	+27%

Source: International Monetary Fund (IMF).

In 2008, the national GDP was 180 per cent higher than in 2002. Despite this substantial improvement, 53 per cent of the total population in Afghanistan still lives below the poverty line . Most of Afghanistan's socio-economic indicators fall far short of the global average.

Afghanistan has historically suffered from underdevelopment which became chronic and finally led to economic regression as various internecine conflicts ravaged the country. In 1980, the national GDP was $ 3.6 billion, while in 2001, it had dropped to $2.4 billion. As of 2002, with a new Afghan Government and substantial support from the international community, the Afghan economy started to grow again. For many Afghans, the growth has, however, been offset by increases in food and oil prices, which are causing a rise in inflation rates. Annual inflation reached 20.7 in 2008 (from March 2007 to March 2008), severely impacting the day-to-day life of most Afghans, and the International Monetary Fund estimates an average consumer price inflation of 24 per cent in 2008/09.[91]

Opium economy

Between 2002 and 2008, Afghan opium farmers earned a total of US$ 6.4 billion while Afghan traffickers earned approximately US$ 18 billion. About 2 million people were involved every year, on average, in opium poppy cultivation in Afghanistan.

After 2003, due to the drop in dry opium prices, the income of Afghan opium poppy cultivating farmers decreased. In 2009, dry opium prices amounted to US$ 64/kg, a 81 per cent decrease from 2002. At the same time, the total export value of opium to neighbouring countries increased due to the rise in production and a relatively smaller decrease in heroin prices.

In 2004, the level of the opiate economy was equal to 61 per cent of the total licit economy in Afghanistan. But this dropped to 33 per cent in 2008.

In 2002, farmers in southern Afghanistan expanded the area under opium poppy cultivation, along with their opium income. In 2009, almost 90 per cent of the total opium income generated in the country was shared among southern Afghanistan farmers. The remaining 10 per cent was shared among farmers in western Afghanistan (9 per cent) and others (1 per cent). In 2003, this picture was remarkably different: 34 per cent of opium income was shared among southern cultivators, another 34 per cent was divided among eastern farmers; 15 per cent among central farmers; 10 per cent among north-eastern farmers; 5 per cent among northern farmers and 1 per cent among farmers in western Afghanistan.

Agriculture is an important income source, but many Afghans in rural areas also rely on diversified livelihood strategies to generate household income. Almost half of Afghan households depend on income from agriculture. Figure 26 shows the distribution of income generation sources for Afghan households.

Income sources and distribution vary from region to region. In southern Afghanistan, 40 per cent of household income

89 *Alternative Livelihood Database Analysis Report*, UNODC, 2008.
90 *Priority needs assessment summary report*, UNODC, 2008.
91 Economist Intelligence Unit country report for Afghanistan, 2008.

Table 46: **Afghan opium export value, 2002-2009**

	2002	2003	2004	2005	2006	2007	2008	2009	Total (2002-2008)	Total (2005-2008)
Total farm gate income (million US$)	1,200	1,534	600	560	760	1,000	732	438	6,386	3,052
Total export value of opium to neighbouring countries	N/A	2,300	2,800	2,700	3,100	4,000	0	N/A	18,300	13,200
Number of persons involved in opium poppy cultivation (million)	N/A	1.7	2.3	2	2.9	3.3	2.4	3.4	-	-

Table 44: **Dry opium farm gate prices in Afghanistan (US$)**

2002	2003	2004	2005	2006	2007	2008	2009	Change between 2002 and 2009 (per cent)
333	425	142	138	125	122	95	64	-81%

Table 45: **Heroin prices at Afghanistan's borders (US$)**

Location	2002	2008	Change
Afghanistan / Iran border	5000	3270	-35%
Afghanistan / Pakistan border	4110	3256	-21%
Afghanistan / Tajikistan border	4540	3150	-31%

Fig. 25: **Share of total opium poppy farm-gate income, by region, 2003-2008**

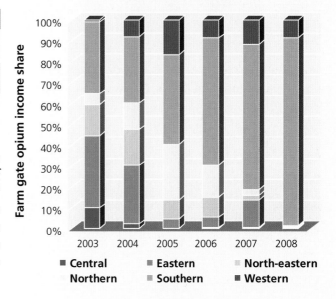

is derived from opium poppy cultivation. This contrasts sharply with central Afghanistan, where only 1 per cent of the total household income comes from opium poppy.[92] The share of opium poppy in total household income has been decreasing for both north and north-eastern farmers in parallel with the decrease in cultivation. A sudden change in income sources may lead to poverty problems similar to

Fig. 24: **Value of the opiate economy compared to the licit economy**

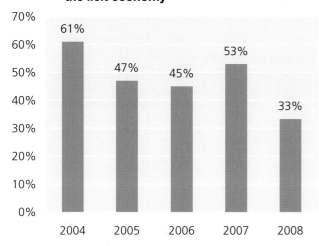

the previously noted situation in Nangarhar province in 2005 after cultivation fell by 96 per cent.

In 2005 and 2006, the vast majority of Nangarhar farmers abstained from cultivating opium poppy but were not able to compensate for the loss in income through other crops. As a result, opium poppy cultivation bounced back to 18,739 ha in 2007. In 2008, cultivation in Nangarhar province was negligible (less than 100 ha). The provision of alternative income sources for Nangarhar farmers may help to sustain the province's opium poppy-free status.

The vast majority of the northern and north-eastern farmers have abandoned opium poppy cultivation. Given the severe drought in these regions in 2008, farmers might face further economic hardship in 2008 and 2009.

Fig. 26: Distribution of income sources for Afghan households (per cent), 2007

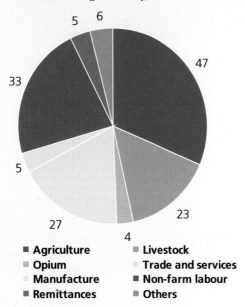

- ■ Agriculture
- ■ Livestock
- ■ Opium
- ■ Trade and services
- ■ Manufacture
- ■ Non-farm labour
- ■ Remittances
- ■ Others

In eastern Afghanistan, average annual income levels do not differ greatly between non-poppy and poppy growing farmers. In central Afghanistan provinces, however, non-poppy growing farmers enjoy higher returns. In this region, farmers are growing poppy mainly for their personal consumption.

In north-eastern Afghanistan, non-poppy growing farmers also earn higher levels of income than poppy growers. This is due to the spike in wheat prices and a decrease in opium prices and opium poppy cultivation.

In western and northern Afghanistan, the income of opium poppy growing farmers is 25 per cent higher than for farmers cultivating other crops. Farmers in the south, whether growing poppy or other crops, generally earn higher incomes than farmers in other regions.

Compared to 2005, farmers' debt decreased in all regions in 2008. The highest decreases were observed in southern Afghanistan (41 per cent) followed by the eastern region (30 per cent), the north-eastern region (30 per cent), the central region (25 per cent) and lastly the northern region (9 per cent). The smallest share was observed in the western region (5 per cent).

The vast majority of Afghans still lack access to electricity, safe drinking water, health systems and education.[93] Only 19 per cent of Afghan households have televisions and six per cent have fridges. Moreover, only 2 per cent of Afghan farmers own tractors.

4. Poverty and motivation behind opium poppy cultivation

Afghanistan remains one of the poorest countries in the world. All its socio-economic indicators are near the bottom of global rankings. But this does not encapsulate all the reasons for opium poppy cultivation in Afghanistan. There are considerable disparities in terms of income levels and land ownership between Afghan regions. Table 50 shows that farmers in southern Afghanistan earn much more and are less indebted than other farmers in the country. The average land owning size is also high for farmers in the

Table 47: Average share of opium poppy income in household income*, 2005-2007

Region	Per cent of opium poppy income in total household income (2005)	Per cent of opium poppy income in total household income (2006)	Per cent of opium poppy income in total household income (2007)
Central	1.6	0.7	1%
Eastern	18.4	12.1	21%
North-eastern	27.7	13.8	3%
Northern	16.8	6.1	1%
Southern	35.2	35.4	40%
Western	14	9.9	10%

* For all households
Source: UNODC.

Table 48: Income of opium poppy growing and non-growing farmers, 2006

Region	Average annual income of opium poppy growing farmers in 2006 ($)	Average annual income of non-opium poppy growing farmers in 2006 ($)
Central	2,357	2,674
Eastern	1,817	1,753
North-eastern	1,970	2,290
Northern	2,270	1,862
Southern	6,194	3,382
Western	2,895	2,273
Overall	5,055	2,370

93 National Risk and Vulnerability Assessment (NRVA) 2005, Central Statistics Office of Afghanistan.

Table 49: Afghan farmers' loans, 2005-2008

Region	Average loan (US$) - 2005	Average loan (US$) - 2006	Average loan (US$) - 2007	Average loan (US$) - 2008	Change 2005-2008 (per cent)
Central	814	806	576	612	-25%
Eastern	861	543	489	593	-31%
North-eastern	474	362	339	333	-30%
Northern	796	708	666	723	-9%
Southern	818	696	787	486	-41%
Western	388	330	318	367	-5%

south, compared to other regions. If poverty were the only reason for opium poppy cultivation in Afghanistan, it would mean that i) Southern Afghanistan farmers became severely impoverished after 2002 after large-scale resumption of cultivation, and ii) other parts of Afghanistan are much richer than southern and western Afghanistan, which does not appear to be the case. Especially in central Afghanistan, farmers are much poorer than in other regions with a comparable level of debt. They do not, however, cultivate opium poppy on the same level as farmers in eastern, north-eastern and northern Afghanistan. In 2006, UNODC published a study about the motivations behind opium poppy cultivation.[94] In this study, the main reasons/ motivations for opium cultivation were summarized as:

i. Lack of rule of law

ii. Insecurity

iii. Lack of off farm employment

iv. Lack of water and agricultural infrastructure

v. Survival – provision of basic needs

vi. External pressure from traffickers and traders

vii. Exaggerated expectations of bilateral assistance through alternative livelihood activities.

viii. Lack of coping strategies without opium poppy income

Table 50: Motivations for opium poppy cultivation by region, 2006

Motivations/ Regions	Central	Northern	North Eastern	Eastern	West	Southern
Role of Islam	Import motivation for not growing poppy	has limited impact on poppy cultivation	has limited impact on poppy cultivation	has limited impact on poppy cultivation	Has no impact	Has no impact
Respect for Government	Respect for Government has a positive impact on stopping poppy cultivation	Respect for Government has a positive impact on stopping poppy cultivation	Respect for Government has a positive impact on stopping poppy cultivation	Respect for Government has a positive impact on stopping poppy cultivation	Lack of respect to Government is one the reason for poppy cultivation	Lack of respect to Government is one the reason for poppy cultivation
Rule of law	Better implementation of rule of law limits/stops poppy cultivation	Better implementation of rule of law limits/stops poppy cultivation	Better implementation of rule of law limits/stops poppy cultivation	Better implementation of rule of law limits/stops poppy cultivation	Lack of rule of law is one of the reason for poppy cultivation	Lack of rule of law is one of the reason for poppy cultivation
Security	Better security helps to stop poppy cultivation	Better security helps to stop poppy cultivation	Better security helps to stop poppy cultivation	Better security helps to stop poppy cultivation	Lack of security results in increase in poppy cultivation	Lack of security results in increase in poppy cultivation
External pressure from drug traffickers and anti government elements	Not applicable	Not applicable	Not applicable	Not applicable	Results in increase in poppy cultivation	Results in increase in poppy cultivation
Lack of provision of basic needs	Does not impact on farmers decisions on poppy cultivation	Has a limited impact on farmers decisions on poppy cultivation	Has an impact on farmers decisions on poppy cultivation	Has an impact on farmers decisions on poppy cultivation	Has an impact on farmers decisions on poppy cultivation	Has an impact on farmers decisions on poppy cultivation
Lack of coping strategies without opium poppy income	No impact on farmers decisions on poppy cultivation	Farmers are not dependent on opium poppy income	Has an impact on farmers decisions on poppy cultivation	Has an impact on farmers decisions on poppy cultivation	Has an impact on farmers decisions on poppy cultivation	Has an impact on farmers decisions on poppy cultivation

94 Factors influencing the variations of opium poppy cultivation in key provinces in Afghanistan, 2006, UNODC.

These reasons/motivations vary between regions. Table 51 presents the main factors influencing opium poppy cultivation in each region in Afghanistan.

5. Farmers` income from opium in Afghanistan

Farmers (sharecroppers or landowners) and drug traffickers benefit most directly from the opium trade in Afghanistan. In addition, a considerable number of rural wage labourers are engaged in and benefit from harvesting opium.

Three persons can harvest one jerib (0.20 ha) of opium poppy-cultivated land in 21 days. This means that annually, the number of individuals needed to harvest the entire opium poppy crop was approximately 2.9 million in 2007 (193,000 ha), 2.4 million in 2008 (157,000 ha) and 1.8 million in 2009 (123,000 ha).

In 2008, a large number of itinerant labourers moved to southern Afghanistan during the poppy harvest season to work as wage labourers (lancing and/or harvesting). Although the typical wage is US$ 5/day, due to labour shortages, daily wage rates were sometimes increased up to US$ 15/day.

In total, 42 per cent of the farmers in Afghanistan began cultivating opium poppy cultivation before the year 2001 and 58 per cent started after 2001. Particularly in 2004 and 2005, a significant number of new farmers began cultivating opium in the country. Only 10 per cent of the total number of opium farmers started cultivation after 2005. This means that long-established opium farmers increased the amount of opium that they cultivated after 2005.

In southern Afghanistan, 56 per cent of opium farmers started poppy cultivation before 2001. 22 per cent of current opium farmers began cultivation in 2004 and 2005. After 2005, existing opium farmers increased the area devoted to poppy cultivation almost threefold. In general, opium farmers in northern, central and western Afghanistan started cultivating after the year 2001. Particularly in western Afghanistan, farmers started to cultivate opium poppy after 2003. In northern and central Afghanistan, after 2001, some farmers wanted to take the advantage of lack of government control and earn easy money by cultivating opium poppy. Later on, instructions from the President to provincial and district government officials led to improvement in these regions as farmers switched to other crops. Since they were not traditionally opium farmers, it

was easier for them to stop cultivating opium. Eastern Afghanistan's farmers, mainly Nangarharies, left opium cultivation in 2005, and having no coping strategy, returned to cultivation in 2006. In 2008, cultivation once again decreased sharply in Nangarhar province.

In 2008, farmers earned US$ 732 million from opium, mainly in southern and western Afghanistan. With the capital gained from opium, farmers reinvest in the formal economy. In this way, the local economy indirectly benefits from the opium economy, and the two are currently inseparable. Another example concerns the sharp decrease in opium cultivation in eastern Afghanistan in 2005 and 2006, which reduced incomes both in the farming sector and in the non-poppy business sector (many shopkeepers were forced to close down their shops).

Opium is a labour-intensive crop which generates jobs in on-farm casual work (for day labourers involved in weeding and harvesting) and in the non-farm rural sector (5.6 jobs per hectare, according to World Bank estimates). Clearly, opium helps sustain the livelihoods of millions of rural Afghans. It is therefore crucial to increase the size of the legal economy in order to isolate the opium economy.

6. Local traders and traffickers` income

Opium is purchased individually from farmers by traders. These traders have close connections with poppy cultivators in villages and, given their ties to the local communities, are approachable by the farmers. Throughout most of Afghanistan, traders work as *Kamishankars*, that is, the people who collect opium (usually small volumes) from farmers to supply to the area/district dealers for a fixed commission. For each opium poppy growing village, depending on the level of cultivation, there can be 2-4 farm-gate traders.[95]

Area/district dealers act as liaison or intermediaries between provincial drug traders and farm-gate traders. They control the farm-gate trading networks in the villages. Depending on the level of cultivation in the area or district, there can be 1-2 traders collecting the opium from farm-gate traders. District traders make cash advances and purchase opium at the farm-gate price. District traders then transfer opium to provincial/zone traders who dominate the trade in bulk purchases at the provincial level. Provincial/zone traders transfer the opium to main market traders.

Each province hosts 1-2 major provincial traders, while

Table 51: Number of people involved in opium poppy cultivation and harvesting, 2003-2009

	2003	2004	2005	2006	2007	2008	2009
Total number of people involved in harvesting	1,200,000	1,965,000	1,560,000	2,475,000	2,895,000	2,355,000	1,845,000

95 *Monitoring of drug flow in Afghanistan*, UNODC, 2007.

Table 52: Farmers' starting year for opium cultivation

	Central	Eastern	North-eastern	Northern	Southern	Western	Total
Before 2001	8%	50%	33%	12%	56%	3%	42%
2002	46%	13%	0%	6%	7%	5%	8%
2003	0%	8%	0%	12%	8%	12%	9%
2004	15%	17%	56%	12%	11%	24%	15%
2005	8%	8%	11%	12%	11%	27%	14%
2006	15%	4%	0%	35%	5%	23%	9%
2007	8%	0%	0%	0%	1%	5%	2%
2008	0%	0%	0%	12%	1%	1%	1%

Source: Afghanistan opium surveys, UNODC.

Table 53: Opium farm-gate income per region (million US$), 2003-2008

Regions	2003	2004	2005	2006	2007	2008	Total
Central	150	12	1	1	3	1	167
Eastern	529	169	25	38	132	4	897
North-eastern	231	103	50	74	24	1	482
Northern	78	76	152	118	28	4	456
Southern	528	191	241	463	701	657	2,782
Western	18	49	95	67	117	62	408
Total	**1,534**	**600**	**560**	**760**	**1,000**	**732**	**5,186**

Source: Afghanistan opium surveys, UNODC.

main market traders mainly operate in Hilmand (Sangin and Musa Qala districts), Kandahar (Kandahar and Andarab districts), Nangarhar (Shinwar district), Hirat (Shindad district) and Badakshan (Faizabad district). These traders maintain strong links with international trading networks and organize processing and trafficking to neighbouring countries where some have tribal and family ties.

Although the above classification seems to indicate rigid market-defined roles, it should be noted that these are often flexible in Afghanistan.

The number of people engaged in the opium trade has increased since Taliban times, due in part to increases in prices and production levels. In Hilmand province alone, the estimated number of traders (all levels) might vary between 600 and 6,000,[96] meaning that hundreds of families derive financial benefit from the opium trade.

The price for high quality (60–80 per cent purity) heroin in Afghanistan is around US$ 2,500/kg. In general, the price of heroin increases the closer it gets to its destination countries, to reach up to $70,000 - $100,000* per kg, which is 30-40 times higher than the price in Afghanistan. The esti-

mated value of opiate trafficking for Afghanistan was US$ 3.4 billion in 2008.[97] The total turn over of the global heroin market is estimated at US$ 65 billion. The total income of Afghan farmers from opium (US$ 0.7 billion) in 2008 is very small in comparison.

From 2002 to 2008, Afghan farmers earned US$ 6.3 billion and Afghan drug traffickers more than US$ 18 billion. Afghan farmers paid 10 per cent of their total income, or US$ 600 million, to the Taliban, warlords, Mullahs or Government officials as tax. Taliban-led insurgents also got other benefits from drug traffickers, like weapons and financial contributions, in return for the provision of security.

---

96   Opium trading systems in Hilmand and Ghor provinces, *Afghanistan drug industry*, World Bank- UNODC pp 98.

97   Afghanistan opium survey, 2008, UNODC.

Fig. 27: The illicit opium trade chain in Afghanistan

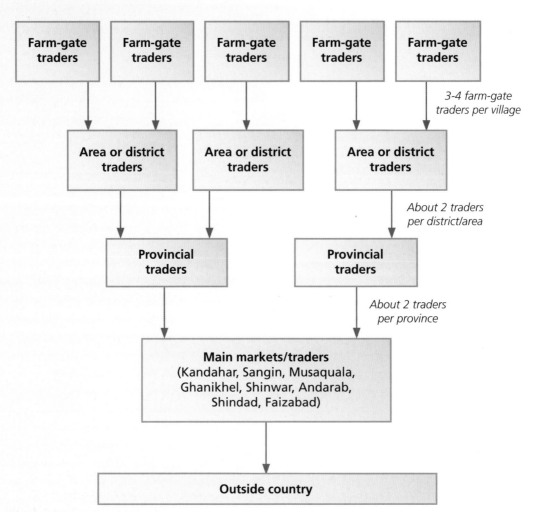

* Street value of heroin.
Source: UNODC Afghanistan Office, *Monitoring of drug flow in Afghanistan*, 2007.

2. THE OPIATE ECONOMY:
A transnational security threat

A. OPIATE ECONOMY AND INSURGENCY

Insurgencies have demonstrated an interest in and capability of using drug money for funding, such as the Islamic Movement of Uzbekistan (IMU) in Central Asia and the FARC (Fuerzas Armadas Revolucionarias de Colombia) in Colombia[1]. The links between anti-government elements in Afghanistan and its drug economy have been well-noted. It has become difficult to distinguish clearly between terrorist movements, insurgencies and organized crime (linked to the drug trade or otherwise), since their tactics and funding sources are increasingly similar.[2]

It can now be said that all actors involved in destabilizing Afghanistan are directly or indirectly linked to the drug economy.[3] Insurgents' access to the opium economy translates into increased military capabilities and prolongs conflict. Opiates also fuel insecurity across Afghanistan as groups fight for control of routes and territory. Finally, the drug trade also indirectly contributes to political instability in Pakistan,[4] Central Asia[5] and the Chinese province of Xinjiang (bordering Central Asia and Afghanistan).[6] These are all consumption markets in their own right, but also transit regions for heroin travelling to western, Chinese and Russian markets, in which organized crime groups control distribution networks.

This section examines interactions between the Afghan drug trade, the Afghanistan-Pakistan insurgency and organized crime. The opiates trade is a major component of Afghanistan's economy, as it has been since the mid-1990s. Insecurity is correlated with the opiate economy, but disentangling cause and effect is difficult. Distinguishing insurgents from drug traffickers is a challenge when these categories overlap in many individuals and groups. These analytical challenges arise because the opiate economy is a central rather than marginal phenomenon in Afghanistan. It is an important source of finance for networks of corrupt government officials and for many insurgent groups.

The term 'anti-government elements' (AGE) permits simultaneous reference to a wide range of actors that are inhibiting the development of the Afghan state. However, it also obscures the varying motivations of AGE and the role shifts of individuals and groups. For example, a wealthy southern landowner may occupy a local government post, preside over sharecroppers who farm opium on his land, and support the insurgency in order to protect his interests from government encroachment. This individual might be considered an official, an insurgent and a drug trader simultaneously. Faced with these category overlaps, it may be more productive to examine how different *behaviours* interact (criminality, insurgency and official governance), rather than how individuals interact.

1   The FARC reportedly taxes coca cultivation and production, earning an estimated $140 million annually; see Michael Renner, T*he anatomy of resource wars, world watch paper 162*, WorldWatch Institute, October 2002.

2   Viatcheslav Avioutskii et al., "The Geopolitics of separatism: genesis of Chechen field commanders", *Central Asia and the Caucasus* 2,20:7-14.

3   Bureau of International Narcotics and Law Enforcement Affairs, *Fighting the Opium Trade in Afghanistan: Myths, Facts and Sound Policy*, http://www.state.gov/p/inl/rls/other/102214.htm, 11 March 2008

4   Pakistani military sources quoted in: Bokhari Laila, "Waziristan- Impact on the Taliban Insurgency and the Stability of Pakistan", *FFI/Rapport*, 2006.

5   The Islamic Movement of Uzbekistan (IMU) profited heavily from the drug trade when it controlled trafficking routes in Tajikistan in the late 1990s, becoming in the eyes of some an organized crime group with a political wing.

6   Ziad Haider, "Politics, Trade, and Islam along the Karakoram Highway",

1. Anti-Government Elements and insecurity in Afghanistan

As a label, 'AGE' brings under one umbrella a complex amalgam of fluid and shifting alliances. This broad mix includes warlords, tribal leaders, religious leaders (mullahs), foreign jihadists, mercenaries/semi-private militias, Pakistani/Afghan Taliban and criminal organizations. Most dedicated insurgents – that is, those who seek to overthrow the government and expel foreign troops – associate themselves with the Taliban or Al-Qaeda, which are the main focus of this section.[7]

The Taliban

"[A] militant outgrowth of radicalized strands of the Pashtun peoples,"[8] the Taliban emerged in southern Afghanistan and from Pakistani *madrassas* (Islamic religious schools) in Afghan refugee camps in 1994. Two years later, the movement gained control over most of Afghanistan, pushing other powers into a corner of the north-east. Following their overthrow by the international coalition and the Northern Alliance in 2001, many Taliban leaders found sanctuary among fellow Pashtuns in Pakistan's tribal areas. From this point, there was heightened operational convergence between an emerging Pakistani Taliban and fleeing Afghan Taliban, with the two groups now planning and launching attacks against both Pakistan and Afghanistan.[9]

Nevertheless, the Taliban movement is not ideologically homogeneous and some members are known to be "reconcilable" through truces and negotiations. As a first step, it is thus important – yet difficult – to distinguish between the Afghan Taliban and the more radical "foreign" Taliban. The latter are mostly graduates of underground madrassa network and are thought to be much more motivated by extremism and sympathy for groups like Al-Qaeda. Research by the Institute for War and Peace Reporting revealed that in provinces like Hilmand, residents were not necessarily troubled by the Afghan Taliban "but from insurgents trained in Pakistan who flow in through the porous border."[10]

The Afghan Taliban include some non-ideological, more "opportunistic" fighters motivated by 1) financial incentives, 2) tribal imperatives, or 3) coalition blunders resulting in civilian casualties. Notably, some semi-autonomous "neo-Taliban" commanders have emerged as a younger generation. They maintain significant operational independence from the Taliban's top leaders in Pakistan, but receive stra-

tegic guidance and occasional orders/assistance in carrying out specific attacks. A number of "neo-Taliban" appear to be opium traffickers and criminal gang members.

Unlike the Al-Qaeda network, the Afghan Taliban is a local insurgent group whose activities and scope are limited to Afghanistan and to a lesser extent the border areas of Pakistan. Although it does receive financial support from AQ and reported by private donors in the Gulf and other regions, much of its funding derives from locals in both countries, delivered from mosque collections, sympathetic businessmen, radical religious parties (in Pakistan) and taxation systems, including those applied to the opiates trade.[11] In addition, locals may provide shelter and sustenance to groups in control of a given area. There is no concrete evidence that the Taliban is currently receiving state funding, and international cooperation continues to put considerable pressure on charities and other non-governmental organizations.

At this stage of its insurgency, the Taliban movement is opportunistic and religiously pragmatic. There seems to be a consensus that growing poppy is religiously proscribed, yet taxing cultivation and trafficking is justified by war imperatives. As discussed below, similar flexibility is evident in the criminal activities of other groups linked to Al-Qaeda. A 2001 UNODC mission evaluating the result of the Taliban ban on cultivation acknowledged its effectiveness. However, the Taliban today again have a tolerance of opium that for some commanders borders on dependence.

Al-Qaeda

Like the Taliban, Al-Qaeda has evolved under international pressure, with more autonomy falling to individual terrorist cells which often have appropriated Al-Qaeda's "brand name". At present, it is highly decentralized, existing as a revolutionary motivation[12] and a loosely affiliated group of individuals based in at least 60 countries. In contrast with the more localized Taliban, Al-Qaeda is a transnational terrorist network. It has operational links with like-minded organizations throughout the world, for which it acts as a focal point or umbrella organization.[13]

Al-Qaeda does not appear to have a direct role in the Afghan opiates trade. Beyond ideological considerations, involvement in drug trafficking would increase the visibility of its secretive core group. Set against this, it may have less access to donations from sympathizers following the September 11 attacks. Extremist groups linked or ideologically aligned with Al-Qaeda have been involved in a wide range

---

7 Some NGOs have identified a "grass roots" insurgency with no ideological links to the Taliban, but like in Iraq made up of disparate groups united with "legitimate grievances" in opposition to foreign troops or the central government.

8 Rodney W. Jones, "Neutralizing Extremism and Insurgency in Afghanistan and Its Borderlands", *Institute of regional studies*, Seminar paper, Islamabad, May 2008.

9 "India and Pakistan in Afghanistan: Hostile Sports", *CSIS*, April 03, 2008

10 IWPR, "Foreign Taleban Rile Hilmand Residents", October 30 2007.

11 Peter Marsden et al. , "An assessment of the Security of Asian Development Bank Projects in Afghanistan", *Asian Development Bank*, March 2007.

12 This doctrine "rejects modernism and emphasizes the concepts of jihad (holy struggle) and takfir (declaring another Muslim an infidel)"; see for example Christopher G. Pernin et al., "Unfolding the Future of the Long War: Motivations, Prospects, and Implications for the U.S. Army", *RAND*, 2008.

13 Examples include the Egyptian al-Gama'a al-Islamiyya, the Islamic Movement of Uzbekistan, and the Harakat ul-Mujahidin of Pakistan.

of illicit activities, including drug trafficking, to finance themselves in such disparate areas as North[14] and South Africa,[15] Southern Europe and Central Asia. The US Central Intelligence Agency has estimated that Al-Qaeda has required some $30 million a year to sustain itself during the period preceding 9/11, but little information exists on its current financial resources.[16] Certainly, it seems to have regained some of its past financial capacity, with some estimates placing the number of Al-Qaeda and Taliban training camps at 157 in the North West Frontier Province.[17]

In Afghanistan, Al-Qaeda does not "control" territory and presumably cannot levy taxes on cultivation or transportation. However, on the Pakistani border, its members are well-placed to participate in low-level drugs and/or arms smuggling. A joint US DEA/FBI investigation in 2001 uncovered a transnational heroin network based in Peshawar and identified money-launderers with alleged ties to Al-Qaeda. Sea-borne trafficking through Pakistan to Europe via the Gulf States seems to have been significant for Al-Qaeda funding – in a two-week period in December-January 2004, the US Navy intercepted four boats carrying tons of hashish, heroin and methamphetamines. The first of these was manned by suspected Al-Qaeda members and was carrying almost two tons of hashish with a street value of US$ 8-10 million.[18]

2. Insurgent groups linked to Al-Qaeda and the Taliban

Hizb-i Islami

Hizb-i Islami (HI, Party of Islam) has members and influence in many areas of Afghanistan, and was an important group during the conflict of the 1990s. It is split into two factions, each led by a former anti-Soviet Mujahedin[19] commander. One is led by Gulbuddin Hekmatyar (HiG) and the other by Anwar ul-Haq Mujahid (HiK), named after its original leader, the late Mawlawi Yonus Khalis. During the Soviet conflict, the Taliban supreme leader had fought under Khalis and HiK was later absorbed by the Taliban in 2003.[20] Hekmatyar's faction seems to be closer to Al-Qaeda groups than the Taliban, and the list maintained by the UN Security Council Al-Qaeda and Taliban Sanctions Committee (1267 Committee) considers Hekmatyar an associate of Al-Qaeda. Its centre of gravity is in eastern Afghanistan,

particularly Kunar, Nuristan and Laghman provinces, drawing on support and sanctuary in adjacent areas of Pakistan such as Dir, Bajaur and Khyber agencies. Hekmatyar also maintains a certain degree of support in his native Kunduz and in western Takhar Province.

HI is dedicated to expelling foreign troops but has varied in its operational and ideological convergence with the Taliban and Al-Qaeda. This was most obvious in the 1990s, when HI directly confronted the Taliban in some areas of Afghanistan. Competition continues today, in places like Wardak and Logar. HiG is not strong in most areas of Afghanistan that cultivate opium, with the important exception of Kunar and Laghman. Given its influence over these provinces, it seems safe to presume that HiG has accommodated itself to cultivation in the areas it controls. Most of its drug-related funding consists of informal taxes in border areas and to a lesser extent involvement in processing. According to some experts, Hekmatyar was the only Mujahedin to exploit opium profits systematically as a basis for a party and a conventional army. Most commanders were content selling raw opium, but Hekmatyar also invested in laboratories, in partnership with Pakistani heroin syndicates.[21] US troops have raided labs linked to HiG in the past[22] and, according to UNAMA analysts, HiG still maintains a number of laboratories in Nangarhar and Badakshan provinces, from which it draws funds for the insurgency.[23]

Haqqani network

The Haqqani network is led by Jalaluddin Haqqani, a noted Mujahedin during the Soviet occupation of Afghanistan. The network is active in south-eastern Afghanistan (mainly Khost and Paktya provinces) and is based in adjacent North Waziristan (Federally Administered Tribal Areas of Pakistan).[24] The Haqqani network maintains strong historical links with the Taliban[25] in Afghanistan and Pakistan, and has established several training camps in North Waziristan. The Haqqani network provides shelter and protection to Al-Qaeda and conducts joint operations with elements of the group. Information from UNAMA suggests that Al-Qaeda favors Haqqani over the Taliban as a 'sub-contractor' for complex and spectacular attacks.

As well as receiving financial support from Al-Qaeda, members of the Haqqani network derive funding from cross-border trade (such as protection payments from opiate/hashish traffickers) and have traditional lines of financing

14 "Al-Qa'ida in the Lands of the Islamic Maghreb (AQIM)", *Australian National Security*, http://www.ag.gov.au/agd/www/nationalsecurity.nsf

15 Global Witness, *For a few dollars more: How al Qaeda moved into the diamond trade*, April 2003.

16 Victor Comras "Al Qaeda Finances and Funding to Affiliated Groups", Strategic Insights, Volume IV, Issue 1 (January 2005).

17 Bill Roggio, "Cross-border strike targets one of the Taliban's 157 training camps in Pakistan's northwest", *The Long War Journal*, August 13, 2008.

18 Navy Makes Persian Gulf Drug Bust , CBS/AP, Dec. 19, 2003.

19 Plural form of the Arabic term for religious or holy warrior.

20 Johnson, T.H., *Understanding the Taliban and Insurgency in Afghanistan*, Orbis (2006).

21 Shahin Eghraghi, "Hekmatyar: The wild card in Afghanistan", *Asia Times Online*, January 2004.

22 Robert Charles, Assistant Secretary of State for International Narcotics and Law Enforcement Affairs, *Testimony Before the House Committee on Government Reform Subcommittee on Criminal Justice, Drug Policy and Human Resources*, April 1, 2004.

23 Interview UNAMA, Kabul, April 2009.

24 Shuja Nawaz, "FATA—A Most Dangerous Place", *Center for Strategic and International Studies*, January 2009.

25 Haqqani was Minister of Tribal Affairs during the Taliban regime.

in the Gulf region. The Haqqani network has more limited territory than the Taliban and its narcotics tariffs are correspondingly lower. However, its control of an area straddling the important trade route from Miram Shah (North Waziristan) through Khost, Paktya and further to Logar and on to Kabul, provides it with significant oversight of a flow of goods to and from Pakistan.

3. Organized crime

Organized crime is a notoriously difficult term to define. However, for the purpose of this research, organized crime is

> a group generally operating under some form of concealment with a structure reflective of the cultural and social stipulations of the societies that generate it; and which has the primary objective to obtain access to wealth and power through the participation in economic activities prohibited by state law.[26]

It is a form of accumulation based on corruption and the use or threat of physical violence.

Criminal groups are the main organizers and beneficiaries of the opium trade in Afghanistan. They are critical to the transportation of drugs, contributing substantially to corruption and undermining state capacity. Many of the criminal industries these groups engage in encourage or require international connections. In addition to drug trafficking, organized criminal syndicates are engaged in arms trafficking, human trafficking and the smuggling of migrants, all activities that tend to be transnational. On a local level, the recent upsurge in violent crime across Afghanistan, including burglary and kidnapping, is viewed by many as an indicator of rising organized crime activity. The emergence of these groups in Afghanistan has been facilitated by several factors, including: a recent and continuing history of conflict which has helped breed an environment conducive to crime; widespread economic hardship; and nepotism/corruption. In short, Afghanistan provides multiple opportunities and few constraints on organized crime growth and activity.

Organized criminal groups in Afghanistan are mostly indigenous, even if some members have their residences in border areas of neighboring countries. Groups appear to be ethnically-based and can generally be classified as small gangs. At the top of the pyramid are organizations with recognizable structures, leaders and established modus operandi, invariably involving transnational linkages into Afghanistan's neighbours and beyond.

The borders between licit and illicit markets in Afghanistan are exceedingly blurry and many of the players involved in both the licit and illicit streams are the same. Afghanistan

Research and Evaluation Unit research suggested that

> [m]any traders, even if they are primarily engaged in activities that could be brought into the formal economy, have a background in and a capital base derived from illicit activities. Even if traders have not themselves been involved in the illicit economy, they require good relationships with those who are because this latter group controls the supply routes and transport systems.[27]

With such a large grey area linking the black and white economies, it can be difficult to home in on the most dangerous forms of criminality.[28]

In the opiate economy, there are two primary types of actors connecting the farm-gate to international trafficking routes:

a. Village traders collect directly from farmers (they are often general shopkeepers, taking opium as credit). They also sell opium to district bazaars or directly to large traders, including inter-provincially.

b. Large traders, who commission collectors, buy directly from village traders and may also be landowners with sharecroppers/tenants that they pay rent in opium. This level of trader has direct links to or owns heroin processing facilities. Most large trafficking networks have responsibilities up to the border, after which internationally-oriented groups take over.[29] However, some large traders also have representation in the Islamic Republic of Iran and Pakistan. For example, the Balochistan capital of Quetta reportedly served as a base for some well-known Afghan traffickers,[30] while members of the large Afghan diaspora in Dubai are useful to traders, both for small-scale trafficking and large financial movements.

There are signs that Afghanistan's opiate markets have been consolidating. An assessment by UNODC in 2005 cites 2003

> as a critical period in the transformation of organized criminal activity in Afghanistan from essentially a relatively fragmented and open market to one where a limited number of operators have begun to dominate.[31]

In 2006, a joint UNODC-World Bank publication concluded that the drug industry in Afghanistan was becoming increasingly consolidated. At the top,

> around 25-30 key traffickers, the majority of them in southern Afghanistan, control major transac-

26   Alfredo Schulte-Bockholt, The politics of organized crime and the organized crime of politics; a study in criminal power, Lexington Books, 2006, p. 13.

27   Sarah Lister and al., "Trading in power: the politics of free markets in Afghanistan", AREU, March 2004.

28   As highlighted in the section on the opiate economy and financial flows.

29   UNODC, Afghanistan Opium Survey 2005, p. 91.

30   U.S. v. B. Noorzai, U.S. District Court, Southern District of New York, S1 05 Cr.19, 04-25, 2005.

31   UNODC Kabul Field Office, Organized crime in Afghanistan: a threat assessment, December 2005.

tions and transfers, working closely with sponsors in top government and political positions.

This concurs with the view of UNAMA analysts that approximately 25 networks or "key traffickers" dominate the Afghan opiate economy.[32] At a lower level, in 2007 UNODC surveyors estimated the total number of mid- and high-level traffickers in Afghanistan to be 800-900, reinforcing the conclusion of the 2006 study that there were "some 200-250 large traffickers nationwide (…) and perhaps some 500-600 mid-level traffickers in the country." AREU's view that in Afghanistan "many markets are dominated by a few very large players at the top" suggests that the structure of opiate trading reflects Afghanistan's broader economic structure.[33]

Organized crime in Afghanistan is a tremendous security threat. In a militarized society, it is unsurprising that organized crime groups thrive through the availability and deployment of weaponry and brutal tactics. UNAMA analysts have suggested that organized crime has sometimes used suicide bombings to eliminate opponents, including competitors and uncooperative government officials.[34] A Finnish delegation uncovered evidence of attacks by local drug lords "to hamper the will of ISAF and local police forces to target the drug business."[35] Some organized crime groups maintain close links with the Taliban and other insurgents, particularly where the latter have territorial control, such as in tribal border areas. Links vary from outright membership of insurgent groups to ties of tribal loyalty and alliances of convenience based on transit and protection fees.[36] For example, in October 2007, a major Afghan trafficker, Haji Baz Mohammad (a native of Nangarhar province), was sentenced to more than 15 years in prison for trafficking millions of dollars worth of heroin into the US. Baz Mohammad's indictment also alleged that he was closely aligned with the Taliban, seemingly a case of convergence between profit and Taliban ideology.

Just as debilitating, organized crime in Afghanistan is heavily intertwined with the state *and* the insurgency, participating in or buying protection from both sides of the conflict. Whether protecting the cultivation of opium or sponsoring trafficking of contraband, crime appears to be a primary survival strategy for many government officials and insurgents. This involves collusion on both sides, but the negative impact on reputation understandably affects the government more. By virtue of being 'the opposition', insurgents benefit by highlighting criminality in the government, leading to further alienation of the public from

formal political institutions. Where it undermines the effectiveness of the government, organized crime erodes popular support and thereby indirectly assists the insurgency. Directly, organized crime generates revenue for the insurgency, supplies it with weapons and partners with it in violent resistance to government encroachment.

Warlords

During the war against the Soviet Union, well-funded, young Mujahedin commanders began to assert their authority to the detriment of traditional local elders and with devastating impact on the Afghan social fabric. After the Soviet withdrawal, infighting amongst commanders ensued, leading to further fragmentation of Afghanistan into numerous fiefdoms under the control of warlords who fought each other for power and influence.

The main Mujahedin groups at the time were heavily involved in the drug trade, reportedly controlling by themselves a total production of over 800 metric tons in 1989.[37] The control of opium fields was a factor in fighting between different Mujahedin groups and confrontations over drug smuggling routes in Nangarhar and Hirat were reported.[38]

The consolidation of Taliban power – facilitated in part by popular reaction to warlord-led insecurity – curbed the influence of many commanders. They either:

1. became integrated into the Taliban movement (mostly Pashtun commanders but also non-Pashtuns who changed their allegiance)[39];

2. faced conquest and marginalization by the Taliban; or

3. joined the anti-Taliban alliance (mostly Tajik, Hazara and Uzbek commanders but also some Pashtuns in the east).[40]

Again the opiate economy played a role, as access to drug profits was a factor in warlords' decisions on alliances and allegiances.[41]

Since the overthrow of the Taliban, many ex-Mujahedin commanders, regardless of previous allegiances, have reasserted themselves, particularly those who backed the winning side in the international coalition's invasion. Some have been able to regain influence,[42] particularly in the north but also to a lesser extent in the east. In 2003, the

---

32 Interview UNAMA, Kabul, September 2008.

33 Anna Paterson, "Going to market: trade and traders in six Afghan sectors:, *AREU*, 2006, p.1.

34 Interview UNAMA, Kabul, July 2008.

35 "Report from a fact-finding mission to Afghanistan", *Finnish Directorate of Immigration*, September 2006.

36 See US indictment against Haji Baz Mohammad, www.usdoj.gov/usao/nys/pressreleases/October07/bazmohammadsentencingpr.pdf.

37 Jonathan Goodhand, "Frontiers and Wars: the Opium Economy in Afghanistan", *Journal of agrarian change*, vol.5 n.2, April 2005, p. 198.

38 Jonathan Goodhand, "Frontiers and Wars: the Opium Economy in Afghanistan", *Journal of agrarian change*, vol.5 n.2, April 2005, p. 203.

39 Chris Johnson, "Hazarajat Baseline Study - Interim Report (Part I)," U.N. Office for the Coordination of Humanitarian Affairs, March 2000, p. 5 and Appendix D.

40 It should be noted that some Pashtun commanders resisted the Taliban particularly in the east, see UNCHR, Situation in Afghanistan, 1998, http://www.unhcr.org/refworld/pdfid/467009322.pdf.

41 Jonathan Goodhand, "Frontiers and Wars: the Opium Economy in Afghanistan", *Journal of agrarian change*, vol.5 n.2, April 2005, p. 200.

42 See Human Rights Watch, "Afghanistan: Return of the Warlords," A Human Rights Watch Briefing Paper, June 2002, available at http://hrw.org/backgrounder/asia/afghanistan/warlords.pdf.

International Crisis Group starkly reported that

> [t]he central government does not exercise effective control over most of the country's territory, which is in the hands of a patchwork of regional commanders, the majority of whom are loosely affiliated with one or other Mujahedin party.

A number of warlords also enjoy a degree of influence within government structures and with international coalition countries. For example, Human Rights Watch estimated that 60 per cent of the Members of Parliament had links to warlordism in 2005. Control over territory or resources is maintained (and legitimized to some extent) when warlords enter the political process and are appointed to key government posts, such as by becoming governors, ministers, police chiefs or military officers.[43] In the south for example, several important governorships, such as in Uruzgan and Hilmand, were granted to prominent commanders. Entry into national politics has done little to curb warlords' power and many consider that they continue to be an obstacle to coherent government control of the country.[44]

The typology of warlords ranges from top-level commanders (many of whom have joined the political process) to a sprinkling of small- and mid-level figures who are more involved in and reliant on illicit economies.[45] The latter have few incentives and few prospects of joining the formal political process and thus have a more immediate stake in the opiate economy. According to high-level officials in the Afghan Security Council, many warlords still have connections to drug trafficking networks, despite significant pressure from the international community.[46] In areas under their control, warlords' profits include a share of both illicit and licit activities. For example, local commanders in the Barge-e-Matal district, Nuristan province, were reported to levy a 10 per cent tax (in kind) on livestock and crops – including opium.[47] With regard to opium, data from UNODC opium poppy surveys suggest that such practices have been ongoing since at least 2003.[48]

As the example of Barge-e-Matal suggests, the opiate trade is for warlords as 'normal' a target for taxation as any other economic activity. In another example, cross-border smuggling of timber and opium in Nangarhar has also been alleged to be controlled by warlords,[49] at a rate of US$4,000 to US$6,000 per timber truck.[50] To protect their business interests, some warlords have also been implicated in attacks on ISAF or Afghan police. This was especially visible in the north of the country in 2006, according to an assessment mission undertaken by a Finnish delegation.[51]

4. The opiate value chain and insecurity

The following sections examine how various links of the opiate value chain are associated with insecurity. A conceptual division is maintained between crime and insurgency, bearing in mind that individuals can exhibit both forms of behavior. Indeed, in the following sections the term 'warlord' is largely omitted: their behavior is insurgent-like when it aims to usurp central government control, but most often it is better defined as organized crime when they accommodate or corrupt government influence without any intention of 'regime change'.

Opium cultivation and insecurity

By most measures, insecurity in Afghanistan has increased. Insecurity has been rising across Afghanistan since 2005, primarily a result of the insurgency's growing strength and improved logistics. Afghan law enforcement and coalition forces are the most popular targets, but there have also been a substantial number of civilian casualties. In 2008, Afghanistan registered a record number of attacks, ranging from suicide bombings to coordinated assaults on military bases and maximum security prisons. Much of the violence occurred in southern Afghanistan, but insecurity has also spread outward from the Taliban's heartland to cover a majority of Afghan provinces.

Insurgency

Areas of opium poppy cultivation and insecurity correlate geographically. In 2008, 98 per cent of opium poppy cultivation took place in southern and western Afghanistan. According to UNDSS, these regions are also the least secure. Even in relatively secure provinces, the areas controlled or heavily influenced by AGEs generally cultivate opium, such as Surobi district in Kabul province.

As it is illegal to cultivate opium, it is hardly surprising that cultivation is more likely to occur in places that the government cannot influence. This creates a symbiosis between insurgent and drug trade activity: drug trading needs to prevent or respond to government attempts to enforce the law; while insurgency is dedicated to minimizing and

---

43 Conrad Schetter et al., "Beyond Warlordism. The Local Security Architecture in Afghanistan", *IPG* 2/2007.

44 Roohullah Rahimi, "Afghanistan: Exploring the Dynamics of Sociopolitical Strife and the Persistence of the Insurgency", *Pearson peacekeeping centre*, occasional paper 2, 2008, p.20.

45 Jonathan Goodhand et al., "Bargain for peace? Aid, conditionalities and reconstruction in Afghanistan", *Netherlands institute of international relations*, August 2006, p.40.

46 Interview, November 2008, Kabul.

47 Bashir Babak et al., "When Cops Become Robbers", *Institute for War and Peace Reporting*, April 2005. Figures as high as 30 per cent-40 per cent of gross farmgate revenue have also been reported – see Jonathan Goodhand, "Frontiers and Wars: the Opium Economy in Afghanistan", *Journal of agrarian change*, vol.5 n.2, April 2005, p. 203; see also UNODC Afghanistan Opium Survey 2004, p.72.

48 UNODC, *Afghanistan Opium Survey 2004*, p.72.

49 Sarah Lister et al., "Understanding markets in Afghanistan: A case study of the market in construction materials", *AREU*, June 2004.

50 UNODC Kabul Field Office, *Organized crime in Afghanistan: a threat assessment*, December 2005.

51 "Report from a fact-finding mission to Afghanistan", *Finnish Directorate of Immigration*, September 2006.

Map 1: Security and opium poppy cultivation, 2009

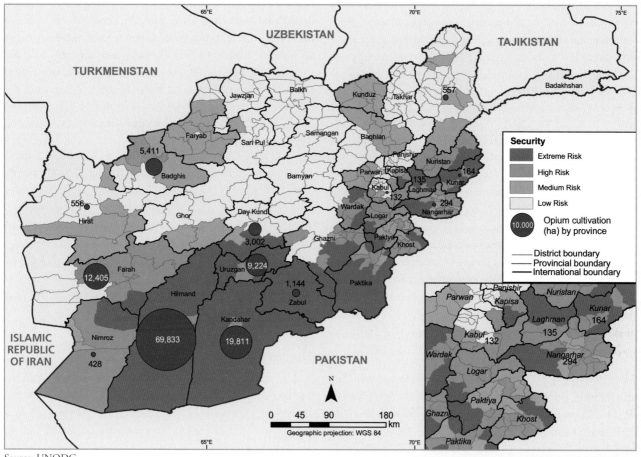

Source: UNODC.

destroying government influence. Cultivation is a particularly difficult part of the opiate trade to conceal, and is a primary livelihood for a large number of people, so the cost-benefit framework favors violent resistance more than, for example, the processing stage.

Primary sources of funding for insurgent activities are:

- Private foreign donations, including diversion and fraud by legitimate charities.

- Taxes levied on the population in areas under their control or influence.

- 'Pure' criminality – trafficking in drugs, arms and humans, among others; kidnappings for ransom and extortion.

In practice, locally-levied taxes and extortion blur together. Some individuals in insurgent-controlled areas give willingly to the cause; others may do so against their will.

Forms of taxation

Two forms of traditional taxation are of particular interest: *Ushr*, a 10 per cent tax on agricultural production; and *Zakat*, a 2.5 per cent wealth tax applied to traders.[52]

According to the 2007 Afghanistan opium survey, almost all opium farmers in southern and western Afghanistan pay the 10 per cent *Ushr*. Depending on the area, this goes to a mixture of mullahs and Taliban,[53] but is less common in northern, north-eastern and central Afghanistan.[54] *Ushr* has an established social and economic pedigree, with the Taliban applying the tax systematically when it ruled Afghanistan between 1996 and 2001. UNODC sources also reported that Taliban commanders usually receive the levy in kind, whereas a cash tax is usually given for licit crops.[55]

The total amount of opium poppy production between 2002 and 2008 was 37,300 tons, with a farm-gate market value of US$ 6.4 billion. Of this amount, approximately US$ 5 billions was shared by southern (US$ 3.4 billion), eastern (US$ 1 billion) and western (US$ 0.5 billion) farmers. The remainder, US$ 1.4 billion, went to farmers in the northern and central regions.

---

52 Adam Bennet, "Reconstructing Afghanistan", *International Monetary Fund* (IMF), 2005.

53 It should be noted that whoever is in a position to exert dominance or authority in any given cultivation area will tax the crop -at varying rates- and this includes some elements within the local Afghan government.

54 The remainder was paid to 'other' – apparently government officials or warlords with varying links to insurgents and who may also be subject to extortion by insurgents.

55 UNODC did not collect systematic information on tax applied to cannabis.

Given that the Taliban have not held sway in the northern and central regions, it is assumed that farmers in these areas have not paid this tax to Taliban insurgents since 2002 (with the possible recent exception of Badghis and Faryab provinces). In addition, until 2005, the Taliban was not very active in Afghanistan and it is assumed that it was not able to levy taxes. To calculate the value of *Ushr* to the insurgency, UNODC combined province-level price data with opium production volumes since 2005.

Between 2005 and 2008, the total estimated farm-gate value of opium produced in southern and western Afghanistan is US$ 2 billion. It is therefore tentatively estimated that approximately US$ 200 million (10 per cent of US$ 2 billion) was paid as *ushr* by farmers. Calculations based on UNODC field surveys suggest that Taliban insurgents receive 30-50 per cent of total *Ushr* levies. This range is also chosen to account for leakage resulting from the tax changing hands, as well as the fact that Taliban has not had total control in the provinces selected. At trader prices, this yields an estimate that Taliban insurgents collected around US$ 60–100 million in farm-gate taxation between 2005 and 2008.

In areas where groups other than the Taliban prevail, they also benefit from *Ushr*. For the amorphous spectrum of AGEs as a whole, therefore, the total funding from *Ushr* increases. However, it is more difficult to determine how much of this money is used for insurgent activity and how much is purely criminal income.

Furthermore, insurgents regularly apply *Ushr* to all crops, not solely opium. Their total tax revenue is therefore greater than the numbers calculated for opium cultivation alone. In principle, reductions in opium cultivation would be expected to undermine insurgent financing only to the extent that the total value of farm production in insurgent-controlled areas drops. However, sustained reductions in opium cultivation would also be expected to feed through into reductions in opiate processing and trafficking; higher levels of the value chain from which insurgents also benefit.

Opiate trafficking and insecurity

The relationship between opium cultivation and insurgency is relatively easy to analyse: it is essentially a matter of insurgents maximizing the economic advantages derived from territorial control, while criminals benefit from insurgents' interference with law enforcement. However, roles and relationships blur further at the trafficking level of the opiate value chain.

One simple interaction is *Zakat*, a 2.5 per cent 'wealth tax'. *Zakat* appears to be applied quite systematically, particularly on low-level traders. As with farmers, it can be presumed that *Zakat* is more or less voluntary, depending on the trader's disposition. Similar to cultivation, the ability to apply *Zakat* gives insurgents an incentive to host and protect trading networks.

A second simple interaction, again based on territorial control, is a fee for passage. Traffickers moving cargo through insurgent-controlled areas pass checkpoints that charge them. Functionally, this is no different from bribes extorted by police officers in areas of government control. It is not clear how systematically insurgents apply such fees. There appears to be a mixture of value-based taxation and flat rates, but in the southern region in 2008 UNODC received multiple reports that opiate consignments were levied at 200 Afs. ($4) per kilogram. This seems analogous to corruption among officers: fees may be greater for high-value/risk shipments, but often there are standard payments for movement. In Taliban areas, such payments usually secure a stamp to allow free passage, although this obviously does not protect traffickers from extortion by any government officials, warlord militias or bandits they may encounter. Moreover, the tax schedule of the Taliban is itself augmented by individual insurgent units on an ad hoc basis, with unsystematic taxes/extortion such as *Baspana*, a so-called "assistance" tax levied in the name of war imperatives.

Roles become more complicated when insurgents act as protection for drug shipments. Some Taliban groups or leaders are involved in joint operations with drug traffickers, transferring opium or heroin to major dealers on the Afghanistan/Pakistan border and sharing the profit.[56] At a lesser level, in 2006, UNODC research suggested that in the southern region

> an alliance has formed between drug traffickers and the Taliban where the drug traffickers provide money, vehicles and subsistence (US$ 4,000 + a Toyota vehicle + subsistence for a 10 man group) to transfer around 2 tons of opium. The amount asked by the Taliban was almost equal to the 2.5-5 per cent of the total value of the opium being trafficked. In return the Taliban protect them and do not interfere with their activities.

When the Taliban act as private bodyguards in this way, it is more accurately considered criminality rather than insurgency.

It appears to be common practice for insurgents to levy taxes not in cash but in kind, which raises the question of how they realize the value of the opium collected. Barter economies are widespread and deeply entrenched in Afghanistan, particularly in rural areas and including the use of opium as value storage and reference currency. Insurgents can therefore exchange taxes collected as opium for subsistence needs. For higher-value purchases, large opiate traders provide cash.

In the latter transactions, insurgents are active participants in the opiate value chain, running from farmer to large trader – who then prepares shipments for export. From one

---

56 Interview with Afghanistan Intelligence unit, Kabul, 2009.

Table 1:   Opium production (2002-2009) and farm-gate income (2003*-2009)

Province	Total opium production for the period (2002-2009) (tons)	Per cent in total	Total farm-gate income (billion of US$) for the period (2003-2009)	Per cent in total
Hilmand	19,620	44 per cent	2,262	38 per cent
Nangarhar	4,035	9 per cent	874	15 per cent
Kandahar	4,007	9 per cent	475	8 per cent
Badakshan	2,581	6 per cent	505	9 per cent
Uruzgan	2,520	6 per cent	356	6 per cent
Farah	2,297	5 per cent	263	4 per cent
Other	9,141	21 per cent	1,165	20 per cent
Total	**44,200**	**100 per cent**	**5,865**	**100 per cent**

* No income data available for 2002.
Source: Afghanistan opium poppy surveys, UNODC.

Table 2:   Distribution of opium farm-gate income by region, 2002-2008

Regions	Per cent in total
Central	3%
Eastern	17%
North-eastern	9%
Northern	9%
Southern	54%
Western	8%
Total	100%

perspective, they continue to act as parasites rather than value-adders. From a different perspective, they provide the nebulous but crucial 'public good' of a space without government interference, in which other opiate traders and traffickers can function more profitably.

In another area of the opiate value-adding chain, some Taliban networks may be involved at the level of precursor procurement. According to South Korean law enforcement, a recent seizure of ten tons of acetic anhydride in South Korea appears to be linked to the Taliban network. A subsequent investigation by Pakistani agencies found that over 50 tons of the substance – linked to the same network - had already been shipped to Afghanistan's southern region disguised as disinfectant (hydrogen peroxide) from April 2007 to March 2008.[57] These recent findings support the assertion that the Taliban network is more involved in drug trafficking than previously thought.

The murkiest arrangements by which insurgents derive funding from trafficking is the revenue provided by large networks. Previous examples of large traders like Haji Juma Khan suggest that such traders give sizeable but ad hoc

donations to the Taliban. The apparently growing fusion between big drug networks and Taliban protection in Taliban-controlled areas indicate that these arrangements are likely to prevail throughout the network. In other words, whether individually or collectively, nodes of such networks are not subject to systematic tax schedules, but do, on aggregate, donate significant funds to the Taliban.

Finally, a different form of synergy between terrorism and the drug trade is evident in the dual use of trafficking networks for militants as well as opiates. Law enforcement sources have contended that in the province of Paktika (south-eastern region linked to Wana in Waziristan, Pakistan) convoys are being used to smuggle drugs out and weapons (and fighters) in.[58] Information on drug routes may therefore have counter-insurgency implications on the Pakistan-Afghanistan border.

To summarize, insurgency overlaps mostly with the minor, middle and macro levels of opiate trafficking, with the major-trader level left mostly to profit-seekers. Macro-level involvement is the 'public good' of freedom from law enforcement. Middle- and minor-level involvement is the transfer of significant quantities of opium from farmers to traders and processors. This does not appear to involve insurgents taking the lead in transferring shipments over long distances or substantial cross-border opiate smuggling. At the major level, insurgents derive benefit from large but generally ad hoc donations from big networks. Lastly, when moonlighting as protection for major trafficking ventures, they are engaged in criminality rather than insurgency.

Opiate processing and insecurity

As with cultivation, there is geographical correlation between areas of insecurity and the location of laboratories. Processing facilities comprise the most geographically con-

---

57   CARICC information bulletin 29, August, 2008.

58   Interview CNPA Nangarhar, October 2008.

Lab interdiction in Afghanistan

Fig. 1: **Opium poppy cultivation in Musa Qala district of Hilmand province (2005-2008)**

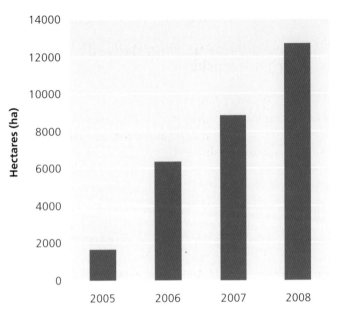

Source: UNODC Afghanistan opium poppy surveys, 2005-2008.

fined aspect of the opiate trade and their effects on security are narrower. While it is difficult to separate them conceptually from trafficking of precursors (in) and heroin (out), practically speaking, the facilities themselves create mostly localized insecurity. UNODC has no evidence that insurgents themselves manage processing facilities. Echoing the discussion of trafficking above, processing management would be a distraction from insurgency and would best be considered crime.

When in power, it appears that the Taliban would in fact levy taxes on laboratories "charging between $50 and 70$ a kilo depending on whether the final product was morphine base or crystal heroin".[59] Recently, an increasing number of reports, particularly from ISAF and UNAMA, have indicated that insurgent groups provide protection for processing facilities. This may be an opportunistic deployment of manpower by commanders and/or a calculated decision to protect a source of tax revenue. It seems that guards are paid in kind, that is, a cut of the processing output. Initially, this would seem quite inefficient, since each guard must then trade the heroin elsewhere. However, lab owners perceive some benefit in avoiding cash movements or payments and guards are able to take advantage of the widespread use of opiates as barter.

The example of Musa Qala

Nowhere is the entanglement of insurgency and crime more evident than in Hilmand. To take the example of Musa Qala district, starting with repeated attacks in May 2006, the Taliban had nearly complete control for most of 2007 and the district became a hub for insurgent activity

across southern Afghanistan. The Taliban established religious courts and presided over a flourishing opium industry, reaping protection money from traffickers and tax revenue from the harvest. At the very least, the Taliban were tolerant of the opium trade, with a new narcotics bazaar constructed and operating openly.[60]

During the rise in insecurity and subsequent Taliban takeover of the district, cultivation figures for Musa Qala went from 1,664 hectares in 2005 to 6,371 and 8,854 in 2006 and 2007, respectively. At 12,687 hectares, the 2008 areas was double that of 2006.[61] Without taking into account other taxes, if insurgents were able to levy Ushr systematically in 2007, they may have earned some US$ 4.3 million.

Following the Taliban takeover, many Afghan traffickers previously living in Quetta, Pakistan and western Iran came to the district and lived in rented houses. There was competition and collusion in increasing control of local markets, including closer relationships with heroin laboratories, at least five of which were functioning.

In December 2007, the Afghan National Army alone reportedly seized 12 tons of opium in Musa Qala.[62] Some interdiction operations also encountered Taliban protecting labs in August 2007.[63] Afghan Special Forces operating in Hilmand also reported that findings in opiate storage/processing compounds suggested a high level of insurgent/trafficker collusion; seizures contained both opiates and

59   Peters Gretchen, *Seeds of Terror: How Heroin Is Bankrolling the Taliban and al Qaeda*, Thomas Dunne Books, 2009, p. 82.

60   Jane's Terrorism and Security Monitor, "The battle for Musa Qala", April 2008.

61   UNODC, *Afghanistan opium survey 2008*.

62   Afghanistan National Development Strategy (ANDS), *Report to the Joint Coordination and Monitoring Board* (JCMB), February 2008.

63   "Afghan, Coalition Forces Destroy Taliban Heroin Lab", *American Forces Press Service*, August 27, 2007.

"sophisticated insurgent materials such as IED (Improvised Explosive Device) manuals one would expect to be circulated to specialist cells rather than Tier Two fighters."[64]

5. Insurgency funding derived from trafficking

Between 2003 and 2008, the total export value of Afghan opiates is estimated at around US$ 18 billion (there is no data for 2002). Between 2002 and 2004, the Taliban had comparatively negligible influence across most of Afghanistan (with the exception of the southern and south-western border areas) but this drastically changed after 2005. As of 2005, Taliban insurgents began to assert control over most of western (Farah and Nimroz provinces – Iran/Afghanistan border) and southern Afghanistan (Hilmand, Kandahar, Uruzgan and Zabul provinces). Between 2005 and 2008, the total export value of Afghan opium is estimated at US$ 13.2 billion. Around 80 per cent of the opiates are trafficked via Afghanistan's borders with Pakistan and the Islamic Republic of Iran, which means that the total export value of opiates trafficked through Taliban-controlled border areas is approximately US$ 10.5 billion.

Similar to the Ushr tax, there are a number of caveats to consider when attempting to quantify Zakat and transit taxes tax. First, the percentage of taxation from drug traffickers varies substantially[65] and taxes are rarely collected uniformly in any given area or region.[66] Second, it is often sporadic rather than systematic. Finally, it is likely that drug traffickers are bribing other elements on the way to the Afghan borders (law enforcement and local commanders, among others).

Using a range that takes into account the uncertainty of the measurement and information collected, it is assumed that insurgents derive 2.5-5 per cent of the total export value (US$ 10.5 billion) as taxation from drug traders and traffickers. This means that between US$ 250-550 million was also expected to be paid in cash -or in kind- (or the equivalent in firearms, vehicles etc.) by drug traffickers to the Taliban in the 2005-2008 period.

In total, including the Ushr from opium farmers (US$ 60–100 million in farm-gate taxation between 2005 and 2008), the Taliban is likely to have pocketed around US$ 350-650 million from the opiate trade between 2005 and 2008 through direct taxation of farmers and traffickers. Per year, this brought Taliban insurgents some US$ 125 million/year from opium/heroin trafficking in Afghanistan. It is important to note that this excludes wages and taxes related

to precursor importation[67] and processing facilities.[68]

Similar to *Ushr*, the Taliban are not only taxing drug convoys but any vehicle which happens to cross one of the checkpoints they have erected along the highways they control.[69] After 2005, some Taliban groups also became directly involved in trafficking of opiates to the Afghanistan/Pakistan border together with drug traffickers. In such cases, Taliban and drug traffickers apparently shared the profit.[70] The net profit of the drug traffickers from opium/heroin trafficking is estimated at US$ 4 billion (besides bribery or taxation etc.), which would also significantly increase Taliban profits over the above estimation.

Afghan drug traffickers hand over the drugs to Baluchi drug traffickers at Afghanistan's borders (Hilmand-Kandahar-Nimroz-Farah provinces) with Pakistan and the Islamic Republic of Iran. From there, Baluch traffickers take over. In Eastern Afghanistan, drugs are trafficked via (Nangarhar-Kunar) into Pakistan's Federally Administered Tribal Areas (FATA). As explained in the next chapter, FATA is mainly controlled by insurgent groups like the Pakistani Taliban and other Al-Qaeda linked groups. Negligible amounts of opium or heroin have been seized in FATA since 2002. At the same time, evidence indicates that Taliban elements are involved in drug trafficking, at least by providing security to the drug traffickers. The total value of the Afghan opium/heroin market in Pakistan is estimated at US$4 billion for the period 2005-2008. There is, however, insufficient evidence on the amount of profits these are generating in Pakistan to draw a conclusion.

6. Taliban financial requirements

According to some sources, there are around 5,000-10,000 armed Taliban fighters[71] in Afghanistan, and around 4,000 Taliban were reportedly killed in 2007.[72] Other estimates put the number of Afghan Taliban at around 30,000, including 15,000 Pakistanis.[73] Regardless of the exact number, any insurgency must be able to replenish and provide for its fighters. Reports from southern districts indicate that the Taliban reportedly pay around US$200-500 per month to young locals, so called "tier-2 fighters."[74] This

---

64 Correspondence with Jane's Intelligence analyst, October 18 2008.

65 CNPA Kandahar reported that in some areas, the Taliban levy a 20 per cent tax on opium (and a 10 per cent tax on wheat); Interview CNPA Kandahar, September 2008.

66 As a general rule, taxes are collected more systematically in southern provinces and less systematically in the provinces bordering Iran in the west.

67 Some revenue is likely drawn from transit tariffs on precursor movements. The funding transfers from large networks to insurgents may also include wealth derived from precursor trafficking profits. However, these are estimated to be very small in Afghanistan relative to drug production and trafficking.

68 Small, intermittent and independent labs are unlikely to be subject to systematic taxation. Large, fixed facilities – the overwhelming majority of which are in southern Afghanistan – are generally thought to be controlled by the big networks that are here assessed to be operating under special arrangements with the Taliban.

69 Seth G. Jones, "The state of the Afghan insurgency", *RAND*, December 2007.

70 Interview with the Afghan Intelligence Unit, Kabul, March 2009.

71 Seth G. Jones, "Counterinsurgency in Afghanistan", *RAND counterinsurgency study volume 4*, http://www.rand.org/pubs/monographs/2008/RAND_MG595.pdf.

72 James Dunnigan "The Taliban Turn Too Tough", *Strategypage*, April 4, 2008.

73 Presentation US Army Training and Doctrine Command (TRADOC) G-2, 2009.

74 H. Mili and J. Townsend "Afghanistan's Drug Trade and How it Funds Tali-

amount is reportedly higher for tier-1 fighters.[75] Across the border in Pakistan, a Taliban recruit reportedly earns PKR 15,000 (approximately US$200) per month.[76]

There has been speculation that Taliban fighters are paid on a regular basis. Others thought the payments to be less regular, and more in line with the immediate needs of a fighter (such as marriage costs and leave pay).[77] Taliban fighters are mostly constituted of small groups (not small armies) designed for hit-and-run attacks and led by an *Amir* (commander) enjoying a large degree of financial and operational autonomy. Financial incentives for some fighters may therefore consist of payment for escorting a convoy, a portion of the booty from the commander, or a share of the *Ushr / Zakat* collected in areas under the group's control (at the commander's discretion). Depending on the relative poverty of an area, some warlords can even employ recruits for as little as a meal a day.[78] In some areas where they enjoy support and can use tribal connections, the Taliban do not pay salaries and can recruit from a pool of willing volunteers.

On top of personnel costs, insurgents need weapons. Set against the potential income from parasitizing the drug trade - let alone other funding sources - these costs are modest. In Kabul, reliable reports indicate that a suicide bomber's family may receive between 600,000-1,000,000 Afghanis (US$ 12,000-20,000) for an attack.[79] Other sources contend that, on average, suicide bombers are paid a more modest $3,000-4,000.[80] With opiate income alone, insurgents can purchase thousands of weapons, fund hundreds of suicide attacks and retain thousands of fighters.

It is estimated that the Taliban need between $800 million and $1 billion per year to finance their operations.[81] Based on the calculations above, 10-15 per cent of their funding could be drawn from the Afghan opiate trade – ignoring any revenue from trafficking through Pakistan that may find its way into Taliban coffers. This is somewhat less than the minimum percentage suggested by some ISAF officials,[82] which ranged from 20-40 per cent of the Afghan Taliban's total income.

7. The opiate economy and the arms trade

There are a handful of warlords that play significant roles in the Afghan arms trade, and their links to the opiate economy warrant attention. Part of their strength lies in possessing experienced private militias and having access to stockpiled weapons from previous conflicts, in particular the remaining weapons depots in northern Afghanistan.

There is a difference in quality between easily-available weapons manufactured in Pakistan and the weapons in northern stockpiles or trafficked from Central Asia. The Tajik-Afghan border regions appear to be important in facilitating the importation of higher quality machine guns and small arms in particular.[83] Significantly, opium is often the surrogate currency. This 'drugs for arms' trade functions in much the same way as it did during the anti-Soviet war, in which "opium was one of the only commodities which could generate enough income for large scale arms purchases."[84]

For example, in May 2005 a joint operation between Afghan law enforcement and the Tajik Drug Control Agency arrested two former Taliban commanders in Kunduz Province. They had been operating a "sizeable" arms and narcotics trafficking network extending into Tajikistan.[85] Across the border, traffickers include individuals who rose to positions of power and wealth in very similar conditions as field commanders during Tajikistan's civil war (1994-1996).More recent information indicates that these routes in Kunduz are still operational, a few miles from the Afghan border and the main crossing at Sher Khan Bandar. From the north, weapons are currently funneled through central routes, from where they are usually transported by truck to the south and east to replenish insurgent stocks. According to reports, in the first stage one kilogram of heroin is exchanged for 15 (new) AK 47s.[86] In the northern region, one AK-47 reportedly fetches 4 kilograms of opium.[87] As they are traded/distributed throughout Afghanistan, weapons and opium are inter-convertible currencies, including their trade for licit goods.

Expensive equipment of Soviet/Russian origin (for example, night vision gear) is also exchanged. According to DIAG (Disarmament of Illegal Armed Groups) analysts interviewed by UNODC, shipments are currently occurring every second day, with an estimate of around 150–200 weapons being shipped into Afghanistan via this route per

ban Operations", *The Jamestown foundation*, May 2007,

75 NATO refers to farmers who may take up arms with the guerrillas as "tier 2 Taliban" to distinguish them from committed, full-time "tier 1" fighters.

76 Shuja Nawaz, "FATA—A Most Dangerous Place", *Center for Strategic and International Studies*, January 2009.

77 Interview with head of counter-terrorism department, Afghanistan Ministry of Interior, November 16 2008.

78 Jonathan Goodhand, "Frontiers and wars: the opium economy in Afghanistan", *Journal of agrarian change*, vol.5 n.2, April 2005, p. 203.

79 Interview CNPA, November 2008, Hirat province, Afghanistan.

80 Interview UNAMA, November 2008.

81 Interview with UNDSS analyst, Kabul, 2009.

82 International Development Committee quoting ISAF sources; see Reconstructing Afghanistan, House of Commons International Development Committee, Fourth Report of Session 2007–08, Volume 1, p. 47.

83 Kyrgyzstan and Kazakhstan inherited small-arms factories from the Soviet Union and conflict in Tajikistan and Afghanistan through the 1990s encouraged imports from all over the world.

84 UNODC, *The opium economy in Afghanistan: An international problem*, 2003, p.88.

85 "RFE/RL Central Asia Report", 29 August 2003.

86 Sayed Yaqub Ibrahimi, "Turning Afghan Heroin Into Kalashnikovs", *Institute for War and Peace Reporting*, ARR No. 295, 30-Jun-08.

87 Information provided by DIAG analysts, July 2008.

shipment. This is supported by research by the Institute for War and Peace that identified a bazaar on the Panj river (the border with Tajikistan), in which "smugglers bring in gemstones and weapons to exchange for high-quality Afghan heroin."[88]

Highlights of the opiate trade and insurgency

At varying levels, the key actors involved in the drug trade have an interest in maintaining an "efficient" level of insecurity.

1. The Taliban-led insurgency is content to reap dividends from the drug economy to finance war expenditures. Their ability to provide protection to farmers and traffickers (preventing interdiction and eradication efforts) delegitimizes the national government and links them with these people's livelihoods.

2. Some warlords use dividends from the drug trade to maintain their power bases and also participate in the opiate trade when offloading weapon stocks to insurgents. Warlords linked to the opium trade may also be orchestrating attacks on international forces or members of the national army and police if they feel their illicit livelihood is threatened.[89] On the whole, however, these are strictly speaking not members of the insurgency.

3. Organized crime groups exploit insecurity and form alliances with insurgents and government officials in order to secure their continued access to regional markets. There are no obvious signs of hostility between the trafficking groups and the Taliban. Coexistence and even cooperation seem to be the norm. In districts of Hilmand where the Taliban achieved sustained control, they did not intervene in the drug trade and reportedly worked with traffickers against the authorities. Criminal groups benefit from insurgent-led insecurity, which ensures the absence of law enforcement in regions like Hilmand and Kandahar. Here also, organized crime elements do not necessarily fit the definition of AGEs/insurgents, largely because of interpenetration with government structures.

This triangular relationship is based on a temporary convergence of interests, chief among them being an interest in a weakened central government unable to enforce its laws and control its borders. The trading of drugs for arms illustrates that these links are direct and mutually reinforcing but also temporal - an alliance of convenience dependent on the continuity of conflict.

The substantial increase in insurgent visibility and mobilization since 2005 coincides spatially and temporally with the concentration of opium production in the south. The continued concentrations of poppies and processing in the south are good illustrations of links between insurgents and the drug trade. However, as opium poppy cultivation concentrates, insecurity increasingly does not, spreading outward to areas that were previously stable, such as parts of north and north-west Afghanistan.

Buttressed by Taliban reinforcements from Pakistan's border areas, which continue to serve as a launching ground as they did during conflict with the then Union of Soviet Socialist Republics (USSR),[90] the Taliban-led insurgency has garnered strength incrementally and is proving a resilient force against the coalition and central government in Kabul. With the shift of violence and reinforcements from Iraq to Afghanistan, this situation is likely to continue in the short to medium term. Based on previous phases of conflict, these trends are likely to enhance the opium economy at all levels of the value chain.

With more than 98 per cent of the country's opium poppies being grown in its most insecure Taliban-influenced areas and an income stream potentially generating US$ 350-650 million (average US$ 125 million/year) since 2005, poppy-dollars may provide the means to foment instability and insecurity in both Afghanistan and Pakistan for years to come. AGE groups thus have a stake in maintaining and expanding the trafficking of narcotics. Furthermore, Afghanistan has started cultivating cannabis on a massive scale and is now a major exporter of the drug. According to the 2007 Afghanistan opium survey, "cannabis cultivation is (…) becoming as lucrative as opium poppy." If so, it will diversify the sources of drug-based finance and further complicate the picture of trafficking flows.[91]

Revenue from drug-related activity must be seen in the context of a broad-based taxation system that covers a wide range of economic activity.[92] Just as importantly, AGEs engage in other forms of crime that can at least match drug-related revenue. For example, one "unplanned" kidnapping of South Korean missionaries in 2007 reportedly netted the Taliban $20 million.[93] Beyond this immediate local funding source, the Taliban are continuing to receive significant funding from private donors all over the world. In the opinion of many experts, this funding contribution dwarfs the proceeds of the opium economy or criminal activity in general.[94] Based on the numbers discussed above, the Taliban must find at least 85 per cent of its funding from non-opium sources. More likely, the total amount of money raised from tax schedules and criminal activity is higher than that required for operations, that is, a portion goes to

88 Sayed Yaqub Ibrahimi, op cit.

89 Peter Mardsen et al., "An Assessment of the Security of Asian Development Bank Projects in Afghanistan", Asian Development Bank, March 2007.

90 Roohullah Rahimi, "Afghanistan: Exploring the Dynamics of Sociopolitical Strife and the Persistence of the Insurgency", Pearson peacekeeping centre, occasional paper 2, 2008.

91 UNODC is conducting its first dedicated cannabis survey in 2009.

92 For example, UNODC surveyors report that in 2009 the Taliban in the southern region are levying 500 Pakistani Rupees from every household connected to the electricity grid.

93 "Taliban say S.Korea paid over $20 mln ransom", Reuters, September 1, 2007.

94 Interview UNAMA analyst, Kabul 2009.

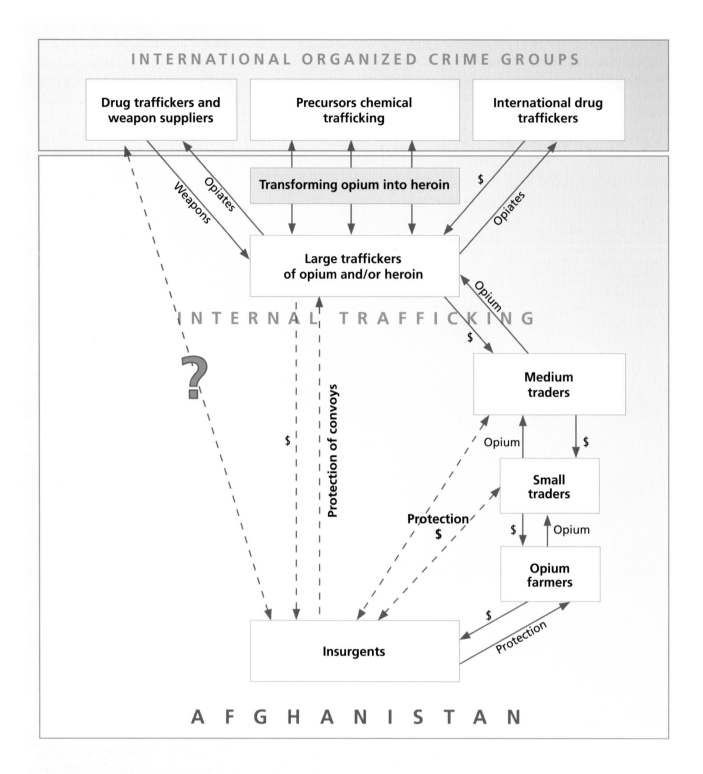

insurgents' personal enjoyment, highlighting again the overlap between criminal and insurgent motivations.

Nevertheless, it is clear from AGEs' approach to the opium economy – including encouragement and protection – that a contraction would have a deleterious impact on the Taliban-led insurgency by disrupting established fundraising methods and blunting a strategic wedge between the population and the Government. Reductions in cultivation, processing and trafficking would erode the financial base of the insurgency, although this would mostly affect the funding that can be derived locally, with minimal impact on the insurgency's strategic threat. Opium is one of many factors influencing the war in Afghanistan, which equally depends on vested regional interests, cross-border sanctuaries, economic disparities, extremist ideologies and long-standing unresolved border claims.

B. FACILITATING CROSS-BORDER TRAFFICKING: TRIBAL LINKS, INSECURITY AND CORRUPTION

Afghanistan and its neighbors are overlaid by a tangled web of intersecting tribal and ethnic allegiances. As the previous section explained, the opium economy is associated with a range of security threats. In all of these, ethnic/tribal links and frictions are important contextual factors.

In examining the importance of ethnic and tribal associations to the opiate trade, a risk exists of rarefying group dynamics and obscuring individual motivations. The discussion below tends to treat tribes as homogenous units. Therefore, it comes with a caveat that these are generalizations rather than strictly causative arguments. Naturally, individuals will sometimes act against their tribe's customs, such as by defying a ban on opiate processing or by trading with members of a rival group.[95] In addition, Afghanistan's recent history has done much to weaken tribal identity and cohesion.

Nevertheless, the strength of tribal identity and accompanying customs of interaction in Afghanistan are such that useful insights can be made by examining ethnicities and tribes. Moreover, some otherwise confusing trends become clear once tribal relations are taken into account. For example, in southern Afghanistan:

> The security and governance structure of each southern town and province largely breaks down along tribal lines, with each tribe affiliated with a commander who usually occupies some official position such as governor, police chief, intelligence chief, or army chief that legitimates his retention of a militia. Towns and provinces are divided, with varying degrees of clarity, among spheres of control by each figure.[96]

Pashtuns are the majority ethnic group in Afghanistan, with approximately 42 per cent of the population (12 million), followed by Tajiks (27 per cent), Hazaras (9 per cent), Uzbeks (9 per cent), Aimak (4 per cent), Turkmen (3 per cent), Baluch (2 per cent) and others (4 per cent).[97] Tribal identity is vitally important for many Afghans, ahead of ideology and for some, nation. Tribal genealogy continues to structure social rank, land use and patterns of inheritance in many areas.[98] In rural areas, tribal identities are the most important points of reference. When this is transferred into formal government positions, it is unsurprising that officials are generally appointed according to tribal population and balances of power.

According to some analyses, most Afghans perceive political parties as vehicles that represent particular ethnic groups, clans or tribes. This could provide a rationale for Afghanistan's unusual choice of electoral system, with its emphasis on individual candidates rather than parties.[99] Following the parliamentary elections in September 2005, a report by AREU provided the figures below for the breakdown of ethnic/religious groups in the newly elected *Wolesi Jirga*.[100]

Groups	WJ seats	Per cent
Pashtun	118	47.4 per cent
Tajik and Aimak	53	21.3 per cent
Hazara	30	12.0 per cent
Uzbek	20	8.0 per cent
Non-Hazara Shi'a	11	4.4 per cent
Turkmen	5	2.0 per cent
Arab	5	2.0 per cent
Ismaili	3	1.2 per cent
Pashai	2	0.8 per cent
Baluch	1	0.4 per cent
Nuristani	1	0.4 per cent

The importance of tribal delineations was also demonstrated in Government sensitivities around the 2004-05 population "approximation" – otherwise known as a sampling census.

Pashtuns

Pashtuns have historically been the strongest ethnic group in Afghanistan and 11 out of 12 rulers prior to 1979 were Pashtun.[101] Pashtuns in Afghanistan can be divided into two large tribal confederations, the Durrani and the Ghilzai (or Ghalji), which between them include approximately 75 per cent of Pashtuns. The other three tribal groupings are the Karlanri (20 per cent of Pashtuns) and the smaller confederations of the Sarbani and Ghurghusht. The Karlanri tribes comprise the majority of the population in the Federally Administered Tribal Areas (FATA) and North Western Frontier Province (NWFP) of Pakistan.

There are significant pockets of Pashtuns throughout Afghanistan. However, Durrani tribes generally dominate in the south-west, from Farah to Kandahar. The Ghilzai primarily reside in the mountainous south-east, from Kandahar to Kabul – Uruzgan, Zabul, Day Kundi and Paktya provinces, and in the Katawaz region of Paktika province. The Ghilzai also have communities in the centre and north of the country (primarily Badghis and Faryab) as a result of resettlement, both forced and encouraged, under Durrani rule in the early twentieth century.[102]

95 For example, Mullah Abdul Salam, a Pirzai (Alizai tribe) defected from the Taliban in Musa Qala and is now its governor; see Jane's Terrorism and Security Monitor, "The battle for Musa Qala", April 2008.

96 International Crisis Group, "Afghanistan: the problem of Pashtun alienation", *ICG Asia Report N°625*, August 2003, p.18.

97 www.cia.gov/library/publications/the-world-factbook/geos/af.html.

98 Jolanta Sierakowska-Dyndo, "Tribalism and Afghan political traditions", Asia & Pacific Studies Nr. 1, January 2003.

99 AREU, "The A to Z Guide to Afghanistan Assistance", 2009.

100 http://www.unhcr.org/refworld/pdfid/447aa6bd4.pdf.

101 Gregory Gajewski et al., "How War, a Tribal Social Structure, and Donor Efforts Shape Institutional Change in Afghanistan: A Case Study of the Roads Sector", *The Louis Berger Group*, September 2007.

102 Roohullah Rahimi, "Afghanistan: Exploring the Dynamics of Sociopolitical

Fig. 2: Pashtun tribal structure

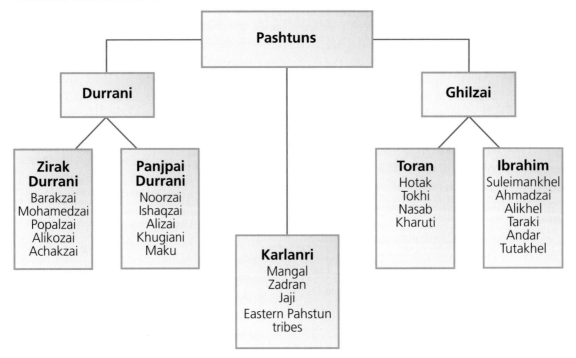

Kandahar may be viewed as the geographical nexus of both the Durrani and Ghilzai confederations, but southern Afghanistan remains the Durranis' traditional heartland, centered on the city of Kandahar, which is where the Durrani dynasty was founded. Consequently, while the Durrani have a traditional geographic base, the Ghilzai in contrast are "scattered all over Afghanistan; thus there is no proper Ghilzai land".[103]

All the above-listed confederations are further divided into tribes and sub-tribes/clans and patriarchal families. Overall there are at least 60 Pashtun tribes[104] and the diagram below charts some of the major divisions.

As previously noted, the Durrani have historically dominated Afghan politics since Ahmad Shah Durrani founded a monarchy in 1747. By contrast, the Ghilzai have been akin to a 'military class', at the forefront of the first and second Anglo-Afghan wars and the 1929 revolt.[105] Later, the Ghilzai provided the largest base for the Mujahedin groups during the Soviet invasion and the Taliban movement thereafter. The original Taliban were mostly comprised of rural Pashtuns from the Ghilzai confederation, with elements from the Kakar tribe of the Ghurghusht

confederation (not shown on chart). Supreme leader Mullah Mohammed Omar Akhund and most of the senior members of the original Taliban are from the Hotak tribe of the Ghilzai confederation.[106]

There are some palpable differences between Pashtun tribes. As a generalization, the structure of social relations among Pashtuns of eastern Afghanistan tends to be flat, whereas in Kandahar hierarchies are more apparent.[107] As an example, in contrast to the south where a fragmentation into small rival groups occurred following the Soviet withdrawal, in the east one witnessed the presence of several strongmen dominating the scene (often reaching power-sharing agreements). Tribes often rallied around a specific Mujahedin leader even if the tribal leader did not. This is likely driven by agricultural practices and the structure of landholdings; it may also transfer directly into differing forms of organized criminal groups based on ethnicity.

General rivalries exist between the Ghilzai and Durrani confederations.[108] Notably, these groups find themselves on either side of the current conflict, with the current Durrani leadership challenged by the Ghilzai-heavy Taliban. Indeed, this stand-off can be traced in part to the favored status of Ghilzai groups in the assistance arrangements implemented by the Pakistani Government to fight the USSR.[109] This placed Ghilzai tribes at the forefront of the resistance, ultimately driving the Taliban takeover of Afghanistan.

Strife and the Persistence of the Insurgency", *Pearson peacekeeping centre*, occasional paper 2, 2008.

103 Bernt Glatzer, "War and Boundaries in Afghanistan: Significance and Relativity of Local and Social Boundaries", *Weld des Islams* 41, 3, 2001, pp 379-399.

104 As shown in the chart, the Durrani confederation has two main braches; Zirak Durrani and Panjpao Durani. The Ghilzai confederation also has two main branches; Toran and Ibrahim. Choosing a precise 'number of tribes' is practically impossible and it should also be noted that large tribes such as the Noorzai may better be disaggregated into sub-tribes, largely based on geography, that are the primary solidarity group reference for members.

105 Thomas J. Barfield, "Weapons of the not so Weak in Afghanistan: Pashtun Agrarian Structure and Tribal Organization for Times of War and Peace", *Agrarian Studies Colloquium Series "Hinterlands, Frontiers, Cities and States: Transactions and Identities"*, Yale University, February 23, 2007.

106 Johnson, T.H., Understanding the Taliban and Insurgency in Afghanistan", *Orbis: A Journal of World Affairs* 51, No. 1, 2007.

107 Conrad Schetter et al., "Beyond Warlordism: the Local Security Architecture in Afghanistan", *International Politics and Security*, Issue 2 , June 2007.

108 Johnson, T.H., op cit.

109 Thomas H. Johnson and M. Chris Mason, "No Sign until the Burst of Fire", *International Security* 32:4, 2008.

Digging beneath this high-level traditional rivalry, strong competition is also evident within confederations. In Kandahar, the rivalry among the major Durrani clans is centuries old,[110] with the long-running feud between the Alizai and Alikozai tribes being just one example. In contrast to these internal rivalries, however, Pashtun unity has generally been strong and quick to achieve in the face of invaders. Furthermore, and despite rivalries, most Pahstun tribes tend to prefer cooperation with other Pashtuns rather than with non-Pashtun groups. In the opiate economy, this creates notable dynamics. For example, intense competition on a local level may become collaborative trading at the wholesale level, depending on how profit shares are expected to affect balances of power. The less directly participants are connected to rivalries, disputes or contested territory, the less their respective tribes' interests will interfere with criminal cooperation.

1. Opium cultivation and the Durrani confederation

The link between opium cultivation and insurgency is commonly noted. At the same time, there appears to be a strong correlation between opium cultivation and the territorial control of the Durrani confederation. As discussed in more detail below, Durrani tribes preside over many of Afghanistan's major opium-producing areas, and around 67 per cent of Afghanistan's opium cultivation occurred in mostly "Durrani territory", the province of Hilmand, in 2008.

Hilmand tribes

The four most prominent tribes in Hilmand (and according to some experts, in the whole of southern Afghanistan) are the Barakzai, Noorzai, Ishaqzai and Alizai (Durrani).

Barakzai

The Barakzai are divided into seven branches and are primarily present in eastern Hilmand, specifically in the districts of Lashkar Gah, Naveh-ye-Barakzi and Nahr-e-Saraj. A landowning tribe, they have been prominent in Afghan political history. The Barakzai also have a strong presence and influence in Kandahar, especially in the Maruf district.[111] The tribe is also present in significant numbers in Farah. There are strong allegations of drug cultivation and trafficking against high-ranking members of the Barakzai tribe.

Alizai

The Alizai tribe belongs to the Durrani confederation[112] and is Hilmand's largest Pashtun group.[113] They control

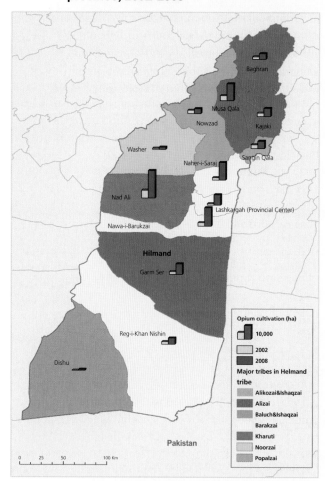

Map 2: **Tribes and opium cultivation in Hilmand province, 2002-2008**

and are numerically dominant in most of northern Hilmand, including the Musa Qala, Baghran and Kajaki districts (hosting roughly a quarter of Hilmand's total population), in which opium poppy cultivation is very intensive. Some important members of the Alizai tribe are known to be Taliban sympathizers and arms smugglers, while also heavily involved in the opiate trade.[114]

The former governor of Hilmand province, an Alizai tribesman named Sher Muhammad Akhundzada, was found with over nine tons of opium at his provincial headquaters by US officials. He was also accused of encouraging farmers to grow poppies (reportedly sparking a 162 per cent rise in cultivation in Hilmand) before he was removed from office in December 2005. Hilmand's strong tribal structures and its relatively concentrated land ownership transform leaders' decisions into practical action quite effectively, which results in close integration of a group's territory and members into the opiate economy.

While the Alizai heartland is the Musa Qala district in Hilmand, the tribe also dominates elsewhere, such as in western Afghanistan. In the last four years, opium poppy

110 Thomas J. Barfield, "Weapons of the not so Weak in Afghanistan: Pashtun Agrarian Structure and Tribal Organization for Times of War and Peace", *Agrarian Studies Colloquium Series "Hinterlands, Frontiers, Cities and States: Transactions and Identities"*, Yale University, February 23, 2007.

111 Naval Postgraduate School, "Kandahar Executive Summary," Program for Culture and Conflict Studies.

112 The Alizai are further subdivided into four tribes: the Jalozai, Hasanzai, Pirzai and Itharzai; see Jane's Terrorism and Security Monitor, "the battle for Musa Qala", April 2008.

113 Antonio Giustozzi and Noor Ullah, "Tribes" and warlords in southern

Afghanistan, 1980-2005, *Crisis States Research Centre*, Working Paper no. 7, September 2006, p.9. Interview, deputy security council, Kabul November 17 2008.

114 www.longwarjournal.org/archives/2007/12/a_chronology_of_the_1.php.

cultivation has been increasing alongside the insurgency in Farah province. Bala Bulok is the most important poppy growing district in Farah province and is dominated by Alizai tribe members. This district is also a major Taliban stronghold, particularly in and around the village of Shaiban.[115] The Alizai in this district were transferred to the area over a century ago from the Musa Qala district of Hilmand and "still maintain close ties with the Musa Qala insurgents."[116] There is also a strong Alizai presence in Kandahar's Maruf districts and the adjoining Pishin district in Balochistan, Pakistan.

Noorzai

The Noorzai are one of the most influential tribes in Afghanistan, with more than a million members in both Afghanistan (south and west) and Pakistan (Balochistan). They own significant swathes of land in the south and are concentrated in Hilmand's Nad Ali district and Kandahar's Spin Boldak district,[117] which straddles the main transportation corridor with Pakistan, and across the border in the Quetta district of Balochistan. They also have large communities in Farah and Hirat provinces. Tribal solidarity is generally strong among the Noorzai, although the large numbers of people under the Noorzai umbrella probably requires a search at the sub-tribe level to find strong community bonds.

In September 2008, the leader of the Noorzai tribe was given a sentence of at least 10 years' imprisonment by a US court for manufacturing and transporting hundreds of kilograms of heroin in Afghanistan and Pakistan, and importing to the USA. According to US court documents, the trafficker was the grandson of Haji Bashir Noorzai, the former chief of the Noorzai tribe.[118] Based in Quetta, he was convicted of involvement in narcotics production and, according to court records, in return for his financial and other support, the Taliban allowed him to continue his drug trafficking activities with impunity. In addition, court documents mentioned that he and his co-conspirators benefited from advance knowledge of the Taliban's 2000 opium ban, and used that information to stockpile opium and sell it at a tremendous profit after the ban caused opium prices to spike.[119]

Court records indicate that Noorzai would sell the opium in Chotu (a large opium market in southern Hilmand) and Maiwand (a Kandahar district bordering Eastern Hilmand). The same sources indicate that Noorzai owned approximately 500 acres of opium fields extending from Kandahar City to Kashkenakhod (Maiwand district). Notably Noorzai testified that the opium would be sold to Baluch tribe members in Kashkenakhod and Kandahar City for further trafficking.[120]

There is reportedly a "close partnership between Noorzai leaders and the Taliban leadership"[121] and some high-ranking leaders of the Noorzai are simultaneously Taliban commanders.[122] There also remain serious allegations of drug trafficking leveled against other powerful members of the Noorzai tribe.

Ishaqzai

The Ishaqzai are part of the Durrani confederation and have strong influence in the Sangin district of Hilmand, one of the most important opium cultivating districts and home to several large heroin processing facilities. The Ishaqzai also live and have influence in Hilmand's Grishk, Nawzad, Lashkar Gah and Garamsir districts. Their strongest influence is, however, in the border districts of Reg and Dishu in southern Hilmand. These districts are located on the border with Pakistan and host major opiate smuggling routes. Dishu is one of the most important havens for drug smugglers and producers in its southern area, particularly in the Baramcha area. The Ishaqzai are numerically the second most important tribe in Dishu after Baluchis.

During 2006, fierce clashes over control of the opium trade pitted them against the Alikozai tribe.[123] One analysis suggests that the Ishaqzai provide the backbone of the Taliban's ethnic support in Hilmand province[124] and one powerful Taliban commander with links to the drug trade is an Ishaqzai.[125]

Other Durrani tribes with an influence in Hilmand:

Alikozai (Alokzai)

This is a land-owning tribe with a presence in Sangin district. The tribe maintains strong links to Pakistan. Moreover, the Alikozai are the biggest tribe in Kandahar, although the killing of several of their high-ranking leaders has weakened their tribally-based governance structures. The Aliko-

115 Waliullah Rahmani, "Farah Province: The New Focus of the Taliban Insurgency", Jamestown Foundation, Terrorism Monitor Volume: 5 Issue: 23, December 10, 2007, http://www.jamestown.org/single/?no_cache=1&tx_ttnews per cent5Btt_news per cent5D=4599.

116 Ibid.

117 All Kandahar lab seizures in 2008 were in Spin Boldak testifying to the importance of the district in processing and trafficking opiates.

118 www.nefafoundation.org/miscellaneous/FeaturedDocs/US_v_Noorzai_GovtMemoOppOmnibusMotion.pdf.

119 http://www.usdoj.gov/dea/pubs/states/newsrel/2008/nyc092408.html.

120 www.nefafoundation.org/miscellaneous/FeaturedDocs/US_v_Noorzai_IntentUseDefendantStments.pdf.

121 Naval Postgraduate School , Kandahar Province: provincial profile, http://www.nps.edu/Programs/CCS/Kandahar.html; see also Peters, Gretchen, "Seeds of Terror: How Heroin Is Bankrolling the Taliban and al Qaeda", Thomas Dunne Books, 2009, p. 198.

122 Giustozzi, Antonio, "Koran, Kalashnikov, and Laptop : The Neo-Taliban Insurgency in Afghanistan", Columbia University Press, London, UK, 2008, p.47.

123 According to a 2006 BBC report, during the Taliban rule the Ishaqzai were favoured; when the Taleban fell the Alikozai re-emerged and "got their revenge by charging high "taxes" on drug smuggling."; see Alastair Leithead, "Unravelling the Helmand impasse" BBC News, 14 July 2006.

124 Conversely, the Ishaqzai were among the Taliban's fiercest opponents in Kandahar in the 1990s; see Afghans in Quetta: Settlements, Livelihoods, Support Networks and Cross-Border Linkages AREU, January 2006, p.17.

125 Interview ISAF analyst, November 2008.

zai maintain some control over trafficking from Hilmand into the Islamic Republic of Iran. There is a historical feud between them and the Ishaqzai.

Achakzai

The Achakzai have an important presence in Kandahar's Spin Boldak district and in Farah province. They have strong links to the Quetta, Qilla Saifullah, Qilla Abdullah and Pishin districts of Balochistan (Pakistan) and are thought to be involved in smuggling networks. The Achakzai are considered one of the traditional leadership tribes of the Afghan south (along with the Barakzai and Popalzai). There is a history of tribal conflict between the Noorzai and Achakzai.

2. Insurgency, tribalism and the drug trade

In many cases, Afghanistan's export-oriented opiate trafficking routes follow centuries-old trading paths. They run along well-established geographical and *social* contours. The strength and flexibility of social structures that support cross-border trading was evident in their adaptation to become Mujahedin supply lines during the Soviet invasion. This is apparent now in their use by drug smuggling networks. Contemporary inter-state borders are virtual lines of demarcation often ignored by peoples that have roamed across them for centuries. In some regions of Afghanistan, such as the south-western provinces of Nimroz and Farah, smuggling is a way of life for tribesmen spanning the borders of the Islamic Republic of Iran, Pakistan and Afghanistan. Smuggling is essentially the modern name for their tradition of trading. Many of them have triple nationalities, which facilitates their smuggling of licit and illicit goods.

Trading opportunities create incentives for territorial control. As discussed in the previous section, maintaining control of smuggling routes can increase revenue. Tribal solidarity becomes both the means of establishing control and the beneficiary of its resulting profit.

Tribal solidarity can only be taken so far, however. Along some routes, ethnic links have been noted to carry contraband great distances from zones of control, such as Baluchi tribesmen from southern Afghanistan with ethnic links in Balochistan and further into Eastern Iran (Sistan-Balochistan province). In most situations, however, links to non-members are required at the edges of zones of control in order to dispose of goods and realize profits. This highlights the profit motive and reinforces a reliance on tribal links. Trust and social sanctions reduce the risks involved in intra-tribal trading, but at the same time the profit from external transactions encourages outward links.

Insurgency and tribalism

Most members of the Taliban are Pashtun, and Pashtuns perceive the Taliban more positively than other ethnic groups. There is a perception among some Pashtuns that the 2001 intervention in Afghanistan deposed a Pashtun government and put in its place a multi-ethnic government "controlled" by the Taliban's traditional enemy, the Tajik-dominated Northern Alliance.[126] The insurgency is partly the result of "inter-ethnic and tribal dynamics that have been antagonized by power distribution at the national level, attempted encroachment on tribal autonomy at the local level, and exploitation of these grievances by ideologically motivated actors at the international level."[127]

These perceptions have been fed and exploited by the Taliban, which "has been able to draw on traditional Pashtun loyalties to support the insurgency."[128] Again, Pashtun solidarity is important, irrespective of the confederation.

As Antonio Giustozzi correctly points out, the majority of the current leaders of the neo-Taliban movement are majority Durrani (and not Ghilzai, as was the case with the original movement).[129] Some insurgents from the Noorzai tribes may also resent being excluded from the government[130] just as some Ghilzai may object to being placed under the control of the rival Durrani. These have opted for anti-government activities, but without 'religious' motives per se.

However, counter-narcotics and counter-insurgency planners must recognize that the Taliban have been most effective in the south of the country not just because of tribal chauvinism. They have also been able to reach across tribal lines to create a rural support base. Part of the explanation for this has been the Taliban's promotion of clerics rather than tribal leaders, encouraging cross-tribal religious affinity instead of inter-tribal rivalries.[131] In both Pakistan and Afghanistan, there has also been a deliberate process of removing (usually killing) tribal leaders who attempt to steer their tribe away from insurgency.

While the Taliban movement exploits tribal differences and resentments to generate antagonism towards the government, they simultaneously stress their religious rather than ethnic motivations. A good example of this was their alliance with Uzbek extremists (of both Afghan and Central Asian origin) of The Islamic Movement of Uzbekistan,[132]

126 K R Singh, "Post-War Afghanistan: Reconstructing a Failed State", Strategic Analysis, Vol. 28, No. 4, 2004., http://www.idsa.in/publications/strategic-analysis/2004/oct/K per cent20R per cent20Singh.pdf.

127 Roohullah Rahimi, "Afghanistan: Exploring the Dynamics of Sociopolitical Strife and the Persistence of the Insurgency" Pearson peacekeeping centre, occasional paper 2, 2008.

128 Magnus Norell, "The Taliban and the Muttahida Majlis-e-Amal (MMA)", China and Eurasia Forum Quarterly, Volume 5, No. 3 (2007).

129 Giustozzi, Antonio, "Koran, Kalashnikov, and Laptop : The Neo-Taliban Insurgency in Afghanistan", Columbia University Press, London, UK., 2008, p.47.

130 Sultan Barakat, "Understanding Afghanistan", *DFID*, November 2008.

131 Thomas J. Barfield, "Weapons of the not so Weak in Afghanistan: Pashtun Agrarian Structure and Tribal Organization for Times of War and Peace", *Agrarian Studies Colloquium Series "Hinterlands, Frontiers, Cities and States: Transactions and Identities"*, Yale University, February 23, 2007.

132 The Islamic Movement of Uzbekistan (IMU) has the declared aim of revolu-

Map 3:   Ethnic map of Afghanistan/Pakistan border

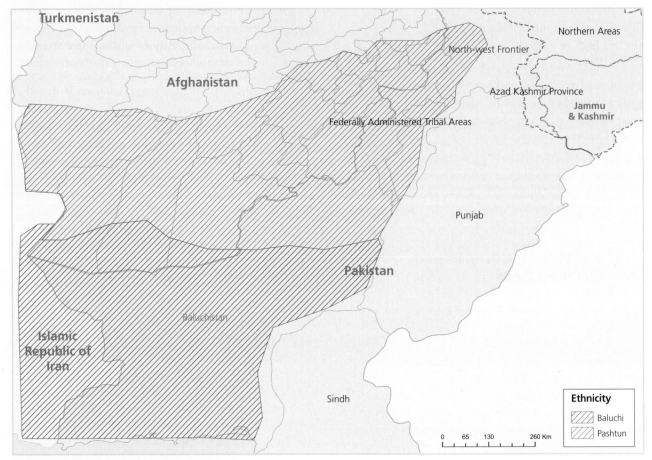

Ethnicity	
▨	Baluchi
▨	Pashtun

Source: UNODC.

despite the historical animosity between Uzbeks and Pashtuns in Afghanistan. The IMU leader, Tahir Yuldash, who pledged allegiance to Mullah Omar, addressed the thorny ethnic issue in a 2004 communiqué that insisted that the Taliban state was not a vehicle for Pashtun power. Although as they were the group who sacrificed the most, the IMU leader stated, it was "right that they should also benefit".[133]

Some ethnic Tajiks and Turkmens (both of Central Asian and Afghan origin) have also been fighting alongside Al-Qaeda and the Taliban in Pakistan[134] and at least one ethnic Tajik is a confirmed Taliban commander in Hirat province. The fact that thousands of non-Pashtuns have affiliated themselves with Mullah Omar indicates that the Taliban movement can in some cases override tribal or ethnic affiliation.[135] One expert of Afghanistan's tribal network describes

a famous insurgent's dual use of tribal and religious affiliation to recruit among Afghans during the Soviet invasion:

> Ethnic and tribal boundaries and identities are not fixed since time immemorial, but are often a matter of negotiation. Whether social action is based on tribal and ethnic criteria depends on opportunities and tactics, and these may change quickly. For example, in his public speeches the Pashtun party leader and warlord Gulbuddin Hekmatyar initially emphasized pan-Islamism and the Muslim solidarity. Boundaries between Muslim states were to become obsolete. Later, during his campaigns for recruitment in Pashtun areas, he appealed to the ethnic and tribal solidarity of the Pashtuns, who must defend their identity and honour against the rest of the world.[136]

3. The Afghan-Pakistani border

Pakistan has a 2,430-km-long border with Afghanistan, punctured by three official crossing points (Torkham in Nangarhar, Ghulam Khan in Khost and Spin Boldak in

---

tionizing the Central Asia region and institute across it a single Islamic state, which would more or less correspond to the boundaries of old Turkestan, including China's Xinjiang province.

133 BBC Today, "Al-Qaida commander speaks", 15 September 2004.

134 Bill Roggio, "Al Qaeda killed in North Waziristan attacks", The Long War Journal, October 11, 2007.

135 Alliances of this sort may only last until the point of victory, after which ethnic rivalries may become important again in dividing the spoils. Johnson and Mason highlight the willingness of Pashtun tribes to unite behind religiously-inspired leaders at times of external pressure. Their traditional tendency to disaggregate once conflict is over is being tested by the relative longevity of jihadist-led action against the Soviets, through the Mujahedin period and

now against the coalition, Afghan and Pakistani governments - "No Sign until the Burst of Fire", 2008.

136 Bernt Glatzer, "War and Boundaries in Afghanistan: Significance and Relativity of Local and Social Boundaries", Weld des Islams 41, 3, 2001, pp 379-399.

Kandahar). The topography of this border area includes numerous north-south mountain ranges, which create natural smuggling routes across the border. In addition, there are hundreds of natural passes, mountain trails and desert roads along the entire border, most of which are unmanned and unsupervised. Many of these are used for the smuggling of illicit goods and weapons using large trucks, pick-ups and pack mules. The potential for high-volume smuggling increases as the eastern border changes from mountainous to open plains near Balochistan province. Control over these trade routes provides a significant revenue stream; for example, the World Bank estimated that the Taliban generated more than US$75 million from taxing Afghanistan-Pakistan trade in 1997.[137]

With the Al-Qaeda and Taliban presence across the Durand Line[138] and a history of cross-border smuggling, this border is of utmost interest to drug control efforts. Upwards of 150 tons of heroin and 80 tons of opium are annually smuggled across the border and trafficked west to the Islamic Republic of Iran, north to the Chinese market or south to the warm water ports of Pakistan where it continues towards the Gulf States, Europe and the USA.

Estimates of the number of Pashtuns in Pakistan range from 25-30 million,[139] not counting Afghan refugee populations (approximately 3 million),[140] of which some 80 per cent are ethnic Pashtuns.[141] Unofficial estimates of the number of Pashtuns in the Federally Administered Tribal Areas range up to four million. Estimates of Pasthun populations in the North West Frontier Province range from approximately 7 million[142] to 16 million.[143] Other areas of high Pashtun concentration are Quetta (Balochistan), with approximately 450,000, Lahore (Punjab province) with one million[144] and Karachi (Sindh province) with an estimated three million.[145] Pashtuns are a majority in Pakistan's tribal areas and dominate regional trade and transport in the

border areas of both Pakistan and Afghanistan.[146] With the exception of Nuristan, all Afghan provinces bordering Pakistan are dominated by Pashtuns (Kunar, Nangarhar, Paktya, Khost, Paktika, Zabul, Kandahar, Hilmand and Nimroz).

The influx of Afghan refugees into Pakistan's tribal areas following the Soviet invasion cemented trade relations[147] and reignited tribal linkages.[148] Weapons and militants are shuttled and drugs and precursor chemicals trafficked across the border. The Durand line thus became (and continues to be) as one researcher put it: "a tactical resource in warfare, a line beyond which one's enemies cannot follow, and the crossing of which offers security for oneself and one's families while offering the chance to find supplies for continuing warfare".[149]

The transnational nature of Afghanistan's insurgency is highlighted by the fact that the Taliban's peak bodies are in Pakistan, where there are reportedly four underground Taliban shuras (councils). The first is in Quetta[150] and directs operations in southern Afghanistan (Zabul, Kandahar, Hilmand and Nimroz). The second is in Miram-shah (North-Waziristan), bordering Afghanistan's Khost province; it is a smaller council responsible for Paktika, Paktya, Khost and Logar provinces. The third is based in Peshawar and directs activity in eastern Afghanistan (Kunar, Nuristan, Nangarhar and Laghman), with attempts to extend to the north of the country and a primary role in operations targeting Kabul. A fourth council was reportedly established outside the tribal areas, in Karachi, and mostly has a political and strategic role.[151]

Each council is subdivided into four 'departments':

1. A military commission, formulating plans for 'normal' insurgent attacks, but also kidnappings and suicide bombings.

2. Financial agency, coordinating donations and organizing purchases to support the other departments.

3. Political commission, taking strategic decisions, including negotiations with external actors.

4. Public information (propaganda, websites etc.).[152]

---

137 Zareen Naqvi, "Afghanistan-Pakistan Trade Relations" World Bank, 1999 in John Solomon, "The Funding Methods of FATA's Terrorists and Insurgents", CTC Sentinel, May 2008, Vol 1, Issue 6.

138 The Durand Line is the term for the 2,640 kilometer (1,610 mile) border. The Durand Line was demarcated by the British and signed into a treaty in 1893 with the Afghan ruler Amir Abdur Rehman Khan.

139 Lisa Curtis et al., "revitalizing US efforts in Afghanistan", *The Heritage Foundation*, October 15 2007,; see also Barnett R. Rubin et al., "Resolving the Pakistan- Afghanistan Stalemate", *United States Institute of Peace*, Special Report 176, October 2006.

140 The current number of Afghan refugees in Afghanistan is approximately three million, down from a peak of five million.

141 Rodney W. Jones, "Neutralizing Extremism and Insurgency in Afghanistan and Its Borderlands", *Institute of regional studies*, Seminar paper, Islamabad, May 2008.

142 Barnett R. Rubin et al., "Resolving the Pakistan- Afghanistan Stalemate", *United States Institute of Peace*, Special Report 176, October 2006.

143 Rodney W. Jones, op. cit.

144 "Traditional Structures in Local Governance for Local Development: A Case Study of Pashtun Residing in NWFP and FATA, Pakistan", info.worldbank. org/etools/docs/library/153053/Pakistan.pdf.

145 Shuja Nawaz, "FATA—A Most Dangerous Place", *Center for Strategic and International Studies*, January 2009.

146 Thomas H. Johnson et al., "Misunderstanding Pakistan's Federally Administered Tribal Area?", *International Security*, Volume 33, Number 3, Winter 2008/09.

147 In similar fashion to the development of links between Central Asian ethnic groups and their Afghan counterparts.

148 In some regions, cross-border trade relations between Pashtun tribes were negligible prior to the Soviet invasion of Afghanistan.

149 Bernt Glatzer, Op. cit.

150 It was previously based in Kandahar; see Seth G. Jones, "the state of the Afghan insurgency", RAND, December 2007.

151 The presence of high-ranking Taliban officials in Sindh province was recently confirmed with the arrest of a significant TTP commander in Karachi, see "Developments in the Jihadi Resurgence in Pakistan", NEFA foundation, January 2008.

152 Interview, head of counter-terrorism department, Ministry of Interior, Kabul, November 16 2008.

Table 3: Federally Administered Tribal Areas (FATA)

Agency	Area (km²)	Population (1998 census)	Density (people/ km²)
Bajaur		595,227	
Khyber		546,730	
Kurram		448,310	
Mohmand		334,453	
North Waziristan		361,246	
Orakzai		225,441	
South Waziristan		429,841	
Six Frontier Regions combined		235,083	
FATA	27,220	3,176,331	117

Source: Pakistan Ministry of Information and Broadcasting, http://www.infopak.gov.pk/districtPK.aspx.

Fig. 3: Average daily vehicle crossing in FATA, 2007-2008

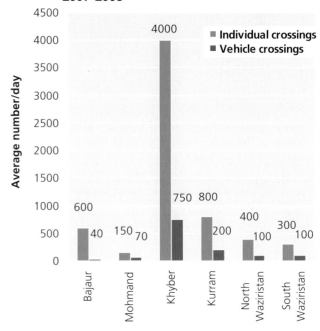

Source: Information provided by Pakistani embassy officials in Kabul.

Regular meetings are reportedly held between all four but most political/strategic decisions regarding Afghanistan are reportedly made in Quetta[153] (followed by Peshawar in order of importance). Jane's Intelligence reported that the Taliban takeover of Musa Qala district in January 2007 occurred pursuant to directives from the Quetta *shura*.

The presence and influence of the Afghan Taliban in FATA and Balochistan has been the transformation of the Pakistani Taliban from a local sub-division of the Afghan Taliban into a fully separate entity organizationally distinct from the Afghan Taliban. Independent of the Afghan Taliban, insurgency activity led by the Pakistani Taliban in Pakistan has continued, both through suicide bombings as well as the evolution of militant organizations. The latter has involved the genesis of new groups as well as the development of established groups that increasingly perceive themselves as part of a global war. The insurgency, or rather insurgencies, in the Pakistan-Afghanistan border areas represent a spectrum of groups and aims, from the local frustrations of Baluchi separatists to global aspirations embodied in the Al-Qaeda ideology.

New groups have emerged in the tribal areas of Pakistan such as *Lashkar-I-Islam* and *Ansar-Ul-Islam*. These are increasingly influenced by the ideology of the Taliban and Al-Qaeda, as are older, more established Punjabi groups. Other groups include the East Turkestan Islamic Movement (ETIM), a Chinese-Uighur group with personnel and logistical links to Pakistan/Central Asia, the Islamic Movement of Uzbekistan (and several offshoots) and smaller, loosely-affiliated Chechen groups. Members of such foreign groups come from almost every ethnic group in Central Asia

(including Western China) and the Caucasus (including a minority of Westerners) but are often numerically dominated by Uzbeks. Whether operating under the Pakistani Taliban umbrella or supported by Al-Qaeda, cross-pollination between the various insurgent groups is increasing and operational links are solidifying.

4. The tribal areas of Pakistan

The FATA borders Afghanistan to the west, the NWFP and Punjab to the east and Balochistan to the south. It consists of seven agencies and six frontier regions. The seven agencies are Bajaur, Kurram, Orakzai, Mohmand, Khyber, North Waziristan and South Waziristan. The six frontier regions are Kohat, Peshawar, Bannu, Lakki, Dera Ismail Khan and Tank. The latter are transition areas between FATA and the adjoining settled districts of the NWFP. They are jointly administered by the NWFP and FATA; according to the 1998 census, they had a combined population of 235,000.[154] Some tribal pockets are kept under the provincial administration as well.

The tribal areas in Balochistan and the NWFP are known as the Provincially Administered Tribal Areas (PATA). In the NWFP, the PATA include the Malakand, Chitral, Dir, Swat, Amb and the tribal areas of Kohistan and Manshehra districts. NWFP inhabitants are ruled by the Pakistani government from the provincial capital in Peshawar. In Balochistan, Zhob and Loralai districts, Dalbandin in Chagai district, Maari and Bugti in Sibi district comprise the PATA. As noted above, the people of the NWFP and the FATA, as

153 Ibid.

154 Some more recent estimates render a combined population of about 275,000; see Hassan Abbas "Profiles of Pakistan's Seven Tribal Agencies", *Jamestown Foundation Terrorism Monitor*, Volume: 4 Issue: 20, October 20, 2006.

Table 4: Tribes and insurgent groups in FATA (Pakistan)

Border agency/ province	Main tribes	Main AGE groups (non-exhaustive)	Cross-border representation and linkages in Afghanistan
Khyber	Shinwari, Afridi	Lashkar I-Islam, Ansar ul Islam, HIG, Tehrik-e-Taliban Pakistan	Shinwari
Kurram	Turi, Mangal, Bangash, Jaji, Moqbil	HIG, Tehrik-e-Taliban Pakistan (TTP)	Jaji, Mangal,Moqbil
Bajaur	Mamunds, Salarzais, Uthman Khel	Tehreek-e-Nafaz-e-Shariat-e-Mohammadi (TNSM), Jamaat-e-Islami (JI), Tehrik-e-Taliban Pakistan (TTP), Al Qaeda, Jaish-e-Islami, Karwan-e-Niamatullah, HIG	Mamunds, Salarzais
North Waziristan	Uthmanzai Wazirs, Gurbuz	Al-Qaeda, IMU and Uzbek splinter groups (e.g. Islamic Jihad Union), Haqqani network, Tehrik-e-Taliban Pakistan (TTP)	Uthmanzai Wazirs, Gurbuz
South Waziristan	Ahmadzai Wazirs, Mehsuds	Al-Qaeda, IMU, Tehrik-e-Taliban Pakistan (TTP)	Ahmadzai Wazirs
Mohmand	Mohmand, Safis	Tehrik-e-Taliban Pakistan (TTP), Al-Qaeda	Mohmand, Safis
Orakzai	Orakzai, Afridi	Lashkar-e-Jhangvi, Tehrik-e-Taliban Pakistan (TTP)	
Balochistan province	Ashaqzai, Alizai, Kakar, Baluch	Afghan Taliban, Balochi separatist groups, Jundullah	Ashaqzai, Alizai, Kakar, Baluch

Source: UNAMA, UNODC, UNDSS, Jamestown Foundation, CTC Sentinel, The Long War Journal.

well as the adjacent eastern, south-eastern and southern regions of Afghanistan, are overwhelmingly Pashtuns, mostly from the Karlanri confederation. Like their cross-border brethren, the Pashtuns of Pakistan's tribal areas take great pride in their history of repelling invaders.

The border between Pakistan and Afghanistan is widely ignored by Pashtuns living on either side. Every day, Pashtuns freely cross the border at hundreds of points, on foot, pack animal and in vehicles.

The Soviet invasion had immense ramifications for the FATA. For example, the impact of that war on the FATA's economy was a shift from "subsistence agriculture and nomadic pastoralism to dependence on the unregulated, cross-border trade of goods, including contraband such as drugs and arms".[155] This trade has continued more or less unabated since the early 1980s as the FATA straddles a major drug route out of Afghanistan, into the NWFP and further to eastern Pakistan.

The current instability in the FATA precludes law enforcement efforts and maintains the border regions' status as de facto sanctuaries for heroin and hashish traffickers (and perhaps minor heroin and opium producers). Pakistan achieved poppy-free status in 1999-2000, but the impact of insecurity may have led to some opium cultivation in Pakistan, albeit on much smaller scale than Afghanistan. According to the US Department of State's International Narcotics Control Strategy Report, after 2002 cultivation picked up in Pakistan in the areas of highest insecurity and bordering Afghanistan: Orakzai, Kurram, North and South Waziris-

tan (FATA) and Gulistan/Qila Abdullah in Balochistan.[156]

While the area cultivated in 2005 (3,145 hectares) was equivalent to only 3 per cent of the area cultivated in Afghanistan, there is a risk that cultivation could increase substantially – especially as a result of displacement from Afghanistan – unless there are sustained efforts to dissuade farmers from planting poppy and to destroy opium crops before they are harvested. The task of eradicating opium cultivation in FATA is complicated by counter-terrorism considerations; in some instances the need to win "hearts and minds" has inhibited action to destroy poppy crops.[157]

The US Department of State's 2008 International Narcotics and Law Enforcement Affairs (INL) Narcotics Strategy Report documents roughly 1,731 ha of opium cultivated land in the area (after eradication), an increase of 200 ha over 2006. The potential production in the tribal areas is reported to be around 4.25 metric tons of opium.

1. The Khyber Agency is named after the Khyber Pass (Torkham border crossing) and provides the most important link between Pakistan and Afghanistan. A majority of consumables in eastern Afghanistan are imported through this agency and it is the coalition's biggest supply route. Once across the border, most goods flow into Jalalabad, the main transit center and distribution point for goods from Pakistan. The importance of cross-border trade with Pakistan is reflected in the fact that Pakistani rupees are the major currency used throughout Nangarhar. The Khyber

155 Barnett R. Rubin et al., "Resolving the Pakistan- Afghanistan Stalemate", *United States Institute of Peace*, Special Report 176, October 2006.

156 International Narcotics Control Strategy Report (INCSR), 2003, United States Department of State.

157 UNODC, Strategic Programme Framework for Pakistan 2007 – 2010, July 2006, p.2.

Map 4: FATA`s seven agencies and Balochistan

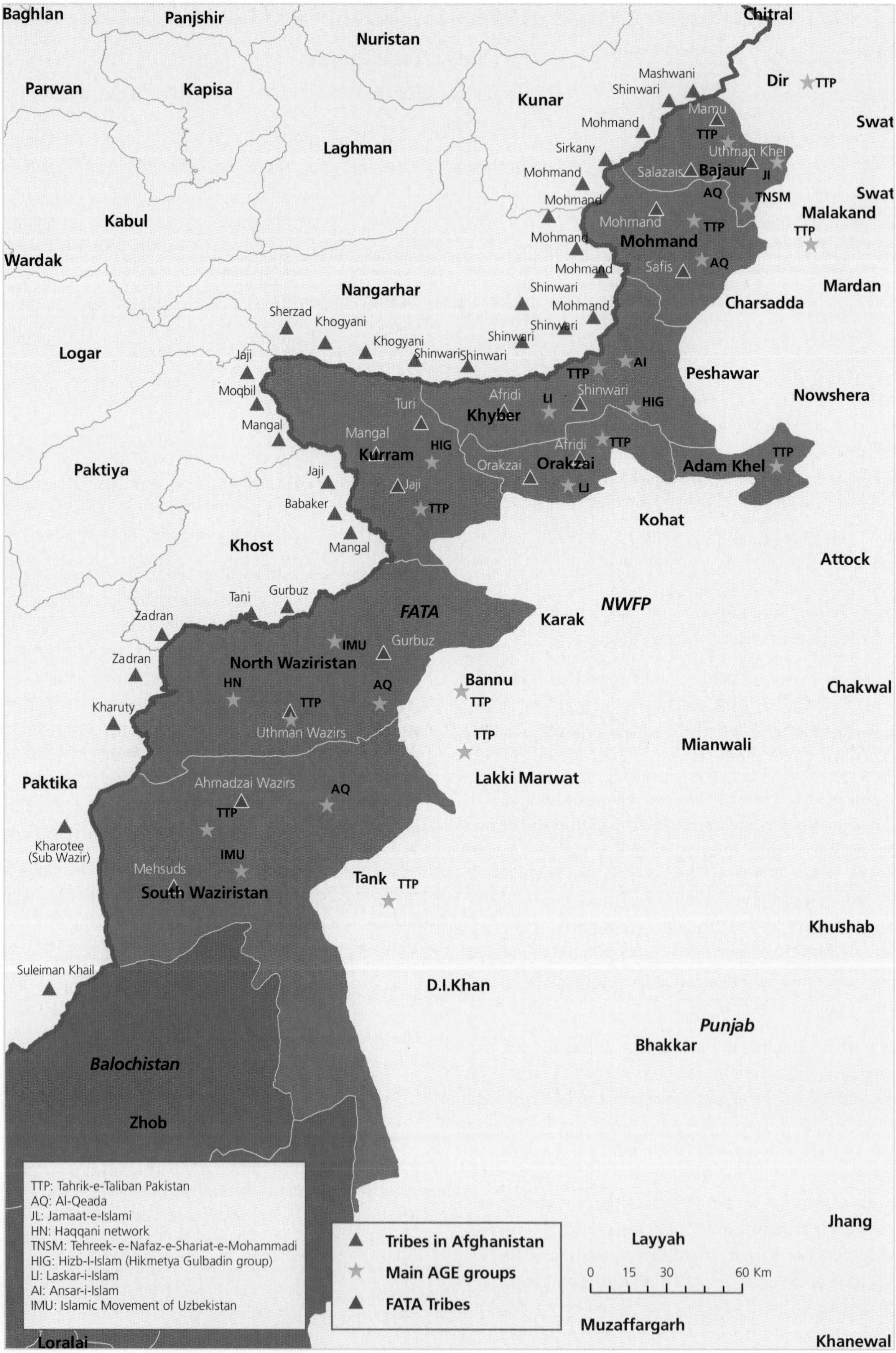

Baghlan
Panjshir
Nuristan
Chitral
Parwan
Kapisa
Kunar
Mashwani
Shinwari
Dir ☆TTP
Mamu
Swat
Laghman
Mohmand
TTP
Uthman Khel
Sirkany
Salazais △Bajaur
JL
Kabul
Mohmand
AQ
TNSM
Swat
Mohmand △
TTP
Malakand
Wardak
Mohmand
Mohmand
Safis △ AQ
TTP
Nangarhar
Mohmand
Charsadda
Mardan
Sherzad
Khogyani
Shinwari
Mohmand
Logar
Jaji
Khogyani
Shinwari
Peshawar
Moqbil
ShinwariShinwari
TTP AI
Nowshera
Mangal
Turi
Afridi
Shinwari
Khyber
LI
HIG
Mangal
Jaji
Mangal △
Afridi
TTP
Paktiya
Jaji
Kurram
HIG
Orakzai △Orakzai
TTP
Babaker
△Jaji
LI
Adam Khel
Kohat
TTP
Khost
Mangal
TTP ☆
Attock
Tani
Gurbuz
FATA
Karak
NWFP
Zadran
IMU
Gurbuz
Zadran
North Waziristan
AQ
Bannu
Chakwal
HN
TTP
Kharuty
TTP
Uthman Wazirs
Lakki Marwat
Mianwali
Paktika
Ahmadzai Wazirs
AQ
TTP
Kharotee
(Sub Wazir)
IMU
Mehsuds
Tank TTP
South Waziristan
Khushab
Suleiman Khail
D.I.Khan
Punjab
Bhakkar
Balochistan
Zhob
Jhang

TTP: Tahrik-e-Taliban Pakistan
AQ: Al-Qeada
JL: Jamaat-e-Islami
HN: Haqqani network
TNSM: Tehreek- e-Nafaz-e-Shariat-e-Mohammadi
HIG: Hizb-I-Islam (Hikmetya Gulbadin group)
LI: Laskar-i-Islam
AI: Ansar-i-Islam
IMU: Islamic Movement of Uzbekistan

▲ Tribes in Afghanistan
☆ Main AGE groups
▲ FATA Tribes

Layyah
0 15 30 60 Km

Muzaffargarh
Loralai
Khanewal

Source: UNODC.

agency is famous for its opium bazaars, which also stock weapons and smuggled goods. The most well-known of these are in Ali Masjeed and Landi Kotal, the latter only 6 km from Torkham. Of note, Hekmatyar's HiK has maintained a base of operations in Khyber (since the Soviet invasion) but it is unclear if the agency is used by this group for operations.

The Khyber agency borders Afghanistan's Nangarhar province in the districts of Kot, Spin Ghar, Achin, Naizian, Dur Baba, Mohmand Dara and southern Lal Pur. Khyber has a population of approximately 500,000, predominately Afridis with significant Shinwari minority and smaller pockets of Orakzais.

The Afridis (Ghilzai confederation) are divided into eight clans[158] and are historically the dominant tribe in Khyber in terms of numbers and influence, constituting about 80 per cent of the population.[159] The tribe is generally oriented towards Sufism, which puts them at odds with more conservative and pro-Taliban groups.[160] Among Afghans, Afridis are well known as traders/smugglers.

Shinwaris (Sarbani confederation), the second largest tribe of Khyber, are also influential, but most of its members (85 per cent) inhabit Nangarhar province,[161] where they are a majority in several border districts (Dih Bala, Spin Ghar, Nazyan, Achin and Dur Baba) and parts of Kunar. They are known as businesspeople, both licit and illicit, a tradition facilitated by their strong links with Pakistani Shinwaris in places like Landi Kotal. In Nangarhar's border areas, they appear to exercise control over the transport business, with a focus on oil tankers, trucks and buses.[162] Across the border in Pakistan, Shinwaris own significant logistics companies, some with offices in Pakistani ports and Dubai.

Tribes such as the Shinwaris (and Khogiani) in Nangarhar are more involved than others in some aspects of the drug trade. They are the historical bearers of opium cultivation knowledge and have played a part in spreading this to other parts of Afghanistan.[163] The Shinwari leadership decision in late 2006 to plant opium was an important driver of the spike in provincial cultivation in 2007. It also resulted in strong resistance to eradication in areas controlled by these tribes.[164]

Higher up the opiate value chain, members of the Shinwari tribes in Nangarhar have held sway over heroin production and processing,[165] with a concentration of laboratories in Shinwari-dominated districts like Achin and Nazyan.[166] Most law enforcement sources believe that the bulk of the incoming precursor chemicals and a portion of outgoing narcotics in Nangarhar are trafficked by pack mules or backpacks through illegal border crossing points in Shinwari territory.[167]

Strong connections between Shinwaris in Nangarhar and Afridis in Khyber are the foundation for drug and precursor trafficking through this area. Afridi networks are reportedly involved in smuggling everything from timber to car parts and narcotics across the Durand Line.[168] The tribe is neatly spread out along the main roads of Khyber.[169] One region almost fully under their control is the strategic Tirah valley (130 km west of the Khyber Pass),[170] a famous drug smuggling route[171] and cannabis cultivation area.[172] There are two main Pakistan/Afghanistan crossings along the Peshawar-Jalalabad route. The most widely used is the Peshawar-Torkham-Jalalabad road. The second border crossing is Peshawar-Ali masjeed Tirah Bazar- Jalalabad. A detour is taken off the Peshawar-Torkham road near Ali Masjeed into the difficult terrain of the Tirah valley. This route is mostly used for smuggling timber and a variety of goods, including opium, from Afghanistan.[173]

In an example of inter-tribal cooperation, there are reports of Shinwari involvement in heroin production in Nangarhar's Spin Ghar district, the product of which is handed over to Pakistani Afridis.[174] For some Afridi traffickers, networks expand far beyond Khyber of even Pakistan. One Drug Enforcement Agency (DEA) operation in 2006 uncovered a Khyber-based Afridi network shipping hundreds of kilograms of heroin to Canada and Africa.[175] An

158 Malikdin Khel, Kuki Khel, Qambar Khel, Sepay, Aka Khel, Adam Khel, Zakah Khel - S. Iftikhar Hussain Shah, "Some major Pukhtoon tribes along the Pak-Afghan border", University of Peshawar and Hanns Seidel Foundation, Germany, 2000, http://www.issi.org.pk/journal/2001_files/no_4/review/3r.htm.

159 Asian Development Bank, "Land Acquisition, Resettlement and Tribal Peoples Plan", June 2007.

160 www.mrt-rrt.gov.au/docs/research/PAK/rr/PAK31546.pdf

161 Naval Postgraduate School, www.nps.edu/Programs/CCS/Docs/Pakistan/Tribes/Shinwari.pdf.

162 Ibid.

163 UNODC, An Analysis of the Process of Expansion of Opium Poppy Cultivation to New Districts in Afghanistan, Strategic study #1: Preliminary Report June 1998.

164 UNODC, Afghanistan opium survey 2007.

165 Interview, July 12 in Kabul.

166 Interview CNPA Nangarhar, October 2008.

167 The flexibility of tribal connections is also suggested by their use for the trade in illegal timber – and most forests in Nangarhar are in Shinwari areas.

168 Naval Postgraduate School, http://www.nps.edu/Programs/CCS/Docs/Pakistan/Tribes/Afridi.pdf; see also Jonathan Goodhand, http://www.gtz.de/de/dokumente/en-opium-economy-2005-afg.pdf.

169 Jonathan Goodhand, http://www.gtz.de/de/dokumente/en-opium-economy-2005-afg.pdf.

170 The Tirah valley lies between the Khyber Pass and the Khanki Valley. It is inhabited by the Afridi and Orakzai tribes but controlled by the former. The Orakzai have always refused the Tirah valley be linked to the rest of the country by a road suitable for motor vehicles, In the 1990s, a government attempt to build a road passing through Shin Qamar, 50 km west of the North-West Frontier Province capital of Peshawar, led to skirmishes between government militias and tribesmen.

171 Sarah Lister et al., "Understanding markets in Afghanistan: A case study of the market in construction materials", AREU, 2004.

172 Muhammad Hamayun et al., "Folk Methodology of Charas (Hashish) Production and Its Marketing at Afridi Tirah, Federally Administered Tribal Areas(FATA), Pakistan".

173 Sarah Lister et al., "Understanding markets in Afghanistan: A case study of the market in construction materials", AREU, 2004.

174 Interview CNPA Nangarhar, October 2008.

175 http://www.usdoj.gov/usao/md.

Durbaba crossing (Nangarhar – Afghanistan/FATA – Pakistan)

Source: Nangarhar Valley Foundation

infamous Afridi tribe member is Haji Ayub Afridi, nicknamed the "Lord of Khyber Pass". He was previously sentenced by both the USA and Pakistan on charges of international drug trafficking.

Khyber straddles a major precursor route and seizure data suggest that most precursor trafficking here occurs along the eastern belt of Paktya and Nangarhar, which border the Khyber and Kurram Agencies of the FATA. From Karachi or Islamabad, precursor routes dedicated to east and north-eastern Afghanistan converge on Peshawar.[176] From there, they travel to Nangarhar – Torkham is 55 km from Peshawar – or Paktya (bordering the Kurram Agency). For those precursors destined for labs in Achin and Nazyan, the majority of their journey is through Afridi territory. There is also information suggesting that Afridi elements have moved some laboratory operations to Badakshan and expanded relations in southern Afghanistan.[177]

In contrast to the general overlap of crime and insurgency, the Shinwaris and Afridis have formed an alliance against insurgent elements. The two tribes have also become increasingly antagonistic to groups such as Lashkar-e-Islam (LI), a local militia trying to implement its own interpretation of religious law but apparently not closely allied to the Paki-

stani Taliban.[178] The LI has reportedly been involved in the destruction of Sufi shrines[179] and claims to fight the drug traffickers,[180] two tendencies that may have provoked a backlash from tribe members (drug-involved or otherwise).

It is worth remembering that the aforementioned anti-insurgency alliance depends on their tribal unity to have any effectiveness. While the Shinwaris seem to act more or less homogeneously in Nangarhar, the Lashkar-e-Islam is in fact dominated by Afridis and led by an Afridi.[181] There are also Afridis reportedly fighting in Taliban ranks (such as from the Shalobar sub-tribe). In fact, the Afridi sub tribes who are confirmed as anti-Taliban are the Mullagori, Zakha and Adam Afridis; other sub-tribes may not have followed suit. This is a prime example of the limits of tribal affiliation, especially in the face of supra-tribal religious extremism.

2. Kurram Agency borders Afghanistan's Nangarhar province in the north-west and Khost and Paktya provinces in the south-west. Comparatively more accessible than other agencies, it has a population of about 500,000 and is home to two tribes – the Turi (Shia Pasthun from the Karlanri confederation) and the Mangal/Bangash (both Sunni and Pashtun), the latter also a part of the Karlanri confederation. Turis account for approximately 40 per cent of Kurram inhabitants[182] and are mostly concentrated in Parachinar (upper Kurram), the area bordering Afghanistan. There are significant minorities of Mangals, Moqbils and Jajis also residing in upper Kurram bordering Paktya province. The latter, the Jajis, are a Khogiani subtribe of the Karlanri confederation, with ethnic links into Nangarhar.

The agency has been the scene of fierce sectarian clashes between the two sects (Shia Turi and Sunni Bangash), particularly in the area of Parachinar, resulting in hundreds of casualties. The conflict is exacerbated by the role of the Sunni Taliban, which has historically been anti-Shia and are reportedly backing the Bangash tribe.[183] This agency has often been considered to be supportive of the Northern Alliance, partly because the Turi tribe (Turkic origin) is thought to be oriented against the Taliban due to these sectarian differences. However, sectarian differences do not seem to prevent good relations between the Turi and the Sunni Jajis in Paktya.[184]

A well-known drugs- and weapons-smuggling route runs between Kurram and Paktya, which was also heavily used during the Soviet invasion. The route travels from Tere Mangle (Kurram) to Kotki, a small town in Paktya province,

176 It is 1,800 km from Karachi to Peshawar and over 1,400 km of the road have been rehabilitated.

177 Interview CNPA Nangarhar, October 2008.

178 "Khyber's Shinwaris, Afridis feel 'humiliated' by LI" Daily Times, December 18 2008.

179 Ibid.

180 "Interview with Mangal Bagh of Lashkar E- Islami" NEFA, May 2008.

181 Lashkar e Islam's leader is Mangal Bagh Afridi. In 2008, LI had control of an abandoned government outpost near the Khyber Pass and has been known to set up checkpoints on the main Torkham-Peshawar road.

182 Shuja Nawaz, "FATA – A Most Dangerous Place", Center for Strategic and International Studies, January 2009, p.14.

183 The Nation, August 24.

184 Interview, Paktya traders Kabul, November 2008.

about 15 kilometres away from the border. In Paktya's border districts, the population is mostly from the Jaji (Karlanri) and Moqbil tribes (Karlanri). Strong cross-border links exist between the Jaji and Turi and the Moqbil and Mangal/ Bangesh. The Moqbil are considered a key cross-border tribe because of their influence over the insurgency.[185]

Kurram also borders three of Nangarhar's districts (Sherzad, Khogiani and Pachir Wa Agam) that are almost entirely inhabited by the Khogiani tribe (Pashtun) and which host a significant number of heroin processing labs. These Khogiani tribesmen have cultivated opium poppy for centuries.[186] The Khogyani district of Pachir Wa Agam is also the only Nangarhar district where coalition forces continued to meet stiff resistance following the 2001 intervention and the ousting of the Taliban. It is also the site of Tora Bora, the cave complex where Al-Qaeda fighters had entrenched themselves.[187]

However, the limited data available does not indicate Khogiani involvement in extensive cross-border smuggling, nor do they appear to have particularly strong links in the FATA. On the other side of the border, insurgents – reportedly able to exert a form of control over cross-border trade by maintaining a presence along these routes - are also able to make use of these to smuggle militants and weapons. A good example is the Sherzad and Hisarak districts, which are historically connected to Kabul by the old silk route (and doubled as a weapons route during the Soviet invasion). Insurgents make use of this route to smuggle militants into Nangarhar and further to adjacent provinces including Kabul.[188]

3. Bajaur Agency is the smallest of the seven and is largely inaccessible due to its mountainous terrain. The population of Bajaur is about 600,000 people. Some of its prominent tribes are the Uthman Khel and the Mamund (Tarkani tribe),[189] although the Salarzai tribe (Tarkani) appear to be the majority.[190] Both the Mamunds and Salarzai have close kin across the border in Kunar province. The Salarzai, Mamund and Uthman Khel tribes have all reportedly founded anti-Taliban militias.

Bajaur borders the Afghan province of Kunar in four districts (southern Sirkanay, Marawara, Shaygal Wa Shitan and Northern Dangam). The tribal composition in Kunar's Marawara district is almost entirely Mohmand, while in Sirkanay district it is split roughly evenly between five tribes

(Safee, Salarzai, Shinwar, Mohmand, Alkozai). The district of Shaygal Wa Shitan has a majority of Shinwaris (70 per cent), followed by an approximately equal number of Mamund and Gujar, with smaller Salarzai and Mashwani presences. Almost half the population of Dangam is Salarzai; the remainder is split equally between the Mashwani and the Mamund tribes.

The crossing point through the Nawa Pass is an unpaved road connecting the Sirkanay district to the Bajaur Agency. It is Kunar's main trade link with Pakistan. Although Kunar's forests are severely depleted and a ban on logging is in place, there continues to be significant timber smuggling into Pakistan. Kunar is also increasingly used as an exit point for opiates, with an apparent shift away from using Shinwari-dominated districts in response to law enforcement efforts in Nangarhar.[191] Outgoing opium is mostly trafficked through the Nawa Pass using pack mules or concealed in timber shipments, with reliable reports that some processing occurs in Bajaur Agency.[192]

4. Orakzai Agency has a population of approximately 240,000 and is primarily inhabited by the Orakzai tribe (Pashtun from the Karlanri confederation). The other important tribe in this area is the Daulatzai.[193] Similar to Kurram, Shiites and Sunnis live side by side in Orakzai and are often in conflict. Regular sectarian clashes have diminished the effectiveness and influence of the Orakzai tribe and extremist organizations such as the Lashkar-e-Jhangvi have been based there for a number of years.[194] This is the only agency that does not border Afghanistan. Despite having a comparatively high literacy rate, the agency was the first to ban NGOs from operating in the area, declaring them anti-Islamic. The possession of televisions has also been declared a crime here as result of influence from the local Taliban.[195]

Darra Adam Khel is a town in Orakzai, located between Peshawar and Kohat, very close to the FATA. The city is a strategic location as it straddles the Indus highway. It is inhabited by Pashtuns of the Afridi clan, the Adam Khel. It is a historical gun manufacturing area[196] and more recently a major drug market. Adam Khel has been the scene of numerous clashes between insurgents and Pakistani forces. In one operation in October 2008, Pakistani security forces reportedly arrested 168 militants,[197] including dozens of

185 Major Darin J. Blatt et al., "Tribal Engagement in Afghanistan", *Special Warfare*, January-February 2009, Volume 22, Issue 1.

186 Sophia F.D. Woodcock, "Socio- Economic and Psychological Assessment of Fluctuations and Variations of Opium Poppy Cultivation in Key Provinces in Afghanistan: Balkh, Kandahar, Nangarhar and Central Provinces", UNODC Kabul field office, December 2006.

187 http://www.aims.org.af/afg/dist_profiles/unhcr_district_profiles/eastern/nangarhar/pachir_wa_agam.pdf.

188 Data provided by UNODC Nangarhar, May 2008.

189 Matt Dupee, "Afghan Taliban leaders nabbed in Pakistan", The long war journal, February 12, 2008.

190 http://www.pbase.com/noorkhan/pakistan.

191 Interview with UNODC surveyor, Kabul, July 27 2008.

192 Interview CNPA Nangarhar, October 2008; Interview UNODC official in Nangarhar, October 2008.

193 The Dalautzai also reside in Balkh and Kabul province; see http://www.encyclo.co.uk/deinfe/Daulatzai.

194 "Developments in the Jihadi Resurgence in Pakistan", NEFA foundation, January 2008.

195 Jamestown Foundation, "Profiles of Pakistan's Seven Tribal Agencies", *Terrorism Monito*r,Volume: 4 Issue: 20October 20, 2006

196 Francis Fukuyama, "The future of the Soviet role in Afghanistan: a trip report", *Rand Corporation*, September 1980, www.rc.rand.org/pubs/notes/2007/N1579.pdf.

197 "Detained Uzbekistani nationals confess to planning suicide attacks at behest

Uzbeks who had reportedly crossed into Pakistan via the Khyber Pass.[198] In July 2008, a *jirga* (grand meeting) of 17 tribes in the Orakzai Agency promised full support to the government should the Taliban attempts to use their territory for attacks on government security forces.[199]

5. North Waziristan Agency is the second-largest agency in terms of area. It borders Afghanistan's Khost province and is a major exit point for narcotics to Pakistan (mainly hashish but also some opiates). The Ghulam Khan official checkpoint is located near Khost city and is linked by road to Miram-Shah (agency center), continuing to Pakistan's Tochi valley (NWFP) and further to Rawalpindi (Punjab province). Some 300-500 vehicles a day are reported to pass through the checkpoint, including an undetermined amount of trucks.[200] As such, North Waziristan straddles a major transportation corridor between Pakistan and Afghanistan. The Pakistani Taliban or Tehrik-e-Taliban Pakistan (TTP) in Miram-Shah reportedly "introduced a formal schedule for taxes and criminal offenses into the area. Truckers (…), are sold six-month or yearlong passes to travel safely through the territory".[201] Miram Shah (and North Waziristan in general) are major hubs for cross-border arms trafficking, perhaps more important than Baramcha (southern Hilmand) in terms of weapons trafficking. The agency also borders Paktika province in the Gayan and Bermel districts.

North Waziristan agency is home to approximately 375,000 people, populated primarily by Utmanzai Wazirs (Karlanri confederation) and a minority of Daurs (in the highlands) and Gurbuz. The tribes maintain a monopoly on the transport business in the region but some elements are more notorious for engaging in kidnapping for ransom. The Wazir tribe has strong representation in Paktika's border district of Barmal, while the Gurbuz have strong links with the Gurbuz district of Khost in Afghanistan. North Waziristan is also the site of the Taliban shura in the town of Miram Shah. It is the Taliban council in charge of operations in Paktika, Paktya, Khost and Logar provinces.

In 2007, the former security chief for Pakistan's tribal regions, estimated that

> about 2,000 foreign militants - mostly hardened Uzbek[202], Chechen and Tajik fighters, along with a sprinkling of Arab financiers and organizers - shelter in North Waziristan, particularly in four villages

south of the town of Mir Ali, and in the territory west of Datta Khel.[203] Others stay in South Waziristan.

The village of Dande Darpa Khel in Miram-Shah is reported to be the main base of the Haqqani network. The network includes Pakistanis, Uzbeks, Chechens, Turks and Middle Easterners within its ranks,[204] but its leadership is dominated by the Zadran[205] (Karlanri confederation), a Pashtun tribe which resides in Paktya's Zadran, Shwak and Zurmat districts as well as Ghazni province.[206] The Zadran are a majority in Khost's border district of Spera[207] and in the Paktika border district of Gayan, where widespread support for the insurgency is observed. The network also maintains a strong presence in Paktya's Zadran district, which is Haqqani's home district.[208] As previously stated, it appears that the Haqqani network is involved in and "deeply dependent on smuggling heroin".[209]

6. South Waziristan Agency is the largest agency by land area, home to around 425,000 people split about evenly between the Mehsud and Ahmadzai Wazir tribes, both belonging to the Karlanri confederation. The tribes are proud of a reputation as warriors and are known for frequent blood feuds. Both tribes also played decisive roles in Afghan armed rebellions as far back as the early twentieth century. The overall political leadership of South Waziristan is dominated by conservative mullahs.

The Mehsud tribe have one of the highest literacy rates in the FATA and have produced many senior civil and military officers. They are, as one author put it "well-placed in the power hierarchy of the state".[210]

Previously the majority tribe in the agency, the Mehsuds are now at the forefront of the insurgency and one of their own is leading the Pakistan Taliban. The involvement of the Mehsud in the insurgency appears to be a recent phenomenon, dating back to 2005.[211] The Ahmadzai Wazir are divided into nine sub-tribes, with the Zali Khel as the most important.[212] Following the 2001 invasion, Al-Qaeda and

of intelligence of neighbourly country", BBC monitoring, October 21 2008

198 It should be noted here that according to Pakistan security sources, the Uzbeks in question were not citizens of Uzbekistan but rather inhabitants of Balkh and Faryab;

199 Federico Carbonari, "Pakistan: the security situation and its impact on Afghanistan", ARGO, September 2008, http://www.argoriente.it/_modules/download/download/pakistan/pakistan-ots-security-afgh-eng.pdf

200 UNAMA, Border Crossing Assessment, 2006.

201 http://www.world-check.com/media/d/content_experttalk_reference/Expert-Talk_Sep08.pdf.

202 "Pakistan detains two Uzbek citizens near Afghan border – agency", Pajhwok Afghan News, 16 February 2006

203 According to some sources, the Datta khel area is a major training ground for suicide bombers; see Presentation "Transnational Threats and International Coordination: Afghanistan in 2008", Ambassador Said T. Jawad, George Washington University, February 20, 2008.

204 Bill Roggio, "Senior leader of Haqqani network killed in Afghanistan", *The long war journal*, November 1 2007.

205 The Zadran are reported to be the largest tribe in southeastern Afghanistan.

206 Naval Postgraduate School, "Paktya Province overview", www.nps.edu/Programs/CCS/PaktyaPaktya.html.

207 Naval Postgraduate School, "Khost Executive Summary," Program for Culture and Conflict Studies, www.nps.edu/programs/ccs/Docs/Executive per cent20-Summaries/Khost per cent20Executive per cent20Summary.pdf.

208 Zadran is the home district of the leader of the Haqqani network Sarajudin Haqqani, see Shuja Nawaz, "FATA—A Most Dangerous Place", *Center for Strategic and International Studies*, January 2009.

209 Peters, Gretchen, "Seeds of Terror: How Heroin Is Bankrolling the Taliban and al Qaeda", Thomas Dunne Books, 2009, p. 37.

210 Shuja Nawaz, "FATA—A Most Dangerous Place", *Center for Strategic and International Studies*, January 2009.

211 Ibid.

212 Rizwan Zeb, "The Wana operation: Pakistan confronts islamic militants in Waziristan", Central Asia and Caucasus Analyst, March 24 2004.

other foreign elements found refuge in South Waziristan, where they developed strong links with the Zali Khel.[213] The late Nek Mohammad, a popular militant leader in the region, belonged to this sub-tribe and led the insurgency during 2003-2004.[214] The Zali Khel sub-tribe maintains a degree of dominance over Wana, the administrative and financial capital of the district. The Ahmadzai Wazir also dominates the western parts of South Waziristan, controlling the economically lucrative border trade and smuggling routes with Afghanistan.

The Wazir tribe (but not the Mehsud) also spill over into Afghanistan, specifically into the Barmal district of Paktika, a remote province where the reach of the Afghan government is very limited, particularly in the border districts. Proximity to South Waziristan has had extensive ramifications for the security in Paktika. The United Nations Department of Safety and Security assesses that most districts in the province are at the highest risk levels and the security situation further deteriorated in 2008.[215]

The town of Wana in South Waziristan is also one of the main drug hubs in the FATA.[216] Notably, the transregional and inter-tribal Tehrik-e-Taliban (TTP) appears to have integrated criminal groups into its ranks[217] and there are reports that the TTP is partly funded from involvement in the drug trade.[218] In fact, a similar strategy as that seen in Afghanistan is being followed in North Waziristan: the creation of alternative government structures complete with tax or "donation" schedules for local businesses.[219]

7. Mohmand Agency takes its name from the Mohmand tribe (Durrani confederation) that resides there and numbers about 350,000.[220] The Mohmand[221] are considered to have a relatively unified tribal structure in both Pakistan and Afghanistan (similar to the Shinwaris). When conflicts cannot be resolved, Mohmand elders from across the border are asked for help. The Mohmands are one of the three biggest tribes[222] by population, but in proportion to this they hold little power. The tribe has a proud history as guerrilla fighters and have fought most of their wars under the leadership of their mullahs.

The Mohmand agency is connected to Kunar's Khas Kunar and Marawa districts, which are majority Mohmand districts. The tribe also has representation in other border districts of Kunar (Sirkanay). The agency borders Nangarhar's districts of Lal Pur and Goshta, where Mohmands make up the overwhelming majority of the population. These Afghan districts straddle major smuggling routes/mountain passes into the Mohmand agency and the Mohmand are heavily involved in Nangarhar's transport business. One of the biggest smuggling routes runs through Goshta, which is close to 100 per cent Mohmand and gives them almost full control over trade there. From Mohmand, opiates or hashish are smuggled to the Punjab region. These same routes are used to shuttle militants from Mohmand agency into Nangarhar/Kunar. Al-Qaeda number two Ayman Al-Zawahiri is reportedly married to a woman from the Mohmand tribe. Both TTP and Al-Qaeda have a presence in Mohmand and Taliban courts have been established in the agency.[223]

A minority of Safis (Durrani confederation) also inhabit the agency,[224] including a high-level TTP leader.[225] The Safi tribe also span both sides of the border and reportedly control a number of crossings.[226]

5. North Western Frontier Province (NWFP)

According to the 1998 census, Pashtuns made up 74 per cent of the NWFP's 17.7 million population. Compared to the FATA, Pashtuns living in the NWFP tend to be more educated and urbanized, and leftist political parties like the Awami National Party (ANP) have had some electoral success there. However, insurgents in the NWFP have targeted law enforcement personnel and threatened judges in attempts to assert their influence over the area. As in the FATA, effective drug control is thus increasingly precluded by the volatile security situation in the NWFP's Provincially Administered Tribal Areas, which include Chitral, Dir, Swat, Amb and the tribal areas in Kohistan and Manshehra districts.

Pakistani Customs acknowledges this on its website: "*In recent times, the turbulent situation in southern North Western Frontier Province (…) due to creeping talibanization from*

213 Shuja Nawaz, "FATA—A Most Dangerous Place", *Center for Strategic and International Studies*, January 2009.

214 Nek Mohammed belonged to the important Yargulkhel clan of the Zalikhel sub-tribe (a traditional leading sub-tribe of the Waziris).

215 UN Department of Safety and Security (UNDSS), Afghanistan Security Report, July 2008.

216 Interview, ABP Nangarhar, October 2008.

217 Shuja Nawaz, "FATA—A Most Dangerous Place", *Center for Strategic and International Studies*, January 2009, p.18.

218 http://www.globalsecurity.org/military/world/para/ttp.htm.

219 Robert C. Martinage, "The global war on terrorism: An assessment", Center for Strategic and Budgetary Assessments, CSBA, 2008, http://www.csbaonline.org/4Publications/PubLibrary/R.20080223.The_Global_War_on_/R.20080223.The_Global_War_on_.pdf.

220 Jamestown Foundation, "Profiles of Pakistan's Seven Tribal Agencies", Terrorism Monitor ,Volume: 4 Issue 20, October 20, 2006.

221 The Mohmands are sub-divided into the Khawezai, Baezai, Halimzai, Tarakzai, Aka Khel, Burhan Khel, Dawezai, and Utmanzai; see S. Iftikhar Hussain Shah, "some major Pukhtoon tribes along the pak-afghan border", *Institute for Strategic Studies*, 2000.

222 There are also pockets of Kodakhels Khugakhels, Musakhels, Isakhels spread out throughout Mohmand; see Brig Mahmood Shah," Tribal Areas of

Pakistan and Afghanistan: Interconnectivity and Spillover Effects", *Institute of regional studies*, Seminar paper, Islamabad, May 2008.

223 Ziad Haider, "Mainstreaming Pakistan's Tribal Belt: A Human Rights and Security Imperative", Discussion paper #09-0, *Belfer Center Student Paper Series*, Harvard Kennedy School, January 2009.

224 Shuja Nawaz, op. cit.

225 "Developments in the Jihadi Resurgence in Pakistan", NEFA foundation, January 2008, http://www1.nefafoundation.org/miscellaneous/nefapakanalysis0308.pdf.

226 Ibid.

Map 5: Tribal connections at Afghanistan/FATA (Pakistan) border

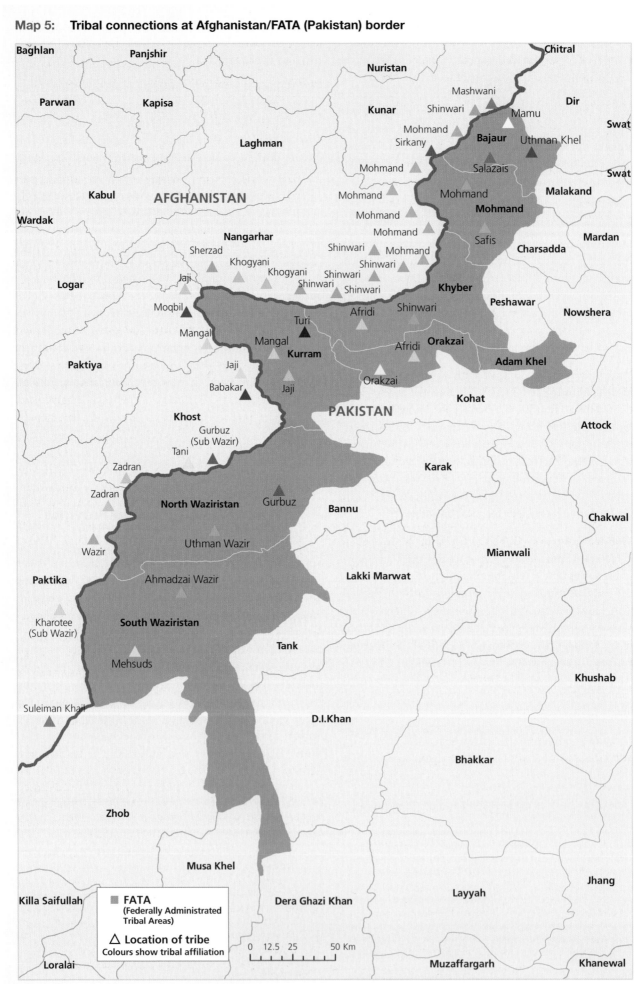

Source: Afghan Opiate Trade Programme, STAS/UNODC.

adjoining tribal areas has literally halted Customs functioning in those areas."[227] Local border controls by the Frontier Corps face similar challenges as most border posts are, in the words of the analyst Shuja Nawaz:

> isolated and poorly manned and cannot be defended against concentrated attacks by militants… [Frontier Corps] soldiers find it wiser sometimes to look the other way when well-armed Taliban bands cross the border near them.[228]

In other words, even where there are manned border posts, the cross-border tide of drugs, militants and weapons proceeds virtually unabated.

6. Balochistan

Balochistan is a mountainous region covering an area of 347,200 square km. It has a population of 7,215,700 (2002 estimate). There are 26 districts in Balochistan and the capital is the city of Quetta (Quetta district). Much of Balochistan is dry and rocky plateau with a rainfall of less than 13 cm a year. Agriculture is an important sector of the local economy, as is mining and the informal sector (smuggling). It is bordered in the east by the Pakistani provinces of Sindh, Punjab and a part of North West Frontier Province. The province has a coastline of 760 km, a 1,160 km border with Afghanistan and 835 km with the Islamic Republic of Iran.[229] Balochistan borders Afghanistan's Nimroz (223 km), Hilmand (163 km), Kandahar and Zabul provinces, as well as the southern part of Paktika. It also borders Afghanistan's largest drug hub, the Baramcha bazaar in the southern Dishu district.

The Baluch, Pashtun, and Brahui[230] are the three main tribal groups in Balochistan. The population is 45 per cent Baluch, 38 per cent Pashtun and 17 per cent others.[231] Unlike the eastern FATA, south Balochistan is not Pashtun-dominated, which has an impact on smuggling networks. Pashtun-dominated districts in Balochistan are in the south, and are generally border districts, including Zhob, Qilla Saifullah, Pishin and Qilla Abdullah.[232]

The Brahui population is estimated at 100,000 and is mostly concentrated south of the provincial capital of Quetta, in Balochistan's Kalat district. It also has strong representation in Afghanistan (mostly southern Kandahar in the border district of Shorabak), with over 250,000 individuals.[233] One important Brahui sub-tribe are the Mohammad Hasni stretching across the Hilmand valley to Nushki (Chagai district) in Balochistan.[234] Opinions differ as to whether Brahuis are ethnic Baluch or a separate group.[235] According to UNODC sources, those in control of the Baramcha drug hub (Hilmand-Dishu district) in 2006 were "Brahui Baluch".[236]

The main Pashtun tribes living along the border, apart from the Baluch tribes in the extreme south, are Mohammad khels, Noorzais, Achakzais, Kakars, and a mixture of Mando khels, Kharotis, Nasirs, and Suleyman khels.[237] Both the Noorzai and Achakzai enjoy strong representation in southern Afghanistan. The movement of refugees from Afghanistan into Balochistan further reinforces cross-border linkages between Pashtuns and many Afghan Pashtuns have Pakistani ID cards.

Cross-border trade relations are strong and most Afghan importers and traders have their offices and establishments in Quetta and other townships close to the Afghan border. There are two main cross-border trade routes passing through Balochistan. One is via Chaman to Afghanistan and the other is via Taftan/Zahedan into the Islamic Republic of Iran. The two routes intersect at Quetta (Balochistan capital) located in the centre of the province. Quetta is linked by rail and road with Karachi in the south, Chaman (Pak-Afghan Border) in the north, Taftan/Zahedan (Islamic Republic of Iran) in the west and with the main rail road network of the country in the east. The Pakistan Railway extends from Quetta to Zahedan (831 km) about 100 km inside Iran.[238]

There are two roads linking Karachi and Quetta. One is direct via Kalat district (672 km), extending up to Chaman on the Pakistani-Afghan Border (129 km). The other is via (Rohri/Sukkur) on the main trunk route that runs across the country from Karachi to Peshawar (859 km). The rail link follows the main trunk road. Afghan transit trade is carried through Chaman (and Torkham in the north), depending upon the destination in Afghanistan, although Chaman provides the shortest distance from Karachi to anywhere in Afghanistan.

Afghanistan's southern drug trafficking route has numerous exit points from Zabul, Kandahar, Hilmand and Nimroz into Balochistan. Drugs are trafficked from this region through Balochistan towards Karachi, the Makran coast

227 http://www.cbr.gov.pk/newcu/Collectorates/Pesh/Peshawar-Collectorate.asp

228 Shuja Nawaz, op. cit.

229 Chronological introduction to Balochistan, prr.hec.gov.pk/Chapters/670-1.pdf.

230 Although a distinct ethnic group, in many regions of Afghanistan and Balochistan the Brahui are virtually indistinguishable from the Baloch; see Naval Postgraduate School, Kandahar Provincial Profile, http://www.nps.edu/Programs/CCS/Kandahar.html.

231 Report of the Parliamentary Committee on Balochistan, November 2005, Report 7. http://www.senate.gov.pk/reports/mushahid/7.pdf.

232 Rodney W. Jones, "Neutralizing Extremism and Insurgency in Afghanistan and Its Borderlands", *Institute of regional studies*, Seminar paper, Islamabad, May 2008, p. 96, http://www.kas.de/wf/doc/kas_14831-544-1-30.pdf.

233 Naval Postgraduate School, Kandahar Provincial Overview, http://www.nps.edu/Programs/CCS/Kandahar.html.

234 Mariam Khan, "Border Tribal Belt: Partnership, Prosperity and Security", December 2008.

235 "Baloch Nationalism its Origin and Development", http://www.balochistan-info.com/200604/BalochNationalismitsOriginandDevelopment.pdf.

236 UNODC Mission to Nimroz province, 2006.

237 Brig. Mahmood Shah," Tribal Areas of Pakistan and Afghanistan: Interconnectivity and Spillover Effects", *Institute of regional studies*, Seminar paper, Islamabad, May 2008.

238 Interview, Abdul Majeed, Transport economist Balochistan, December 2008.

Map 6:   Afghanistan/Pakistan border: Balochistan province

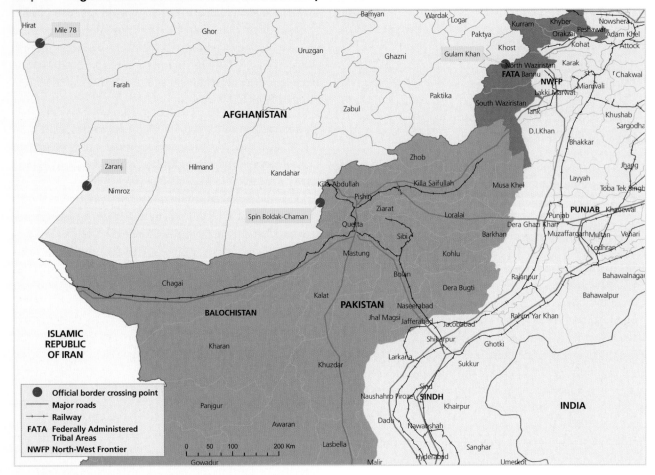

and western Iran by road. There is one official border crossing point at Spin Boldak (Kandahar), which links with the Pakistani town of Chaman. However, dozens of 'semi-official' and unofficial crossing points are also used. The Spin Boldak crossing averages 300 trucks[239] and 30,000 people crossing per day. The area called Registan (including the southern border districts of Dishu and Reg in Hilmand, Reg in Kandahar and southern Nimroz) is nearly all desert and essentially devoid of law enforcement or international presence. It is replete with insurgents and smugglers, both of whom use the numerous illegal crossing points to move back and forth across the border.

Baluch tribe

The Baluch are a Sunni Muslim people who live in eastern Iran, southern Afghanistan and western Pakistan. They are a distinct ethnic group with their own language and strong tribal traditions which tend to prevail over religious identity. The tribal system within the Baluch is quite strong and there are few faultlines among the various sub-tribes of the Baluch. Compared to most Pashtun tribes, the Baluch tribes are hierarchical, including the appointment of chiefs (*sardars*), who tend to possess more power than leaders of Pashtun tribes. There are numerous Baluch tribes, each with its own clan subdivisions. Two Baluch sub-tribes of

particular importance in terms of numbers and cross-border influence are the Rakhshanis who have representation in Iran, Pakistan and Afghanistan and the Sanjrani Baluch who are present in Dalbandin up to Robat-I-Jali and into Nimroz province.[240]

Estimates of the number of Baluch in the Islamic Republic of Iran range from 1–4 million, nearly all of whom are Sunni Muslims (in contrast to other Iranians, who are overwhelmingly Shia).[241] These are concentrated in the province of Sistan-Balochistan and Zabol, the latter mostly in border areas.[242] In Pakistan, the total Baluch population is approximately 6 million, mostly concentrated in Balochistan.[243] In neighbouring Afghanistan, the Baluch account for 2 per cent of the population, or about 0.7 million people.[244]

There are pockets of Baluch settlements in the Afghan provinces of Farah, Hirat, Badghis, Faryab and Jawzjan. Most Afghan Baluch, however, live in the border areas of

239 Asian Development Bank, *Brief description of border posts and ICD's*, 2006.

240 Mariam Khan, "Border Tribal Belt: Partnership, Prosperity and Security", December 2008.

241 "Balochi Nationalists Intensify Violent Rebellion in Iran", *Jamestown Foundation*, Terrorism Monitor Volume: 7 Issue: 3, February 9, 2009 .

242 John R. Bradley, "Iran's ethnic tinderbox", *The Washington Quarterly*, Winter 2006-07.

243 United States Central Intelligence Agency, "Pakistan," The World Factbook, April 9, 2009.

244 Institute for the study of war, "Pakistan and Afghanistan", http://www.understandingwar.org/print/647, April 15 2009.

Nimroz, Hilmand and Kandahar. In Afghanistan's Nimroz province, the Baluch are the majority ethnic group. According to USAID, less than a quarter of Nimroz's trade with Iran is legal and more than 70 per cent of the local population participates in smuggling activities.[245] Baluchis in Nimroz are very closely oriented to Zabol and the Iranian province of Sistani-Balochistan and, to a lesser degree, Pakistan's Balochistan province.

The border district of Chahar Burjah in Nimroz is overwhelmingly Baluch and many reportedly own property in Iran's adjacent Zabol province. In 2006, UNODC surveyed Shirabad,[246] a small town in the Islamic Republic of Iran near the Sistan-Balochistan provincial capital of Zahedan and close to Nimroz province. 40-60 per cent of residents earned their living either by smuggling goods between Iran and Pakistan or by providing logistical support to local drug traffickers.[247] In Hilmand, the drug hub of Baramcha was reportedly founded by an ethnic Brahui/Baluch, the drug kingpin Haji Juma Khan, who was recently convicted by a US court.

Narcotics cross from southern Hilmand (for example, Baramcha bazaar), southern Nimroz (Robat-I-Jali bazaar) or Kandahar into Balochistan before heading west towards the Iranian province of Sistan-Balochistan for onward transport towards Turkey and western markets. Drug convoys in Balochistan are mostly (but not exclusively) manned by Baluch tribesmen. The convoys are usually comprised of 2-3 vehicles, although larger convoys are not uncommon). Convoys often possess heavy weaponry, including reports of surface-to-air missiles.[248] Motorcyclists act as scouts for these convoys and satellite phones are used for early warnings and to arrange passage. Sand dunes and desolate terrain give traffickers a good chance of moving undetected and convoys transit from one staging area to another at night. When these mostly nocturnal smuggling operations are discovered by law enforcement, firefights almost always ensue as traffickers are unwilling to give up their cargo and have good reason to believe that they can outgun the authorities.[249] Of note, the Baluch also control trade routes in the reverse direction, such as fuel import from Iran to the southern Hilmand districts by the route of Taftan.

As the drugs change hands, smuggling methods diversify. Crossing into the Islamic Republic of Iran, many traffickers use camel caravans to avoid raising law enforcement suspicion, but also because of the nature of the terrain. Another established route transports drugs to the southern Qasim port (international container port), smaller fishing ports and open areas of the Makran coast, for onward shipment to the Gulf states, East Africa and Europe. Karachi port is especially important, according to a 2007 UNODC report, as most narcotics entering Karachi come from Balochistan.[250] A reverse route from Karachi transports precursors towards Kandahar and Hilmand.

To summarize, the Baluch depend heavily on smuggling income and run the dominant smuggling networks heading south-west from Afghanistan. However, very little opium cultivation occurs on Baluch land, primarily because they inhabit mostly non-arable land. Therefore, while not traditionally interested in Pashtun-led insurgency, the Baluch depend on relations with Pashtuns to generate most of their drug-related profits. For drug trafficking, by volume, the interface between Baluch and Pashtun tribes is probably the most significant one between any two ethnic groups in the world.

Chagai district

Chagai is perhaps the most important of Pakistan's districts in terms of opiate trafficking. It borders the three key provinces of Hilmand, Kandahar and Nimroz, and large quantities of drugs are transported through the district center and main bazaar, Dalbandin. Much of the land in the areas from and around Nokkundi to Dalbandin is reportedly owned by the Sanjrani, a Baluch tribe with links to Afghanistan.[251] The area has long been known as a major transit point for Afghan opiates traveling from Hilmand and Kandahar to the Makran coast or to the Islamic Republic of Iran.[252]

In June 2006, Pakistan's ANF reported the destruction of nine laboratories in the area of Malgai, about 800 meters away from the Pakistan-Afghan border in the Chagai district, seizing 2,137 kg of morphine base, 50 kg of ammonium chloride and huge quantities of arms and ammunition. Large seizures in Chagai are mostly related to opium poppy cultivation in Hilmand and arrive from the Baramcha opiate market in Hilmand's adjoining Dishu district. That district is 80 per cent Pashtun and 20 per cent Baluch, the latter mostly present in the border areas.[253] A 2002 UNHCR report estimated that 10 per cent of the population in

245 USAID, "The Contribution of Regional Markets to Afghan Wheat Supplies", May 2007.

246 It is estimated that out of Shirabad's 55,000 inhabitants, 20-30 per cent are Afghan refugees; see Nahidsiam doust ,"Women in Iran Gain From Community approach",http://www.undp.org.sa/Reports/Choices per cent20Sep per cent2004.pdf., September 2004.

247 "Drug Supply Reduction: An overview of drug supply and trafficking in Iran", http://www.unodc.org/pdf/iran/drug_crime_situation/dsr/Supply_Reduction_trends_and_trafficking.pdf.

248 UNODC office Pakistan, Project document 2003.

249 Iran, for example, has suffered considerable human and financial costs in responding to both direct traffic from Afghanistan and the substantial opiate shipments arriving via Pakistan (losing 3,500 officers in 20 years). In response to increased trafficking, the Iranian government has reportedly spent upwards of $600 million to strengthen its border with Pakistan, using ditches, barbwire fences and numerous armed checkpoints.

250 Eisa Nang, UNODC mission report to Pakistan, 21 April – 2 May 2007, p.5.

251 http://www.paktribune.com/news/index.shtml?179172.

252 Pierre Arnaud Chouvy, Opium Smuggling routes from Afghanistan to Europe and Asia, Jane's Intelligence Review, March 1 2003, http://www.geopium.org/JIR3.htm.

253 UNHCR Sub-Office Kandahar, "District profile: Helmand", 2002, http://83.138.163.176/afg/dist_profiles/unhcr_district_profiles/southern/helmand/dishu.pdf.

Dishu was involved in smuggling (mostly opiates), while 80 per cent are labor migrants in Pakistan, the Islamic Republic of Iran and southern Afghanistan.[254]

The "Baramcha route" is of utmost importance to trafficking because of its numerous laboratories, its location on the border and large opiates stocks. The main drug hub in the area (indeed in all of Afghanistan) is located in this village, which straddles the Pakistan-Afghanistan border. Baramcha is frequently accessed from Nimroz along the Hilmand river into Dishu district and is linked by trade routes to the Dalbandin bazaar in Balochistan. Hilmand's labs are fed by the same route flowing in the reverse direction and the Afghan Border Police officers in Nimroz assessed that most precursor chemicals enter Hilmand through Baramcha.[255]

Chagai also borders Nimroz. In September 2006, a UNODC mission to Nimroz province reported no border posts on the entire length of the Nimroz/Pakistan border (and only one post on the southernmost 100 km on the Iranian border), leaving approximately 300 km of porous border for smuggling. ANP officers interviewed during this mission stated that the 223 km border with Pakistan is an "ideal smuggling route." The province remains virtually isolated from the country's security apparatus and the 5th ABP brigade is reported to be the only government presence, as neither ISAF nor the ANA maintain a base in Nimroz. Like much of Afghanistan, Nimroz has been experiencing rising insecurity since 2005, particularly around Zaranj city and the neighbouring district of Khash Rod.[256] ANP officers interviewed in 2006 were reporting persistent and growing Taliban activity with extensive links to drug trafficking networks,[257] a nexus which has intensified in the last two years.

Another of Chagai's neighboring provinces, Kandahar, is dominated by Pashtuns, with minorities of Baluch nomads in the south-west Reg district.[258] Chagai's border with the Reg district contains a number of well-established smuggling routes, controlled by Baluch tribesmen with strong links to their kin in Balochistan, Nimroz and Sistan-Balochistan (Iran). Chagai also borders the southern part of Kandahar's Shorabak district, populated almost exclusively by the Bares (Barech, Bareq), a Pashtun tribe of the smaller Sarbani confederation,[259] reported to be significantly involved in narcotics trafficking (and other forms of smuggling).

Qilla Abdullah district

Qilla Abdullah borders Kandahar's districts of Spin Boldak, Arghestan, as well as parts of Maruf and Shurabak. The population of Qilla Abdullah district was estimated to be over 400,000 in 2005, predominantly of the Achakzai Pashtun tribe,[260] which has a strong presence in Chaman and across the border in Kandahar, particularly in the Spin Boldak area.[261] The Pakistani Achakzais reportedly control large sections of the transportation sector in Balochistan[262] and maintain strong links with their brethren in Kandahar. The Achakzai and Noorzai tribes also maintain close cross-border economic ties, again around the strategic Spin Boldak/Chaman area.

In an illustration of how widespread and accepted the smuggling activities are, the government of Balochistan's own webpage describes the area of Chaman as "the major centre for smuggling activities. It is a paradise for smugglers from both sides of the border".[263] In fact, the entire district of Qilla Abdullah is one giant smuggling route for hashish and opiates. Other research corroborates this – for example, in 2006, researchers for the Asian Development Bank observed similar phenomena in the adjacent border crossing area of Spin Boldak: "Trucks and cargo as well as people and non-motorized vehicle move across the border through authorized and unauthorized route going in all directions avoiding capture by customs control which is a small temporary shed in front of the border gate or even by customs police control a few hundred yards down the road."[264]

A large seizure in December 2008 involved a train of donkeys carrying more than 550 kg of hashish in the Gulistan area.[265] The same method was recorded in a similar seizure in the same area in July 2008 where 730 kg of hashish had been loaded onto pack mules.[266] Another large seizure - 1,200 kg of opium - occurred in the same district in November 2008. From this district, narcotics can travel west towards the Islamic Republic of Iran but also travel directly to Karachi. As an example, in October 2008 the Pakistani Coast Guard recovered 220 kg of hashish from a vehicle outbound from Qilla Abdullah on its way to Karachi using the main RDC (N-25) highway.[267]

---

254 Ibid.

255 Phone interview with Nimroz border official, September 14 2008.

256 Matt DuPee, "Coalition and Insurgents vie for control of southwestern Afghanistan Part 1- Nimroz Province", the Long War Journal, May 25 2008.

257 UNODC mission to Nimroz, 2006.

258 As well as Hazara, Hindu and Uzbek minorities.

259 http://www.khyber.org/pashtotribes/b/barak.shtml.

260 The Achakzai tribe are further divided into into two large sub-groupings, the Gujanzais and the Badinzais. They have two major clans living in Qila Abdullah, the Mallezai and Ashemi. The Mallezais (and some Asherzais) are native to Baluchistan, while most of the Asherzais migrated from neighboring Kandahar and other southern provinces of Afghanistan, first in the 1950s and later in the 1980s. They have since settled permanently in Chaman and other parts of the Qilla Abdullah and adjacent Pishin districts.

261 Naval Postgraduate School, Kandahar Provincial Overview, www.nps.edu/Programs/CCS/Kandahar.html.

262 "Afghans in Quetta: Settlements, Livelihoods, Support Networks and Cross-Border Linkages" AREU, January 2006, p.17.

263 http://www.balochistan.gov.pk/New Folder/Social Killa Abdulla.htm.

264 Asian Development Bank, "Islamic Republic of Afghanistan Ministry of Public Works/Asian Development Bank cross border trade and transport facilitation", Draft Final Report, June 2006, p.43.

265 Associated Press of Pakistan news agency, 02 December 2008.

266 Associated Press of Pakistan news agency, 30 July 2008.

267 Associated Press of Pakistan news agency, 14 October 2008.

Terrain on Kandahar's southern border with Pakistan

Source: UNODC provincial office in Kandahar.

Qilla Saifullah district

This district is centrally located between Quetta and Zhob to the north and east, Loralai district to the south and to the west by Pishin district and Afghanistan (Kandahar province, Maruf district). The district limits start some 88 km from Quetta on the Quetta- Zhob-Dera Ismail Khan road.[268] The district sits on a road junction, the Quetta-Zhob-Dera Ismail Khan (N-50) and the Qilla Saifullah-Loralai-Dera Ghazi Khan (N-70). It has a total population of 200,000 and most of its inhabitants are Pashtuns from the Kakar tribe.

Zhob district

Zhob is bounded by Afghanistan and South Waziristan (FATA) to the north, to the east by the tribal area adjoining Dera-Ismail-Khan district of the NWFP and Musakhel district, and to the south and south-west by Loralai and Qilla Saifullah districts. This district borders the Afghan provinces of Paktika and Zabul (45 km border). Zhob district is inhabited mostly by Kakars (Ghurghusht confederation),[269] Suleymankhels (Ghilzai), Nasirs (Ghilzai), Kharotis (Ghilzai). Across the border in Zabul, Ghilzais also constitute a majority (over 90 per cent) in the Shamulzayi border district and the adjacent Atghar district. The major ethnic groups living in adjacent Zabul province are Tohki (Ghilzai), Hotak (Ghilzai), Suleymankhels, Kakars, Popalzai (Durrani), Nasirs and Shamulzai (Ghilzai).[270]

Zhob connects to Afghanistan through a number of cross-border trails, including at Badini (a village straddling the border and connecting with Zinzeer in Pakistan). From Zhob, insurgents enter Zabul's Shalmuzai district, which acts as a major militant inflow route into Afghanistan. The province has been the site of numerous AGE attacks.[271]

Reliable sources assess that in Zabul's border district (Shalmuzai) the local insurgency (composed almost totally of the Shalmulzai and Hotak tribes) enjoys significant control outside the district centre.[272] On the border with Paktika, UNAMA reports that Taliban insurgents "are believed to be running checkpoints opposite Terwa district (Paktika), where they host/train foreign fighters, including Kashmiris."[273] This same route is identified as a narcotics smuggling route.

Although the district has historically been an important inter-provincial and international route of illicit trafficking,[274] law enforcement officers interviewed by UNODC did not believe Zhob to be a significant cross-border smuggling point due to the poor road infrastructure on both sides of the border. It was suggested that Zabul's crossing points may not be used by traffickers because of the reported difficult mountainous terrain (although less so than border provinces in eastern Afghanistan), which gradually becomes less challenging as the border slopes further south toward Kandahar. Even so, UNAMA reports indicate that 100-150 cars and trucks illegally cross the Zabul-Pakistan border on a busy day,[275] suggesting that, as in the east, trade networks are undaunted by difficult terrain. This is logical, since much of Zabul's economy is linked with Pakistan, specifically the Pakistani markets of Muslimbagh (district Qilla Saifullah) and Pishin district,[276] to which many crossing points lead. Nevertheless Zhob district does not seem to be a major trafficking area when compared with Balochistan's other districts.

Pishin district

This district borders parts of Kandahar's Shorabak and Maruf districts. The population is estimated at around 400,000 and approximately 150,000 Afghan refugees also reside in Pishin.[277] The major tribes in the district are Kakars, Achakzais and Sayeed and Alizai.[278] It is the site of the Jungle Pir Alizai camp (reportedly closed down in 2007), home to some 35,000 Afghan refugees in 2007. The camp was established following the Soviet invasion in 1979 and, like Gardi Jangle, it has been described by Pakistani officials as a hub for militants and drug traffickers.[279] Pishin straddles the main transport corridor linking Spin Boldak to Quetta to Karachi (National Highway Quetta-Khuzdar-Karachi) and as such is a major transit district for a significant portion of Karachi-bound narcotics.

per cent5C11 per cent5C10 per cent5Cstory_10-11-2006_pg7_11.

272 Interview CNPA Kabul, November 2008.

273 UNAMA Border Crossing Assessment, 2006.

274 S. M. H. Zaidi et al., Programme development of drug abuse control in Baluchistan, Pakistan".

275 UNAMA Border Crossing Assessment, 2006.

276 Personal communication with traders based in Zabul, Kabul, July 2008.

277 http://drought.iucnp.org/fertile.htm.

278 District Profile: Northern Balochistan – Pishin, Dawn, http://www.dawn.com.pk/weekly/herald/herald90.htm.

279 "Afghanistan: After Mullah Dadullah", South Asia Conflict Report: May 2007, June 11 2007, Pakistan Institute for Peace Studies.

268 cmsdata.iucn.org/downloads/pk_idv_qillasaifullah.pdf.

269 As well as with Mandokhels, and Sheranis, Haripals, Babars, Lawoons, Khosty and Sayeds ; see Chronological introduction to Balochistan, prr.hec.gov.pk/Chapters/670-1.pdf.

270 In addition to pockets of Ludin and Kuchi nomads; see Zabul Provincial profile. UNAMA, 2006.

271 "Taliban fighters talk tactics while safe in Pakistan?", Daily Times Monitor, November 10, 2006 http://www.dailytimes.com.pk/default.asp?page=2006

7. Refugee camps

Millions of Afghans moved to Pakistan after the Soviet invasion, with more joining them during the civil war (1994-1996) and the war with the Taliban (2001). Although refugees have started to move back to Afghanistan, according to UNHCR, there were around three million Afghan refugees in Pakistan in 2005. According to UNHCR's 2005 census, there are 783,545 Afghan refugees in Balochistan, and the majority of them are Pashtuns. Most Pashtuns live in Quetta or adjoining areas, although there are dispersed pockets close to the border with Afghanistan. According to UNHCR, Afghan Pashtuns make up 27 per cent of the population in Quetta and 20 per cent of the total population in the Chagai district (approximately 25,000).[280]

Conditions in refugee camps are very difficult. Economic and social deprivation among young refugees creates fertile ground for recruiting insurgents and encouraging extremist doctrines.[281] The Pakistani government has contended that four camps in particular had become sanctuaries for cross-border insurgents, these are: the Kacha Gari and Jalozai camps in NWFP (reportedly closed in 2008) and the Pir Alizai and Gardi Jangle in Balochistan.[282] Data collected by UNAMA and UNDSS suggest that some suicide bombers are Afghan refugees settled in Pakistan. According to some sources, elements based in the Gardi Jangle camp and the adjacent Baramcha bazaar (Hilmand province) provided training for suicide bombers.[283] In 2002, Gardi Jangle also reportedly hosted some fleeing high-ranking Taliban officials.[284] Of importance to this research, a minority of the camps are also said to be used by drug traffickers to store narcotics and consolidate shipments.[285] The two camps most often connected to drug traffickers are Pir Alizai (Pishin district) and Gardi Jangle (Chagai district), both in Balochistan.[286]

Afghanistan's most prominent drug hub in Baramcha connects with Gardi Jangle in the Dalbandin area of Chagai district.[287]

Gardi Jangle is located on the main road between Dalban-

din and the Afghanistan border. It is viewed by many experts as a consolidation and transshipment point for narcotics and may also be a processing area. The Gardi Jangle camp was reportedly closed in 2007 by the Pakistani government, which cited trafficking as the reason for its closure.[288] Although it is located in a remote area and difficult to access, it has been the site of some large seizures, including 700 kilograms of morphine in 2002 and 574 kilograms of hashish in February 2005. One of the most significant seizures took place in 2004 and involved 1,600 kilograms of heroin found buried in the Baramcha area (Pakistani side) in Amuri village.[289] From Gardi Jangle narcotics are transported to various Pakistani seaports and further to Gulf countries or into Iran's Sistan-Balochistan province. ABP officers interviewed by UNODC have also asserted that Gardi Jangle was the main precursor transit point supplying southern labs.[290] The deputy of the Afghan Security Council also assessed that many Afghan had used the camp as a base.[291] Indeed, there appears to be consensus among Afghan and Pakistani sources that Gardi Jangle is a narcotics hub and useful to the insurgency. As previously mentioned, another probable drug hub is the old refugee camp of Pir Alizai (Pishin district), located 62 km west of Quetta on the Quetta-Chaman road, populated by a tribe of the same name (a sub-tribe of the Achakzai). Jane's Intelligence reports also that many itinerant harvesters come to Hilmand during harvest time (May-June) from Gardi Jangle.[292]

Highlights of tribal links with opiate trade

The interspersion of ethnic and tribal groups across Afghanistan's borders provides a conducive social environment for drug trafficking. This section has highlighted these interactions on the Pakistan-Afghanistan border, but similar conditions occur on all of Afghanistan's borders, with similar effects on each smuggling route.

The opium economy presents clear examples of inter-ethnic cooperation, such as Pashtun and Baluch traffickers in the south. By contrast, in the east, cross-border trafficking is a Pashtun affair, sometimes centred on a single tribe, such as in Nangarhar, where several border districts are uniquely inhabited by one tribe. While some tribes have taken decisions against involvement in the opiate trade, most communities in border areas rely to a greater or lesser extent on smuggling and irregular migration. The profit motive should not be downplayed, but the strength of the tribe as a political unit makes it an important element of analysis of trafficking flows, particularly in southern and eastern Afghanistan. Indeed, tribalism and the profit motive are not mutually exclusive – tribal connections are a vehicle to

280 http://www.unhcr.org/cgi-bin/texis/vtx/home/opendoc.pdf?tbl=SUBSITES&id=464dca012.

281 It is worth remembering that the Taliban movement partly grew out of Afghan refugee camps in Pakistan.

282 Although slated to close in 2008, at the time of this writing the status of Pir Alizai and Gardi Jangle remains unclear.

283 Said T. Jawad, Presentation "Transnational Threats and International Coordination: Afghanistan in 2008", George Washington University, February 20, 2008, http://www.gwumc.edu/hspi/ART/AfghanPresentation.pdf.

284 Ilene R. Prusher and Philip Smucker "Al Qaeda quietly slipping into Iran, Pakistan", the Christian Science Monitor, January 14, 2002.

285 "Afghan refugees concerned over imminent closure of two camps in Balochistan", IRIN, May 6 2007.

286 Shahzadi Beg, "The Ideological Battle", p. 171, Institute of regional studies, Seminar paper, Islamabad, May 2008.

287 There are reportedly some 43,000 residents still inhabiting the camp. Source: Thomas H. Johnson, On the Edge of the Big Muddy: The Taliban Resurgence in Afghanistan, China and Eurasia Forum Quarterly, Volume 5, No. 2 (2007) p. 93-129.

288 BAAG Afghanistan Monthly Review, July 2005, http://www.baag.org.uk/downloads/monthly per cent20review per cent2005/61 per cent20June per cent20 per cent2005.pdf.

289 RILO Monthly Bulletin for Asia and the Pacific, January 2004.

290 UN Mission to Afghanistan Mazar-Sharif and Hairatan, (25-27 March 2008).

291 Interview, deputy security council, November 17 2008.

292 The changing structure of the Afghan opium trade, Jane's intelligence 2006

Map 7: Refugee camps and heroin seizure locations in Balochistan, 2002-2008

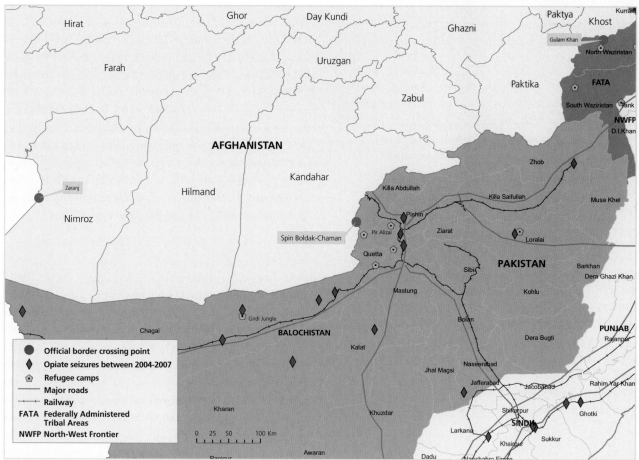

Source: UNODC individual drug seizure database.

reduce risk and increase profit, which in turn bolsters the strength of tribal connections.

Cross-border ethnic links in the north and west of Afghanistan – for example among Tajiks – facilitate crime in a way familiar from organized crime groups around the world. Shared ethnicity creates opportunities for collaboration and some social enforcement mechanisms that enhance trust. However, in tribal parts of Afghanistan and Pakistan – primarily rural Pashtun areas - these mechanisms are stronger to the point of becoming qualitatively different. The prominence of tribal relations in communal politics means that involvement in crime is just one decision in a long list that is mediated and enforced by custom. This tends to tie individual tribal members more closely to criminality – even when not personally involved – and encourages them to defend their brethren assiduously, with correspondingly greater benefits to traffickers than the more commercial relationships among trafficking groups that rely on ethnicity in the north and west.

The importance of smuggling to many border communities' economies suggests that a nuanced approach to counter-narcotics is required. It is more difficult for tribal leaders to defend a reliance on drug income and it is less threatening to focus on counter-narcotics rather than irregular trading more broadly, particularly by engaging through tribal

structures. Recognizing the significance of tribal politics can thereby enable effective responses at the most relevant social center of gravity in many of Afghanistan's prime opiate exit points and precursor import routes.

8. Corruption

Afghanistan currently ranks in the second lowest percentile on the World Bank's corruption index.[293] A significant component of this index is based on the activities of corruption prone government agencies. Survey after survey reveals the Afghan perception of law enforcement and courts as among the most corrupt institutions in the country.[294] A 2006 poll by the Asia Foundation found that 77 per cent of Afghans believed corruption was a problem at the national level.[295]

In Afghanistan, there is corruption among low level law enforcement officers, but also members of the judiciary and senior government officials. As one author put it "There are government officials at the district, provincial, and national levels involved in drug-trafficking, who are more interested

293 http://info.worldbank.org/governance.

294 UNDP, Afghan Human Development Report, 2007.

295 *Asia Foundation*, "Afghanistan in 2006: A Survey of the Afghan People", 2008.

in making money than in serving their populations". [296] In other words, there are serious accusations that officials are receiving kickbacks from organized crime groups in return for protection and some may have a direct involvement in the drug trade.

At the outset, it is important to make a rough functional distinction between low-level/common corruption and high-level so-called "grand corruption" in Afghanistan. The majority of corruption in Afghanistan is low-level, such as "gift payments" to public officials (such as law enforcement and court officers) and to other service providers, including in the private sector. Related to the opium economy, it involves *inter alia* bribes on the roads and/or border crossings. The use of the adjective "low-level" does not mean harmless, This corruption of course has a negative impact/ In the above examples it drives up the costs of transportation and deprives the Afghan government of much needed funds.

High-level or "grand" corruption refers to corrupt acts performed by politicians and other top state officials (including those in administrative positions). In the Afghan context, segments of the state apparatus have effectively been "captured" by a specific client group, organized crime. In this sense it is "not only a failure of state institutions but also a means for enrichment and empowerment of political elites." [297]

Low-level corruption

Most interactions with government services in Afghanistan generally involve some form of bribery. [298] A survey conducted by Integrity Watch Afghanistan in 2006 revealed that nearly half of Afghan households had paid an average of US$ 100 in bribes that year. [299]

A 2006 poll by the Asia Foundation revealed that 36 per cent of Afghans said they had had to bribe a police officer at some point. [300] There have also been allegations of possible collusion with the drug trade. In 2006, the CNPA arrested a former police officer for selling two kilograms of heroin to a law enforcement informant. The accused had previously directed a special narcotics unit within the Ministry of Interior. There have also been cases of drugs concealed and moved in official police vehicles. Similar allegations have been made about other agencies such as the Afghan National Army (ANA). [301]

Logistics companies and locals confirmed the existence of illegal payment systems across Afghanistan. Interviews with truck drivers in Jalalabad revealed that unofficial customs and other taxes were routine at Torkham (Nangarhar-Pakistan border) and a number of other crossing points. [302] In 2006, researchers for the ADB made the following observations: "According to trader sources, there are some 15 check points between Torkham and Jalalabad charging anywhere between $10-100 per container. Similar assertions have been made about other border link roads. During field mission by road the team observed numerous check points at various points along the road especially at entry and exit of all cities and towns with personnel collecting 'fees' from all moving vehicles especially trucks, buses and taxis." [303] In some eastern border provinces, district authorities levy an illegal tax on each truck crossing into Afghanistan. [304]

In the case of trade, both licit and illicit, this involves payment to law enforcement/ANA officers. Rates increase when the goods are moved across legal entry points where custom officials are the main beneficiaries. Afghan Border Police (ABP) and ANA officers frequently accept bribes but also demand illegal payments from licit traders and travellers. As the Afghan Research and Evaluation Unit (AREU) interviews with truckers revealed: "You can fill a truck with bricks or for that matter anything else and bribe your way from Peshawar to Jalalabad without any documentation." [305] It should be noted that, in many cases, border control officers often accept bribes without knowing what commodity is being smuggled into the country.

The bribes are not confined to border areas. Indeed, they extend to all of Afghanistan's roads where various law enforcement agencies (and warlords) engage in what has been termed the "stop-and-bribe." For example, in July 2008, a BBC report investigating this practice found that the typical two-hour journey from Torkham crossing point to Jalalabad (Nangarhar province) was completed in four hours due to the number of checkpoints/bribes along the way. [306]

This practice also exists on a regional level and bribes can cost long-distance drivers up to $10,000 a year: "Hauling freight across the country, say from Iran to Pakistan's Khyber Pass, a truck could be stopped 400 times." [307] In response to informal payments to customs/ABP, many small traders prefer to use illegal border crossing points and seek the help of specialized smuggling networks to move their commodities. Of course, other traders simply wish to avoid paying

296 Seth G. Jones, "the state of the Afghan insurgency", RAND, December 2007.

297 UNODC et al., "fighting corruption in Afghanistan: a roadmap for strategy and action", February 2007.

298 UNDP, "Afghan human development report", 2007.

299 Integrity Watch Afghanistan (IWA), a Survey report, March 2007, Kabul; in UNDP, "Afghan human development report", 2007.

300 Asia Foundation, *Afghanistan in 2006: A Survey of the Afghan People*, October 2006

301 Naval Postgraduate School, "Summary of Afghan National Army" Program for Culture and Conflict Studies, http://www.nps.edu/programs/ccs

302 Interview, Nangarhar, October 2008.

303 Asian Development Bank, "Islamic Republic of Afghanistan Ministry of Public Works/Asian Development Bank cross border trade and transport facilitation", Draft Final Report, June 2006, p.41.

304 Interview, Nangarhar, October 2008.

305 Sarah Lister et al., "Understanding markets in Afghanistan: A case study of the market in construction materials", AREU, June 2004.

306 Bilal Sarwary, *"Bribery rules on Afghan roads"* July 29 2008, http://www.news.bbc.co.uk/2/hi/south_asia/7519189.stm.

307 Arthur Kent, "Covering up Karzai & Co.", *Policy options*, Institute for research on public policy, July 2007, http://www.irpp.org/po/archive/jul07/kent.pdf.

legal taxes and circumvent export bans (such as in Pakistan). According to customs officers in Kabul, at least US$ 400 million (which is 3.5 per cent of Afghanistan's 2008 GDP) in tax revenue was thus lost in 2008.[308]

The impact on Afghanistan's economy is obvious and the main complaint among the business community remains the corruption of personnel at border crossings[309] and on the many checkpoints (official or unofficial) which impede commerce and "do nothing to stop the drug business." In April 2007, this continuing practice led to a strike by Afghan truckers.

The opium impact on licit trade is also detrimental to the perception of Afghan traders in international commerce. The ministry of Commerce and Industry acknowledges this in its 2007 strategy paper: "It must be noted also that the level of confidence concerning Afghan traders and transport operators is very low due to historic perception that many shippers in Afghanistan are involved in smuggling or trafficking in illegal drugs."

Motivations: Official and unofficial salaries

Much of this corruption is the outcome of great economic hardship. Although there have been significant material improvements, the country has not recovered from the severe economic crises brought about by 30 years of conflict. Afghanistan's per capita income (US$ 415) put it near the bottom of the world's states in 2008.

The resulting low salaries of Afghan law enforcement officials may contribute to fostering an environment in which corruption readily occurs. The average salary of civil servants in Afghanistan is often insufficient to meet basic needs and some corruption is clearly a means to supplement the low incomes. An Afghan National Army (ANA) recruit typically earns only US$ 70 a month[310] while judges in the provinces reportedly receive around $35-50 per month.[311] All but the most senior law enforcement personnel are poorly paid and may thus be susceptible to bribes from drug traffickers and others.

It should be noted, however, that research has not found a significant relationship between these two variables (corruption and low salaries). Additionally, increasing salaries may not necessarily provide the most adequate solution. In an attempt to stamp out corruption, the Taliban regime reportedly raised judges' salaries ten times. This initiative only led to higher bribes and gave judges "the double benefit of raising the salary".[312]

The issue of salaries notwithstanding, the incentives for corrupt behaviour are huge, especially when taking into account the amount of drug money circulating outside financial structures. One related indicator is the widespread knowledge that postings to lucrative border crossings are organized by payments to superiors. In Nimroz province, prospective border guards apparently have to pay upwards of US$ 30,000 to be appointed to work at the border where an officer may make US$ 50,000 a month in illegal payments.[313] In Badakshan province, the bribe for getting hired as chief of police in border districts was reported to be upwards of US$ 20,000.[314] This is further corroborated by a report from Jane's Intelligence Review which found that in 2006, a mid-level position in the highway police was purchased for US$ 25,000.[315] Research by UNODC in Central Asia mirrors these findings. For example, a 2006 UNODC study of the Central Asia-China and Central Asia-Afghanistan borders found that border guards had to pay large bribes to superiors in order to be posted at major crossing points.[316]

Smuggling and "grand corruption"

There are strong incentives to use illegal border crossings and avoid the main roads for low-level licit and illicit traders. Larger, well-connected trafficking networks, however, can count on contacts - and/or afford the bribes needed - to move opiates/precursors within and out of Afghanistan. These contacts are high-level officials who ensure safe passage for drug convoys. Once inside the country, the same procedures apply, as demonstrated by a 2007 UNODC study on opiates flows inside Afghanistan which concluded that "approximately 70 per cent of drug trafficking takes place along the main roads, sustained by the strong support and involvement of the governmental authorities".[317] One UNODC surveyor summed it up succinctly "Big dealers use big roads, small dealers use small roads".[318]

Corrupt government or law enforcement officials thus facilitate the opium chain by enabling smooth trafficking operations and neutralizing law enforcement. While there are intermittent reports of high-level traffickers being arrested on drug-related charges, these are rarely prosecuted or dismissed.[319] Successful prosecutions of any significant traffickers are often overturned by a simple bribe or protection from above.

The establishment of the Criminal Justice Task Force (CJTF) in May 2005 was partially a response to this

308 Interview with Afghan customs officials, Kabul, March 2009.

309 ADB, "Afghanistan's trade with CARECC neighbors: evidence from surveys of broder crossing points in Hairatan and Sher Khan Bandar", 2008.

310 Laura Schuurmans, "Peace and Stability, Good Governance and Development in Afghanistan", *Institute of regional studies*, Seminar paper, Islamabad, May 2008, http://www.kas.de/wf/doc/kas_14831-544-1-30.pdf.

311 "Afghanistan justice sector overview", UNAMA, April 2007.

312 Johann Wagner, Interview with Ministry of Justice official, Kabul, UNODC, 17.02.2005.

313 Telephone interviews, Nimroz ABP, July and October 2008..

314 Telephone interview, Nangarhar ABP, October 2008.

315 "The changing structure of the Afghan opium trade", *Jane's Intelligence Review*, 2006.

316 UNODC, "Precursor Control on Central Asia's Borders with Afghanistan", 2006.

317 UNODC, Monitoring of drug flows in Afghanistan, October 2007.

318 Interview September 2008.

319 Although there have been a number of high-level extraditions to the US.

problem. According to the CJTF, since April 2007, "The number of cases involving middle or high-value targets has increased by over 300 per cent in the last year to reach 10 per cent of the total number of cases. Those prosecuted have included a provincial deputy head of the CNPA, senior civil servants, former anti-Russian commanders and officers in the ANA, ANP, NDS and the Border Police".[320]

Prosecuting high-level targets may also be a deadly endeavour. Those law enforcement or judiciary officials not connected are reportedly often threatened and sometimes killed for interfering with the trade.[321]

Corruption and opium poppy cultivation...

Corruption impacts all levels of the opium economy, including the production stage. For example, in 2006, the Ministry of Interior dismissed a district governor and district chief of police after they failed to assist in the pre-planting campaigns against poppy cultivation. The provincial governor alleged that the two were corrupt and involved in narcotics trafficking and cultivation. There are also consistent reports that eradication police officers negotiate agreements with villagers not to eradicate the poppy fields or eradicate the failed crops in exchange for a bribe. UNODC weekly eradication reports show that on average, only 46 per cent of the existing poppy fields were eradicated in each village visited by Afghan governor eradication teams in 2008.

...and security

In the above example, corruption invariably affects the poorer segments of Afghan society disproportionally. Those who cannot bribe their way out of eradication are the poorer farmers who lose their only cash crop while well-connected or richer landowners go unscathed. In the words of a high-ranking CNPA official, "the government is more likely to seize or eradicate the poppy while the insurgents only tax".[322] This statement was echoed in various forms in several interviews in 2008. This has a positive impact on the general population's perception of insurgents, who are seen as protectors of the population's basic livelihood against the central government and the international coalition. An official from the Ministry of Interior indicated a burgeoning alliance between local farmers and insurgent elements to jointly resist Afghan Eradication Force (AEF) Activities"[323]; a phenomenon observed in Badghis and other provinces.

The previous example illustrates how the precarious security conditions undermine eradication (but also interdiction) efforts. Given the security situation, it has become virtually impossible to conduct eradication operations in

districts under the Taliban, which penalizes farmers in pro-government districts. These districts are mostly located in the south of the country where it is increasingly obvious that high corruption is geographically correlated with areas of drug production, trafficking and insecurity. Police corruption was, according to one study, more pronounced in the south and west of the country than in the centre and north. In interviews conducted in the spring and summer of 2005, more than 90 per cent of respondents in the south and west preferred the local militias (*Arbakee*) to state police, who are often seen as corrupt and ineffective.[324] As discussed above, the average Afghans deal with day-to-day corruption on a daily basis and in some areas in the south there is growing support for the Taliban, which is viewed as a preferable alternative to corruption and rampant crime.

Particularly at the lower levels of government, corruption is the carrot and violence the stick offered by traffickers to induce compliance from officials. When officials facilitate or directly engage in trafficking, it is unavoidably a drain on public resources, just as trafficking is a distraction from insurgency for the Taliban.

However, for insurgents this poses no greater risk than an occasional diversion of time and men. For the government, in contrast, opiate-related corruption is a strategic threat. It undermines effectiveness and reduces public trust in the middle of a war with insurgents who are most fondly remembered for straightforward law and order. This brings us full circle: opiate trafficking is an overwhelmingly criminal affair, sometimes recruiting insurgents but of greatest threat to Afghanistan in crippling government functions and eroding popular support.

Corruption also has a more direct impact on insecurity, as many weapons shipments travel "undetected" across illegal border crossing points with the help of a small bribe. Related to this, officers of the ANA have been caught smuggling weapons to insurgents in Logar Province.[325] That 2006 case is on the borderline between wilful official ignorance of transnational threat activity and active participation.

Corruption along drug trafficking routes

Corruption is of course not limited to Afghanistan. Transnational trafficking networks have so far been able to take advantage of lax border controls and corruption worldwide to transport tens of thousands of metric tons of precursors into Afghanistan and ship hundreds of tons of opiates across into Europe and through the Islamic Republic of Iran, Pakistan, Turkey and Central Asia.

Corruption is a critical link in the trafficking chain, espe-

320 Information provided by CJTF official in the briefing "The criminal Justice Task Force – A year of advances", 2009.

321 Interview with customs enforcement official, Kabul, September 2008; Ethirajan Anbarasan, "The leading anti-drugs judge in Afghanistan has been killed", *BBC*, 05-09-2008.

322 Interview, Nangarhar, October 2008.

323 Interview, Kabul, 2008.

324 Gregory Gajewski et al., "How War, a Tribal Social Structure, and Donor Efforts Shape Institutional Change in Afghanistan: A Case Study of the Roads Sector", *The Louis Berger Group*, September 2007.

325 Samuel Chan, "Sentinels of Afghan Democracy: The Afghan National Army", *S. Rajarathnam School of International Studies*, Singapore, June 1 2007.

cially as the number of borders to cross increases. It is the major facilitating factor all along the drug trafficking routes out of Afghanistan and into the European and Asian markets. Afghanistan ranks as the 176th country out of 180 according to the 2008 Transparency International corruption perception index (CPI)[326]. Neighbouring countries face similar problems, as shown in table 63. The CPI is particularly low in Afghanistan and its border countries (except China) compared to the world average (average CPI = 4 for 180 countries in 2008).

Afghan opiates are trafficked to Europe via the so called Balkan route (Afghanistan, the Islamic Republic of Iran, Turkey, Bulgaria, Greece, Albania and beyond) and the Central Asia route (Afghanistan–Turkmenistan/Uzbekistan/Tajikistan-Kyrgyzstan/Kazakhstan-the Russian Federation).

Table 5: **CPI* index value for Afghanistan and its neighbours**

Country	2008
Afghanistan	1.7
Iran	2.4
Pakistan	2.5
Tajikistan	2.1
Turkmenistan	1.9
Uzbekistan	1.9

* CPI ranges between 10 (highly clean) and 0 (highly corrupt).

Tajikistan is the most important country in terms of trafficking of Afghan heroin to Russia and beyond. Heroin is being trafficked from Tajikistan to Kyrgyzstan (mainly) or Uzbekistan or direct to Russia (by air). Kazakhstan is a hub country for Afghan heroin to be trafficked to Russia. The CPI for both Kazakhstan and Tajikistanis is very low. In Kyrgyzstan the CPI was 1.8 in 2008, and in Kazakhstan, 2.2. That Central Asian states are still in transition from the Soviet period has created a favorable environment for thriving organized crime and corruption. At the destination point, Russia is an important country for the trafficking of Afghan heroin as consumer (mainly) and transit country. The CPI was also very low for Russia in 2008 (2.1).

On the Balkan route, the CPI for Turkey is 4.6 and for Greece 4.7, which is slightly more than the world average in 2008. Bulgaria (CPI = 3.6) and Albania (CPI = 3.4) had lower CPIs than the world average in 2008.

Corruption is not a problem limited to Afghanistan. It extends across the region and beyond, including to destination countries. Corruption poses major challenges to drug

control efforts, but also facilitates all types of transnational trafficking apart from opiates; from human beings and weapons to smuggled goods and resources such as fuel and precious gems.

Corruption has clearly affected the morale and motivation of Afghans. While this study is in no position to assess the reliability of all allegations of corruption, one fact remains clear: there is palpable general distrust of government and its institutions (particularly law enforcement) among the Afghan public.

Insurgents are eager to use this disenchantment through information operations and propaganda, but corruption has done more damage to the government's image (and by extension the coalition and the international community) than any Taliban propaganda campaign. In a sense, the Taliban/insurgents derive both financial and political capital from the opium economy.

The "corruption problem" in Afghanistan may potentially take more time to tackle than the drug culture as the former predates the latter. It will necessitate sustained effort and the refocusing of significant energy on the part of international donors.

---

326 The CPI Score relates to perceptions of the degree of corruption as seen by business people and country analysts; see United Nations "Afghanistan: Public Administration Country Profile, January 2006; see also www.transparency.org/news_room/in_focus/2008/cpi2008/cpi_2008_table.

CONCLUDING REMARKS

Between 2002 and 2008, Afghan farmers earned a total of about US$ 6.4 billion from opium poppy cultivation, and Afghan traffickers approximately US$ 18 billion from local opiate processing and trading. During the same seven-year period, the transnational trade in Afghan opiates produced a total turn over of US$ 400 to 500 billion. Arrests figures suggest that there may be around 1 million traffickers involved in bringing opiates to some 16 million opiate users across the world every year. The source of the trade is in Afghanistan, but its bulk takes place outside that country.

The difficulties to eliminate opium production in Afghanistan and the global dimensions and transnational structure of the opiate trade it fuels, clearly suggest that the solution to this transnational threat cannot be found in Afghanistan alone. With a view to tackle the problem in its broad dimensions, the international community and UNODC have launched a number of regional and international initiatives, such as the Paris Pact and UNODC's Rainbow strategy. These efforts must be actively supported and expanded to continue strengthening a strategic response that is based on (a) a growing understanding of the patterns and dynamics of the transnational Afghan opiate trade, and (b) on a targeted, sequenced and cost-effective mix of interventions.

To continue advancing our understanding of the transnational Afghan opiate trade, some of the priorities for further research include:

- more and better data on opiate demand, purity and prices to improve the mapping of opiate flows in the world; priority South-East Asia, East Asia, Africa, Central Asia, Middle East and South-East Europe (regions/subregions); India, China, the Islamic Republic of Iran and Iraq (countries);

- the involvement of insurgent and organized crimes groups in heroin/opium trafficking in Afghanistan and Pakistan;

- money flows related to the transnational Afghan opiate trade;

- the role of organized crime groups in running the trade along the Balkan and Northern routes;

- the growing trade of Afghan opiates in South-East and East Asia's retail markets.